D1617605

INFANT MEMORY

Its Relation to Normal
and Pathological Memory
in Humans and Other Animals

ADVANCES IN THE STUDY OF COMMUNICATION AND AFFECT

A Continuation Order Plan is available for this series. A continuation order will bring delivery of each new volume immediately upon publication. Volumes are billed only upon actual shipment. For further information please contact the publisher.

ADVANCES IN THE STUDY OF
COMMUNICATION AND AFFECT

Volume 9

INFANT MEMORY

Its Relation to Normal and Pathological Memory in Humans and Other Animals

Edited by

Morris Moscovitch

Erindale College
Mississauga, Ontario, Canada

BF
720
.m45
I54
1984
West

PLENUM PRESS • NEW YORK AND LONDON

Arizona State Univ.
West Campus Library

Library of Congress Cataloging in Publication Data

Main entry under title:

Infant memory.

(Advances in the study of communication and affect; v. 9)
Versions of the papers presented at the Erindale Symposium on Infant Memory.
Includes bibliographies and index.
1. Memory in children — Congresses. 2. Infant psychology — Congresses. 3. Memory,
Disorders of — Congresses. 4. Psychology, Comparative — Congresses. I. Moscovitch,
Morris, 1945–   . II. Erindale Symposium on Infant Memory. III. Series. [DNLM: 1.
Memory — in infancy & childhood — congresses. 2. Child Development — congresses.
W1 AD8801 v.9 / WS 105.5.M2 I43 1982]
BF720.M45I54   1984   155.4′22   84-9844
ISBN 0-306-41588-7

© 1984 Plenum Press, New York
A Division of Plenum Publishing Corporation
233 Spring Street, New York, N.Y. 10013

All rights reserved

No part of this book may be reproduced, stored in a retrieval system, or transmitted,
in any form or by any means, electronic, mechanical, photocopying, microfilming,
recording, or otherwise, without written permission from the Publisher

Printed in the United States of America

To Herman and Margareta Moscovici, my parents,
Jill, my wife,
and Elana and David, my children

Contributors

JOSEPH F. FAGAN III
Department of Psychology, Case Western Reserve University, Cleveland, Ohio

ROBERT S. LOCKHART
Department of Psychology, University of Toronto, Toronto, Ontario, Canada

JEAN M. MANDLER
Department of Psychology, University of California at San Diego, La Jolla, California

MORRIS MOSCOVITCH
Department of Psychology, Erindale College, University of Toronto, Mississauga, Ontario, Canada

LYNN NADEL
Cognitive Science Program, School of Social Sciences, University of California, Irvine, California

KATHERINE NELSON
Graduate School and University Center, City University of New York, New York, New York

GARY M. OLSON
Department of Psychology, University of Michigan, Ann Arbor, Michigan

HOLLY A. RUFF
Department of Pediatrics, Albert Einstein College of Medicine, The Bronx, New York

DANIEL L. SCHACTER
Department of Psychology, University of Toronto, Toronto, Ontario, Canada

MARK S. STRAUSS
Department of Psychology, University of Pittsburgh, Pittsburgh, Pennsylvania

STUART ZOLA-MORGAN
Veterans Administration Medical Center and Department of Psychiatry, School of Medicine, University of California at San Diego, La Jolla, California

Preface

The study of infant memory has flourished in the past decade for a number of reasons, not the least of which is the tremendous growth of interest in normal and pathological adult memory that began in the late fifties. Despite its common lineage to other areas of memory research, however, infant memory has perhaps been the least integrated into the mainstream. In reading the literature, one gets a sense of discontinuity between the study of infant memory and memory at all other stages of development from childhood to old age. The reasons for this are not hard to find. The techniques used to study memory in infants are usually very different from those typically used even in children. These techniques often limit the kind of inferences one can draw about the nature of the memory systems under investigation. Even when terms, concepts, and theories from the adult literature are applied to infants, they often bear only a loose relationship to their original usage. For example, an infant who stares longer at a new pattern than an old one is said to "recognize" the old one and to have a memory system that shares many characteristics with a memory system that makes recognition possible in adults. Similarly, an infant who emits a previously learned response, such as a leg kick, to an old stimulus is said to "recall" that response and to be engaged in processes similar to those of adults who are recalling past events. A further reason for the discontinuity is that studies of infant memory are (or should be) closely linked to issues related to the cognitive capacities of the child. Studies of adult memory are not always linked in such a way; all too often, memory in adulthood is seen simply as the acquisition of new information. It is difficult to maintain such a narrow view of memory in infants. One can legitimately argue that in infants, memory supports all cognitive development.

One of the purposes of the Erindale Symposium on Infant Memory was to find ways to eliminate the discontinuity between infant memory and the mainstream of memory research. Afterall, because infant memory abilities develop into adult memory abilities, the field should reflect this continuity. The papers delivered at the symposium and the discussions that followed centered on this theme, although many other interesting issues were taken up and some were much more focused on particular research problems. As a whole, the chapters collected in this book, which are versions of the papers presented at the symposium, capture the central theme as well as most of the additional concerns of the symposium. Significantly, attempts at an integration between infant memory and mainstream memory research did not involve the wholesale immersion of the former into the latter. What emerged, instead, was the view that memory is not unitary even in adulthood. Many memory phenomena seen in infancy may survive relatively unaltered into adulthood. Similarly, the types of memory phenomena one associates with adulthood have closely related precursors in infancy. The transition between one and the other, though not fully documented, may not be as abrupt as it once seemed.

Because I am new to the area of infant memory, I organized the conference, in part, as a set of tutorials that were meant primarily to educate a neuropsychologist whose research interests include normal and pathological forms of adult memory and to inform students of infant memory of some interesting developments in human and animal neuropsychology. Although the conference and the chapters in this book served this purpose well, the participants in the conference, happily, had their own, much more ambitious priorities. The result is a book that I hope both novices and experts will find valuable.

I would like to thank various people and organizations for their support at various stages of the project. The symposium was funded jointly by the Natural Sciences and Engineering Research Council of Canada and by Erindale College. Sherri McKay-Soroka, Carl Corter, and Sandra Trehub suggested the topic of the conference, helped me select speakers, and even provided me with a reading list on infant memory. Maureen Patchett and Patti Livingstone provided invaluable assistance during every stage of organizing and running the conference and preparing this volume.

MORRIS MOSCOVITCH

Contents

CHAPTER 6

What Do Infants Remember? 131

ROBERT S. LOCKHART

CHAPTER 7

Infantile Amnesia: A Neurobiological Perspective 145

LYNN NADEL AND STUART ZOLA-MORGAN

CHAPTER 1

Infant Memory
History, Current Trends, Relations to Cognitive Psychology

Joseph F. Fagan III

Department of Psychology
Case Western Reserve University
Cleveland, Ohio

Overview

This chapter has two purposes. The first is to present a historically organized summary of the basic findings on the visual recognition memory
of infants and to note current empirical trends in the area. The second
purpose is to illustrate the manner in which research on infant memory
may be integrated with research in the general area of cognitive psychology.

The chapter begins by noting that visual perception is defined by the
infant's tendency to devote more fixation time to some stimuli than to
others and that the infant's devotion of unequal attention to novel and
previously seen targets defines recognition memory. Following a summary
of paradigms developed to test the infant's differential response to novel
and previously seen targets, it is shown that recognition is possible at any
age, but the kind of information that is encoded by the infant varies with
age. Consideration is then given to evidence for long-term memory and
for forgetting and to the effects of study time on recognition. The focus
then shifts to a survey of how recognition testing has been used to study

The preparation of this chapter was supported, in part, by Major Research Project
Grant HD-11089 from the National Institute of Child Health and Human Development.

1

the infant's perceptual and conceptual world. In the next section of the overview of infant memory studies, data indicating a link between early recognition memory and later intelligence are examined. The survey concludes with a discussion of current trends in the area of infant visual recognition memory.

To accomplish the second purpose of the chapter, points of integration between research and thought on infant memory and the general area of cognitive psychology are noted through a discussion of the circumscribed issues of mutual concern to students of infant memory and students of child and adult cognition. Specific examples of such issues from the areas of memory and categorization are given, followed by a final discussion.

Infant Visual Recognition Memory

The earliest studies of infant visual recognition memory, conducted from 1964 to 1970, focused on the development of a rationale by which infant memory could be inferred and on the translation of that rationale into specific paradigms. Methodological developments were followed by studies which sought to explore the parameters controlling infant memory. Emphasis on the parametric study of infant memory was strongest from 1970 to 1978. The use of visual recognition testing to explore general issues in early perceptual-cognitive development began in 1964 but became increasingly prominent from about 1972 on. Studies of perceptual-cognitive development now comprise the bulk of systematic work on infant memory. A final trend in research on infant visual recognition memory has been the attempt to link individual differences in early recognition memory to later variations in intelligence. Such attempts began as early as 1967 but have been most prevalent since 1979. The following sections on methods and parameters, perceptual-cognitive development, and early intelligence are arranged in historical sequence. For the most part, citation of studies is arranged chronologically within each section. The concluding section presents a brief discussion of current trends in the study of infant memory in the context of the main divisions comprising the history of the area.

Methods and Parameters

By 1970, three major techniques had been developed to assess the visual recognition capabilities of infants. All three techniques are based on the assumption that recognition memory is indicated by differential responsiveness to a novel and a previously exposed stimulus. Tests of infant visual recognition memory were preceded by the development of a technique to measure infant visual perception. That technique, known as the *visual interest test*, was developed by Fantz in 1956 and assumes that if an infant looks more at one stimulus than at another, the infant must be able to differentiate between the two targets. The procedure for determining the infant's visual fixation is to place the infant in front of a "stage" on which targets are secured. An observer, looking through a peephole centered between the targets, observes the corneal reflection of a target over the pupils of the infant's eyes and records the length of fixation paid to each stimulus.

Based on the visual interest test, two paradigms have been developed to test infant recognition. In one procedure the same stimulus is presented for a number of trials, followed by a new stimulus. Typically, the infant's response to the repeatedly exposed target declines or "habituates" over trials but returns to its initial level or "dishabituates" when the novel target is introduced. The habituation–dishabituation sequence is taken as an indication that the infant has stored some information about the repeatedly exposed stimulus. If, following the initial decline and recovery of response, the old target is reintroduced and the infant's response again declines, there is some indication of delayed recognition. The habituation–dishabituation paradigm came into use as a measure of memory following demonstrations of its utility by Lewis, Fadel, Bartels, and Campbell (1966), R. Caron and Caron (1968), and Pancratz and Cohen (1970).

A second paradigm developed to test visual recognition memory, also based on the visual interest test, is to expose the infant to a target for a certain period of time (e.g., 1–2 min) and then to present him with the recently exposed and novel target simultaneously. Infants typically devote the greater part of their visual fixation to the novel target when tested with this paired-comparison approach. Delayed recognition memory is easily tested by varying the time that elapses between the end of the study period and the presentation of the test pairing. Early tests of memory in which a novel and a previously exposed target were paired were carried out by Fantz (1964), Saayman, Ames, and Moffett (1964), Fantz and Nevis (1967), and Fagan (1970).

Both the habituation–dishabituation and paired comparison paradigms employ direct measurement of the infant's visual interest or differential looking. The third paradigm developed to test infant memory provides an indirect estimate of visual interest by measuring instead the infant's rate of sucking, in which sucking is employed as an instrumental response by the infant to produce visual stimulation. Specifically, in the high-amplitude sucking paradigm used to test visual recognition and developed by Siqueland and Delucia in 1969, a visual stimulus is brought into focus as a contingent reinforcement for high-amplitude sucking. As the infant habituates to the repeated target, sucking declines. After the infant reaches some criterion of habituation, a new target is introduced. If the sucking response returns to its previous high amplitude in the presence of the novel target, recognition is inferred.

Methodological accomplishments were followed by studies that focused on parameters thought to influence early recognition memory. The major parameters included the age of the infant, the length of the retention interval, and the amount of study time allowed prior to recognition testing.

Age. Early studies by Fantz and Nevis (1967), Fagan, Fantz, and Miranda (1971), and Wetherford and Cohen (1973) sought to discover the age at which recognition memory is first exhibited. None found evidence for visual recognition in infants younger than 10–12 weeks. Subsequent studies by Friedman (1972), Friedman, Bruno, and Vietze (1974), Milewski and Siqueland (1975), and Milewski (1978), however, showed that visual recognition memory is possible during the first month of life.

The studies that found evidence for visual recognition memory under 3 months differed from those that did not in the interdiscriminability of the previously exposed and novel targets and in the length of study time allowed prior to recognition testing. Studies that found evidence for early recognition employed widely discrepant stimuli that were easily scanned and varied along multiple dimensions known to be discriminable to neonates, such as brightness, size, number, and contour of elements. In addition, study times in such experiments ranged from 2–5 min. Studies finding no evidence for recognition under 3 months employed stimuli that were less easily scanned and that varied along fewer dimensions. Moreover, study time in these experiments was typically 80 sec or less. In effect, one would expect that highly discrepant stimuli may be differentiated on a recognition test following lengthy study time at very early ages. Such a demonstration of early recognition is provided in a study by Werner and Siqueland (1978), who employed the high-amplitude sucking paradigm to test 6-day-old infants who had been born 5 weeks prior to term. Following at least 5 min of study, the neonates in Werner and Siqueland's experiments were able to differentiate between novel and previously exposed checkerboards that varied in size and in number of pattern elements as well as in hue and brightness.

In summary, visual recognition memory may be demonstrated at any age during infancy depending on the discriminability of the previously exposed and novel targets with which the infant is faced. Length of study time allowed also determines whether recognition will occur. Generally, targets differing along many dimensions following lengthy study are differentiated on a recognition test at an early age.

Long-Term Memory. The question of whether novelty preferences would be demonstrated following retention intervals of hours, days, or weeks following original study attracted the immediate attention of investigators. A study by Fagan (1970, Experiment II) provided direct support for 2-hr retention and (Experiment I) some indirect support for the existance of 24–48-hour retention of information gained from exposure to abstract patterns on the part of 5-month-old infants. A direct test of long-term memory for abstract patterns was made in a study by Fagan (1973), in which infants 5–6 months of age recognized, after 2 days, which member of a pair of targets they had originally studied. A second experiment in the Fagan (1973) study demonstrated delayed recognition for photos of faces at intervals of 3 hr, 1, 2, 7, and 14 days on the part of 5-month-old infants. The main findings from the 1970 and 1973 studies by Fagan have been confirmed in subsequent investigations. Martin (1975), and Strauss and Cohen (1980) demonstrated 24-hr retention of the information conveyed in abstract forms on the part of 5-month-olds. One to two week retention for abstract patterns at 7 months has been reported by Topinka and Steinberg (1978). Finally, 5- to 6-month infants showed 48-hr memory for abstract patterns and face photos when examined for a "savings" effect in a study by Cornell (1979).

Attempts to find disruption of memory also attracted the attention of investigators. In a study by Fagan (1971) both immediate and minutes-delayed recognition tests were made for each of three sets of abstract black and white patterns administered during a single test session. The 5-month infants in the Fagan (1971) study demonstrated immediate and delayed recognition for each of three problems and gave no evidence of disruption of memory. In addition, a series of experiments by Fagan (1973, 1977a) sought to induce 5-month-old infants to forget which face photo they had seen before providing the infants with interference from other face photos or line drawings of faces during a 2-min retention interval. The general results of the Fagan (1973, 1977a) experiments were that highly similar intervening targets could, if presented soon after study, lead to loss of recognition. The effects of such intervention were quite limited with recovery of recognition occurring after a 1-min rest or memory loss being easily prevented by a further, brief exposure to the previously studied target. Findings similar to Fagan's (1973, 1977a) with regard to the infant's resistance to interference have been reported by Bornstein (1976) for retention of color, by McCall, Kennedy, and Dodds (1977) using form–color patterns, and by Cohen, DeLoache, and Pearl (1977) for faces.

In summary, the existence of long-term recognition memory on the order of days and even weeks on the part of 5–7-month infants has been confirmed in various studies. Moreover, such memory is robust, with forgetting occurring only under very circumscribed conditions (see Chapter 8 for discussion).

Study Time. An experiment by Fagan (1974) was the first that sought to discover the amount of study fixation prior to recognition testing that would be effective in allowing the infant's novelty preference to emerge. A related question was whether longer study was needed for more difficult discriminations. Difficulty of discrimination was indexed by the age at which recognition memory had been first evidenced for a particular discrimination. Among the tasks included in the Fagan (1974) study were pairs of abstract stimuli varying along a number of dimensions, abstract targets varying only in pattern arrangement, and photos of faces. Amount of study time necessary to elicit a novelty preference on recognition testing for 5-month-olds varied over tasks. As little as 4 sec of prior study time was needed to differentiate a novel from a previously seen target when the targets varied widely. Novelty preferences were not in evidence for pairs of targets differing solely on patterning unless 17 sec had been spent studying the to-be-familiar target. Distinctions among faces required from 20–30 sec of prior study. Variations in the amount of prior study needed to solve each task corresponded to age-related differences in ease of discrimination, with tasks requiring little study also being the tasks solved at an earlier age.

Since 1974, the efficacy of brief study times and the interaction of study time with target discriminability have been reported by a number of investigators. Studies by Cornell (1979), Rose (1980, 1981), and Lasky and Spiro (1980) have confirmed the fact that widely varying abstract patterns may be differentiated following as little as 5–10 sec of study time. As was the case in the Fagan (1974) study, infants tested by Fagan (1977b), Cornell (1979) or Lasky (1980) on abstract patterns that differed only in arrangements of elements required 15–20 sec of study before one pattern was distinguished from the other. Finally, novelty preference for photos of faces, as in the Fagan (1974) report, emerged after 20–30 sec of familiarization for infants tested by Cornell (1979), Lasky (1980), and Rose (1980, 1981).

Some limits on the efficacy of brief study for later recognition have also been found. Rose (1980, 1981), for example, has shown that brief study may be sufficient to produce immediate recognition of abstract patterns but is not sufficient for retention of that same information over a 2- or 3-min interval. Similarly, Lasky and Spiro (1980) note that memory for abstract patterns following brief study of from 4–5-sec may be disrupted by masking targets interpolated within the first 2 sec following study.

In short, infants at 5–6 months are able to recognize a target immediately following a relatively brief exposure to that stimulus. The more similar the to-be-remembered stimulus is to the novel target, the more study time is required to elicit a novelty preference. Moreover, it is possible to recapture the order of emergence of novelty preferences for particular tasks over age by varying study time at a single age. The latter conclusion implies that manipulation of study time and task difficulty at a later age may provide investigators with a simple empirical means for generating and checking hypotheses about the earlier course of perceptual development.

Summary. The infant's tendency to devote more fixation to a novel than to a previously exposed target serves as an operational definition of visual recognition memory. Infants, from birth, are able to differentiate among highly discriminable targets on an immediate recognition test following lengthy study of the to-be-remembered stimulus. Successively finer distinctions are made with increasing maturational level. The infant, at least from 5 months, requires relatively little study of a target for subsequent immediate recognition, with more or less study needed to encode different kinds of information. Also by 5 months, given sufficient time to study the to-be-remembered target, the infant's recognition memory is long lasting and is not easily disrupted.

Perceptual-Cognitive Development

Historically, students of infant memory have been less concerned with memory *per se* than they have with the information that tests of visual recognition provide on the perceptual-cognitive world of the infant. By controlling the manner in which a novel and a previously exposed target vary, inferences can be made as to which characteristics of a stimulus were encoded during study to serve as the basis of the infant's response on recognition testing. Thus, investigators have explored the ability of the infant to perceive such aspects of the visual world as shape (Cohen, Gelber & Lazar, 1971; Saayman *et al.*, 1964), color (Bornstein, 1976; Cohen *et al.*, 1971; Fagan, 1977b; Saayman *et al.*, 1964), the arrangement of elements in a pattern (Fagan, 1970; 1973; 1974; 1977b), the orientation of a pattern (Cornell, 1975; McGurk, 1970) and facial patterning (A. Caron, Caron, Caldwell, & Weiss, 1973; Cornell, 1974; Fagan, 1972, 1973, 1974, 1976; McGurk, 1970).

By varying age and target differences, investigators have been able to chart theoretically interesting instances of early perceptual development. For example, in a recent study, Fagan and Shepherd (1979) explored the development of the 4- to 6-month infant's ability to recognize facial orientation. Recognition was inferred from the infant's preference for a novel target. The particular orientations that infants were asked to identify on a recognition test were chosen to test Braine's (1978) theory of the development of orientation perception. By combining their recognition test results with those of others (Fagan, 1972; McGurk, 1970; Watson, 1966), Fagan and Shepherd provided a summary of the distinctions among facial orientations that are or are not accomplished from 4–6 months of age, noting the correspondence of the empirical evidence to Braine's theory. The results of Fagan and Shepherd, taken together with earlier work, confirm Braine's assumption that distinctions among orientations of a face develop in a particular sequence such that a differentiation of upright from non-upright precedes distinctions among non-uprights, which, in turn, are solved earlier than are left-right discriminations. (A discussion of orientation perception is beyond the scope of the present chapter.) The point of the illustration is that investigators have underemployed recognition testing to provide a description of the kinds of information that infants encode over age and may use such descriptions in evaluating theories of perceptual development.

The study of responsiveness to novelty has also made it possible to discover whether specific features of a previously exposed target are perceived as invariant by the infant. In a study by Fagan (1977b), for example, 5-month infants were allowed to study a form–color compound and were then presented with a familiar and a novel cue along one dimension and the same two novel cues along the other. For example, the infant might study a red diamond and then be tested on the pairing red square versus green square. Since, in this example, the only dimension containing a familiar and a novel cue is color, a reliable preference for novelty would indicate that color had been coded as an invariant feature during study. Fagan (1977b) found that infants were able to encode either the invariant form or color of a target as a basis for later recognition.

Many experiments have demonstrated that infants are able to detect features of a stimulus that remain invariant from study to test. McGurk (1972), using an habituation–dishabituation procedure, showed that 6-month-old infants recognize the form of a simple stick figure despite discriminable changes in its orientation. Verification of McGurk's finding that infants faced with abstract figures can detect invariance in patterning over changes in orientation has been provided in studies employing a paired-comparison approach by Cornell (1975) and Fagan (1979) for infants 4–5 months old. The infant's ability to recognize invariant characteristics of a pattern is also true for facial representation. A study by Fagan (1976) showed that 7-month-old infants recognized a man as familiar during testing even though that man had appeared in a different pose during study (Fagan, 1976, Experiment 3) and even though such a change in pose could be easily discriminated (Fagan, 1976, Experiment 2). Additional demonstrations of the infant's ability to recognize invariant aspects of faces have been provided by Cohen and Strauss (1979), and Nelson, Morse, and Leavitt (1979).

Tests of visual recognition have also found that infants are able to transfer information from one representation to another or from one modality to another. By 5 months, for example, infants are able to recognize information common to an object and a picture of that object (Deloache, Strauss, & Maynard, 1979; Dirks & Gibson, 1977) and, by 1 year, can employ information gained by study in one modality to solve a recognition test given in another modality (Gottfried, Rose, & Bridger, 1977, 1978; Rose, Gottfried, & Bridger, 1978). Additional examples might be given of the kinds of information that infants encode, but such detail would go beyond the scope of the present chapter. The point is simply that tests of visual recognition have been employed to inform us about the infant's developing ability to perceive, to abstract invariant features, to transfer information, and, in effect, to categorize the visual world.

Early Intelligence

The possibility that individual differences in visual recognition memory during infancy might be linked to later differences in intelligence was raised by Fantz and Nevis in 1967. In the Fantz and Nevis study, 10 home-reared offspring of highly intelligent parents were compared with institution-reared offspring of women of average intelligence. Fantz and Nevis measured the infant's differential responsiveness to a novel target paired with a previously exposed target by pairing abstract black and white patterns on an immediate recognition test. The sample as a whole showed a preference for novel targets beginning at about 2–3 months. The preference developed earlier in age on the part of the offspring of the highly intelligent parents, 8 out of 10 of whom preferred the novel target on all tests after 2 months of age. A novelty preference was not shown by the infants of mothers of average intelligence until about 3 months.

Since 1967 many studies have been undertaken in which groups of infants expected or suspected to differ in intelligence later in life have been compared for their ability to recognize a familiar visual stimulus. With few exceptions (Cohen, 1981; Fagan, Fantz, & Miranda, 1971) such studies have shown that groups of infants expected to differ in intelligence later in life also differ in their ability to recognize a familiar visual target. Such a conclusion is true not only for offspring of highly intelligent parents as compared to offspring of women of average intelligence (Fantz & Nevis, 1967) but also for normal as compared to Down's syndrome infants (Cohen, 1981; Miranda & Fantz, 1974) and for full-term as compared to preterm infants (A. Caron & Caron, 1981; Rose, 1980; Rose, Gottfried, & Bridger, 1978; Sigman & Parmalee, 1974).

Presumably, such group differences early in life are based on differences among individuals that are valid predictors of later intellectual functioning. In fact, tests of infant visual recognition memory have proven to be valid in predicting a child's later intellectual level. Five published reports are available in which the relationship between tests of infant visual recognition memory and later intelligence have been explored for individuals. These studies by Yarrow, Klein, Lomonaco, and Morgan (1975), Fagan (1981), Fagan and McGrath (1981), Lewis and Brooks-Gunn (1981), and Fagan and Singer (1983) include tests of predictive validity for 12 samples of children. Each of the 12 samples have yielded significant associations between early recognition memory and later intelligence. Preferences for visual novelty during infancy have yielded moderate predictive validity coefficients ranging from .33 to .66 across the 12 samples with a mean of .44 (*SD* .09). The associations between early novelty preferences and later IQ pertain to blacks as well as to whites, for a variety of early recognition memory tasks, across different paradigms for assessing infant memory, for initial tests made between 3 and 7 months, and for intelligence measured from 2 through 7 years.

There are at least three ways to assess the relative magnitude of the relation of .44 thus far found between early memory and later IQ. The first is to note that the average value of .44 is significantly greater than the predictive validity coefficients obtained for conventional tests of infant sensorimotor development such as the Bayley Scales. A second way of assessing the scope of the average correlation of .44 between infants' novelty preferences and later IQ is to note that it compares favorably in magnitude to predictive validity coefficients of more well-established tests. The correlation between scores on the Stanford–Binet Intelligence Test and tests of academic achievement, for example, is .50. A third method of assessing the relative value of the mean coefficient of .44 is to note that all of the 12 correlations obtained thus far very likely underestimate the predictive validity of infant memory tests. Attenuation of the correlations was due to two factors. The first source of attenuation was a restricted range of intelligence within which predictions were made from sample to sample. One would expect higher validity coefficients when a wider range of intellectual functioning is tapped. A second source of attenuation of predictive validity was the relatively low reliability of the tests of infant memory employed in each study. Low reliability was due to the small number of visual novelty preferences (from one to five tests of preference) upon which the memory scores were based from study to study. In future studies, tests of infant memory based on more pairings of previously exposed and novel targets should yield higher predictive validity coefficients.

In summary, there is support for the assumption that differences in early visual recognition memory represent and predict variations in intelligent functioning. The demonstration of continuity between early visual recognition memory and later intelligence raises the question of the basis for such continuity, a question to which we shall return. Our present purpose, however, is simply to note that links between early visual memory and later intelligence have been demonstrated.

Current Trends

At the Third International Conference on Infant Studies, which was held in Austin from March 18 to 21, 1982, 35 papers on infant visual recognition memory were presented. Six of the 35 studies focused primarily on temporal parameters controlling recognition memory, such as order of problem input, amount of study time, or length of retention interval. Another 5 of the 35 investigators concentrated on the measurement of individual differences in early recognition memory between groups or among individuals that were expected to vary in later intelligence. The majority (24 out of 35, or 68%) of the studies, however, employed visual recognition testing to explore various aspects of early perceptual-cognitive development. Some 11 of those 24 studies were devoted to the study of the infant's ability to distinguish among cues along a single dimension such as shape or number. The remaining 13 studies had as their focus either the study of the infant's ability to perceive invariant aspects of changing visual displays or the ability to recognize invariant information common to two modalities. Thus, the study of visual recognition memory in the infant currently serves mainly as a vehicle to explore early perceptual-cognitive functioning. As noted above, such a focus has always been a major trend in the history of infant memory research.

With the exception of a growing reliance on the Gibsonian view of perceptual development to guide research in early visual recognition (see Chapter 3), perhaps the fairest statement with regard to conceptual trends that can be made at the present time is that the study of infant recognition memory has been and remains primarily *atheoretical*. In effect, investigators of infant memory have been more concerned with developing a methodology and building a data base than with dealing systematically with broad theoretical issues. At the same time, students of infant memory recognize that the practical issues which they address have their empirical or conceptual counterparts in studies of child and adult cognition, issues to which we shall now turn our attention.

Integration of Infant Memory and General Cognitive Psychology

Two general examples of the manner in which research in infant memory may be integrated with research in general cognitive psychology are given in this section. The first approach is to locate similar phenomena that may be demonstrated across areas, noting that similar phenomena

require a common explanation. The specific examples of similar phenomena I have chosen have to do with context effects in memory. The second
approach to integration is to show how questions posed in one area may
be cogently answered in another. Illustrations here are based on the question of how best to answer questions posed by students of categorization.

Context Effects in Memory

Students of adult memory have long been aware that manipulations
of the context in which an item is encoded or the context in which it is
retrieved have powerful effects on later recognition or recall (e.g., Craik
& Lockhart, 1972; Craik & Tulving, 1975; Hyde and Jenkins, 1969;
Thompson & Tulving, 1970; Tulving & Osler, 1968). They may not be
aware, however, that the manipulation of encoding or retrieval contexts
also has effects on the recognition memory performance of infants.

As to encoding context, certain conditions of study are more apt to
result in the infant's recognition of a target than are others. Specifically,
recognition may be facilitated by allowing the infant to study a related
target as well as the to-be-remembered target prior to recognition testing.
The initial demonstration of the fact that provision of related instances
of a target during study may aid later recognition was provided in a study
by Fagan (1976) that investigated whether an infant would choose a female
face as novel on pairings of a male and female face even though a different
male face had been shown for study. The 7-month infants in the Fagan
(1976) study did identify the male face as familiar but only when at least
two other males had been shown prior to recognition testing. A second
study (Fagan, 1978) tested the replication of the original finding (Fagan,
1976) that exposing the infant to related instances of a face during study
aids later recognition of that face. In confirmation of the earlier result,
Fagan (1978) found that the 7-month infant's recognition memory for a
man's face (when that man was to be differentiated from another man)
was improved by allowing the infant prior study of various poses of the
to-be-remembered man.

A third experiment in Fagan (1978) found that the provision of related
instances of a target during study facilitates not only facial recognition
but the recognition of abstract patterns as well. As an illustration of how
manipulation of study context may alter the infant's recognition of a target
let us consider the third experiment in Fagan (1978) in some detail. As
an aid to discussion, the design and results of this experiment are pictured
in Figure 1. Figure 1 presents the pairs of targets shown during study,
the amount of fixation paid to each target during study, the pair of targets
presented on the recognition test, and the percentage of total fixation paid

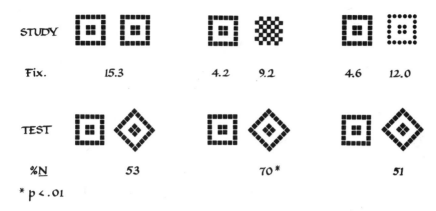

Fig. 1. Results taken from the third experiment in Fagan (1978), including fixation time and percentage of total fixation time.

to the novel stimulus on the test for each of three groups of 7-month infants. The abstract patterns chosen as discriminanda on the recognition tests were selected on the basis of past research (Fagan, 1974) in which recognition of a pattern was shown to be dependent on length of study time. The general approach was to show a control group a pattern paired with itself for a particular length of study, a length insufficient for the demonstration of recognition. The control group was compared with infants allowed the same length of study but who were presented with two different but related patterns during study. The kind of related target presented with the to-be-remembered pattern during study was varied for two experimental groups.

As one can see from Figure 1, recognition memory varied by study conditions. As expected, the 15 sec of fixation spent by the control group shown identical patterns during study proved too brief a study time to allow a reliable novelty preference to emerge on recognition testing. For experimental groups allowed to see related instances of a pattern during study, evidence of recognition depended on the context provided. Infants who studied pairings of the square and the checkerboard, a pairing in which the form of the internal elements (small squares) of each pattern remained invariant, demonstrated a high and reliable preference for the novel pattern on recognition testing. Such recognition was evident even though actual study time for the to-be-remembered target was minimal (4.2 sec). Conversely, those infants exposed to a pair of patterns that were invariant in overall arrangement of elements, that is, those given squares and circles to study, failed to demonstrate any recognition of the square on the test.

In summary, the results of Experiment 3 (Fagan, 1978) tell us that infants' recognition of abstract patterns may be facilitated by providing related instances of a to-be-remembered pattern during study with the kind of related instance presented during study determining whether or not facilitation of recognition will occur.

Aside from the studies by Fagan (1976, 1978), instances of facilitation of infants' recognition due to manipulation of study context are contained in reports by Ruff (1978), Olson (1979), and Nelson, Morse, and Leavitt (1979). In the Ruff (1978) experiment, 9-month infants' recognition of the form of an object was enhanced by allowing the infant to study paired instances of that object identical in form but varying in color, size, and orientation. Olson (1979) found memory for abstract designs to be facilitated when 4- to 5-month infants were shown multiple items from the same category of patterns prior to recognition testing. Finally Nelson *et al.* found that 7-month infants could demonstrate generalized recognition of facial expression only when they had been exposed to the to-be-remembered expression posed by at least two different models during study. Thus, manipulation of encoding context by permitting the infant to see related instances of a to-be-remembered target during study may facilitate the later recognition of the particular target, whether it is a face (Fagan, 1978) or an abstract pattern (Fagan, 1978; Olson, 1979). Moreover, such study conditions may also facilitate the recognition of an invariant feature of a target, such as the sex of a face (Fagan, 1976), the expression of a face (Nelson *et al.*, 1979), or the form of an object (Ruff, 1978).

More recently, Rolfe and Day (1981), and Ruff (1981) have found that the degree of similarity in context between conditions of encoding and conditions of retrieval has a strong effect on infants' recognition memory. In the Ruff study, 6-month infants were allowed to look at and handle objects during study. Half the infants were also allowed to look at and handle objects on recognition testing. The other infants could only look at the objects on recognition testing. In the Rolfe and Day experiment, 6-month infants were familiarized with objects either unimodally (seeing or handling) or bimodally (seeing and handling), with subsequent recognition tests for half the infants that either duplicate study conditions (e.g., bimodal test following bimodal study) or did not duplicate study conditions (e.g., bimodal study followed by unimodal test). In each experiment, recognition memory was either superior or evident only in those conditions in which the context remained the same from study to test.

The purpose of this brief review has been to point out that variations in context during encoding and retrieval influence the recognition memory performance of infants much as such variations change memory performance in adults. The exploration of the parameters surrounding the effects of study or retrieval context on recognition and the suggestion of possible mechanisms that may account for the effects of context on memory remain key empirical and theoretical issues in the area of infant memory. The study of how recognition may be facilitated will probably receive increasing attention from investigators of infant memory, since a great deal of both theoretical and practical benefit can come from knowing how to insure that particular information will be encoded by an infant.

Context effects are not the only phenomena common to studies of infant and adult memory. Two recent studies by Cornell (Cornell, 1980; Cornell & Bergstrom, 1982), for example, have shown that well-established phenomena in the adult literature, such as the distribution effect (distributed study superior to massed study for later recognition) and the serial position effect (primacy and recency effects plus labile recency effect over delay), are present at 6 months. In each study, Cornell notes that explanations of such effects in adults that rely on automatic rather than on strategic processes also serve as appropriate explanations of the performance of infants.

If adults and infants respond in the same manner following particular manipulations, it seems reasonable to suppose that common mechanisms, invariant over age, underlie those behaviors. Theoretical explanations of such behaviors that require processes available at one age but not at another (e.g., a network of verbal associations) seem less desirable than explanations that identify processes available at each age (e.g., sensitivity to context). In effect, the fact that phenomena found in adult memory may be duplicated during infancy raises the possibility that there may be a set of memory processes fundamental to humans that are continuous over age. If such a possibility exists, how pervasive are such processes (i.e., which adult memory phenomena can be duplicated in infancy)? Furthermore, how may such processes be modeled or explained? Such empirical and theoretical questions remain to be answered, but their pursuit should aid in integrating our understanding of infant memory into general cognitive psychology, and consequentially each area should be enriched.

Categorization

In a recent review, Mervis and Rosch (1981) list a number of theoretical questions currently being pursued by investigators interested in the manner in which children and adults categorize natural objects. As the present section suggests, many of the issues noted by Mervis and Rosch may be also addressed, and perhaps more cogently answered, by considering the infant's ability to categorize, which may be tapped by appropriate tests of recognition memory. Specifically, three theoretical questions posed by Mervis and Rosch are considered. Those questions have to do with the order in which hierarchical levels of categories are acquired with age, the decomposability of categories into primitive elements, and the separability of attributes.

Categorization and Age. According to Mervis and Rosch, objects may be categorized (i.e., treated as equivalent even though they are discriminable) at different hierarchical levels. Certain levels of categorization are considered "basic." A basic-level category consists of objects with maximal similarity relative to the similarity of those objects with objects from another (related) category. Chairs, for example, are a basic-level category within the superordinate category of furniture, and rocking chairs constitute a subordinate category within chairs.

Mervis and Rosch hypothesize that basic-level categories are the first to be acquired over age followed by superordinate and then by subordinate categories. Order of acquisition of category levels is inferred from the manner in which children and adults perform when asked to sort items into groups using examples drawn from either natural or artificial categories (e.g., Mervis and Crisafi, 1982; Rosch, Mervis, Gray, Johnson, & Boyes-Braem, 1976). Although it may be that children and adults sort items into category levels in the same order in which the levels were acquired, it is possible that such a sorting is made on a basis other than age at which the category level is acquired. To discover if the performance of children and adults on sorting tasks mirrors order of acquisition over age, it seems desirable to employ items from categories for which the order of acquisition of category levels is known.

The suggestion made here is that the use of items drawn from category levels developed during infancy would provide a relevant test of whether or not later categorization performance on a sorting task reflects age of category level acquisition. As noted earlier (p. 8), infants are able to identify previously seen targets on a recognition test even though those targets have been changed from study to test and even though such changes are discriminable. In other words, infants are able to treat two or more distinguishable objects as equivalent, which is Mervis and Rosch's operational definition of categorization.

Moreover, the order in which items from categories familiar to adults have been progressively differentiated during the early months of life has been explored in tests of infant recognition memory. As noted earlier (p. 8), Fagan and Shepherd (1979) traced the development of the infant's differentiation among various facial orientations from 4–6 months. In a recent review, Fagan and Shepherd (1982) present a rough sketch of the growth of facial pattern differentiation during the first 7 months of life, noting that the growth of facial pattern perception seems to involve four successive differentiations among faces, each more refined than the next.

The first two stages appear to reflect the identification of faces in general and the second two of the faces in particular. The initial differentiation made in the first week of life is a general discrimination of facelike from nonfacial patterns. A more refined distinction of proper from altered facelike patterns appears at 4 months. By 5 months, differentiations among individual faces are accomplished as long as the faces vary by age or sex (e.g., man from baby, or man from woman). Finally, at 6–7 months distinctions are made among faces of the same age or sex (e.g., one man from another).

Additional examples of the growth of differentiation among categorizable objects over the first year of life may be given, but such elaboration is unnecessary. The point is that infants do categorize and do demonstrate progressively refined distinctions over age among items that children and adults would identify as belonging to various hierarchical levels. Hence, it should be possible to make a direct test of the hypothesis that later categorization on sorting tasks recapitulates initial acquisition, such that acquisition occurs for a basic-level category followed by the acquisition of superordinate and then by subordinate categories.

Primitive Elements. Mervis and Rosch point out that categories may be decomposed into smaller and smaller sets of elements, but that at some point certain sets of elements must be considered "primitive" (i.e., functionally undecomposable). Perhaps a delineation of interrelated sets of features defining a category that should be considered "primitive" can be accomplished by retracing the order in which infants differentiate among elements in a category. Consider the category of faces, for example. We know from the work of Fagan and Singer (1979) that those combinations of features that identify a particular man (e.g., his hair length, eye width, etc.) are not as primitive as those feature combinations that distinguish a man from a woman, because men are distinguished from women at an earlier age (5 months) than one man is distinguished from another (about 7 months). Similarly, the set of features that defines the sex of a face are not as primitive as those defining proper arrangement of facial features, the latter being distinguished at 4 months (Fagan, 1972). Features signaling proper facial arrangement, in turn, are not as primitive as those indicating "facelikeness," that is, the combination of a certain size and number of curved and straight elements in an oval that tend, from birth, to be visually preferred to various other collections of features.

Ultimately, then, the "primitives" of a face include a collection of stimulus characteristics that elicit the neonate's attention (i.e., large elements, numerous elements, many curved contours, and elements of sufficient contrast and separation to be easily detected). Attention to these primitives results in the abstraction of the customary arrangement of the elements by 4 months. Once customary arrangement is encoded, it would appear that feature combinations that define the sex of a face are abstracted and relied on for recognition. My goal, however, is not to give an extensive lesson on early face perception, but rather to illustrate that it should be possible to define the primitive elements of various categories by tracing the order in which infants differentiate among elements in a category over age.

Separable Attributes. Items within a category (or those between a category) may be grouped together (or distinguished from one another) on the basis of particular attributes such as form, color, and size. The ability to combine attributes, when necessary, is basic to the formation of categories. One developmental question raised by Shepp (e.g., Shepp and Swartz, 1976) and noted by Mervis and Rosch (1981) with regard to the nature of attributes is whether or not young children perceive particular combinations of attributes (e.g., form and color) as separable. The question of the origins of the child's ability to distinguish among dimensions (e.g., to know that a red diamond is both red in color and diamond shaped) has typically been approached by observing the behavior of children 4 years or older on discrimination tasks or on sorting problems (e.g., Shepp, 1978). On a discrimination task, for example, the child faced with a red square and a green square may solve the problem by separating color from form and by picking the correct color cue (e.g., red). Alternately, the child could solve the problem by compounding the attributes of form and color and by picking the red square. The problem of distinguishing between component and compound solutions is also present in studies of infant recognition whenever the stimulus used during study also appears on the test. If, for example, the infant devotes more fixation to a red square than to a green square, we might infer that he or she had been attending either to the component dimension of color (red versus green) that he or she sees as separable from form or to the compound dimension of form–color (red square versus green square).

The problem of deciding whether the infant sees form and color as separable dimensions may be solved by controlling conditions so that attention to a compound dimension can be separated from attention to component dimensions. Investigators of discrimination learning solve the problem by preserving or destroying stimulus compounds from trial to trial and by testing for gain or loss in performance. Similarly, Fagan (1977b) tested attention to component or separable dimensions by familiarizing the infant with a form–color compound and then presenting a pair of targets with a familiar and a novel cue along one dimension and the same two novel cues along the other. To test whether the component dimension of color was separable from form and served as a basis for recognition, for example, the infant might be shown a red diamond during study and then tested on the pairing red square versus green square.

Because the only stimultaneous pairing of a novel and a previously exposed cue is the pairing red versus green, a reliable preference for the novel color cue (green) would indicate that color had provided a component solution and that form and color were separable dimensions. In Fagan (1977b), infants at 5 months proved capable of attending to form and color as separable dimensions. Moreover, further tests were made by Fagan (1977b) in which the dimensions of both form and color were allowed to provide a simultaneous basis for recognition (e.g., study a red diamond, then test for recognition by pairing the red diamond with a green square). Such tests were combined with a formal mathematical model to discover that the 5-month infant combines the attributes of form and color in an additive manner.

More recent work by Mundy (1982), employing the same experimental design as Fagan (1977b), has indicated that form and color may not be separable dimensions for the 3-month-old infant. The specification of exactly when particular dimensions are first treated as separable is a subject for further study. The point is, however, that fundamental questions about the nature of attributes such as their separability may be approached in the first few months of life through the study of visual recognition memory.

Summary. Examples have been given of the manner in which the exploration of basic questions posed by students of child and adult categorization can be facilitated by considering the perceptual-cognitive functioning of infants. Additional examples of the interplay of ideas between the fields of infant memory and adult categorization are provided by Strauss (1979), and Cohen and Younger (1981). In effect, the presence of so many theoretical concerns common to students of infant memory and adult categorization should insure the further integration of ideas and data on infant memory into the field of child and adult cognition via the study of categorization.

Discussion

The origins of memory may be studied by observing the infant's visual behavior in the presence of a novel and a previously exposed stimulus. Infants, from birth, are able to remember some of the things they have seen. Tests of infant recognition memory have been employed to chart instances of perceptual development that are of interest to theory and to assess the infant's level of cognitive functioning.

Various phenomena found in studies of adult memory have been demonstrated with infants. The recognition memory of infants, like that of adults, varies with the length of study time allowed prior to recognition testing and with the nature of the distinction to be made between novel and previously exposed targets. Memory, when evidenced, is usually long lasting and is not easily disrupted. Additional memory phenomena common to infants and adults include the effects of encoding and retrieval context on memory, the form of the serial position effect, and variations in performance due to distribution of practice. In the future, explanations of memory phenomena that take into account those abilities common to infants and adults may lead to the specification of a limited set of memory processes fundamental to humans and continuous over age.

The study of infant visual recognition memory may also be employed to provide cogent answers to questions raised by students of categorization. Specifically, tests of memory during infancy may aid in discovering whether the order in which hierarchies of categories were originally formed may be recaptured at a later age by studies of sorting behavior. The specification of the primitive elements in a category and the question of the separability of attributes were also noted as amenable to test through studies of early recognition memory.

In closing, I would like to mention an additional approach to the integration of the areas of infant memory and adult cognition. That approach consists of bringing findings and concepts in each area to bear on the solution of a common theoretical problem. The theoretical problem I have in mind is the explanation of the nature of intelligence. As noted earlier (pp. 9–10), there is some evidence that individual differences in recognition memory during infancy may be predictive of later intellectual functioning. The chief theoretical implication of such a finding is that the growth of intelligence may be seen as continuous. Evidence for the continuity in intelligence raises the question of the basis for such continuity. I would like to suggest that efforts by students of infancy to explain the basis of continuity in intelligence may be linked to current work by cognitive psychologists, such as Jensen (1979), Sternberg (1981), and others, who are seeking to explicate the nature of the general factor in intelligence (g). In other words, I am hypothesizing that the search for the basis of intellectual continuity over age is formally the same as the search for the basis of g and that findings and explanations in each sphere of endeavor will be of mutual benefit.

To understand how the search for the basis of intellectual continuity and the explication of g may combine to allow a more complete explanation of intelligence, it is necessary to sketch out a theory of intelligence. Let us assume, in the same spirit as theorists such as Cattell (1963) and Hebb (1972), that intelligence may be looked at in two ways. The first way is to view intelligence as a small set of basic processes for the acquisition of knowledge, processes that are largely innate, dependent on neural integrity, and continuous with age. The second way is to view intelligence as the body of knowledge that is the cumulative result of the action of the basic processes for acquiring knowledge on the environment to which the person has access. Further, let us adopt the working hypothesis that people vary in the speed with which they execute those basic processes of knowledge acquisition such that acquisition of knowledge proceeds at a more rapid rate and, thus, amount of knowledge cumulates faster for one person than for another. When intelligence tests are administered at a later age, speed of knowledge acquisition may be measured to the extent that new tasks are present and new information is being acquired. But what we are primarily measuring on later intelligence tests is the result of the interaction of speed of knowledge processing with the environment the person has been allowed to process. Given such assumptions, correlations among the subtests of an intelligence scale are primarily due to hypothesized differences in speed of knowledge acquisition either directly (i.e., the rate at which new information is being processed) or indirectly (i.e., the faster processor has acquired more vocabulary knowledge, more knowledge of arithmetic, etc.). Because correlations among subtests are typically taken as the empirical definition of the general factor in intelligence, I am equating variations in g with variations in speed of knowledge acquisition. In effect, what I am suggesting is that there exists a small set of processes for knowledge acquisition that are innate, that underlie g, and that provide the basis for continuity in intellectual functioning during development.

An important step, then, in the explanation of the nature of intelligence would be the measurement and identification of the set of basic processes for knowledge acquisition postulated to underlie g and providing developmental continuity. One way of measuring the output of such processes would be to estimate variations in speed of acquisition of knowledge from individual to individual where the effects of interindividual differences in environment are either held constant or have been minimized. At least three approaches to minimizing environmental influences while measuring speed of acquisition are possible. One is to employ a task so simple that all subjects know how to perform the task. Another is to employ tasks that are novel for all subjects. A third is to test speed of processing at a very early age, before a substantial body of knowledge has been acquired. Each approach is currently in use. Jensen (1979), for example, finds that individual differences in response and in movement speed on simple reaction time tests correlate with measured intelligence. Sternberg (1981) finds a relationship between measured intelligence and performance on novel or "nonentrenched" tasks. Fagan and Singer (1983) summarize the results of a number of studies indicating that early differences in visual recognition memory are correlated with later intelligence. Once measurement of speed of knowledge acquisition has been approached via simple, novel, or early tasks, identification of the basic processes of knowledge acquisition would proceed in two steps. The first would be to construct models and to conduct appropriate tests so that each simple, nonentrenched, or early task might be reduced to its constituent component processes. Once such componential analyses have been carried out, the final step would be to note those components which are invariant over the three kinds of tasks.

To summarize, I have discussed the manner in which research on infant memory and research on the nature of the general factor in intelligence on the part of investigators of adult cognition might be combined to arrive at a more complete explanation of intelligence. Students of adult memory might find such an exercise interesting but of limited relevance for their own theoretical concerns. I would like to suggest that the explanation of the nature of intelligence, as I have outlined the problem, is of direct relevance to a central question in the area of adult memory; that is, How do the specific events we experience become translated into general knowledge (e.g., Brown, 1979)? My suggestion is that the processes by which information in memory is abstracted to form meaning may well be the same processes that form the basis of intelligence. Thus, the pursuit of the laws underlying human memory may ultimately result in resolving the nature of intelligence. It is my hope that the study of infant memory will play an important role in the formulation of the laws of human memory and in the explanation of the nature of intelligence.

In closing, I would like to briefly address an issue raised during the 1982 Erindale Symposium on Infant Memory. The issue is theoretical and has to do with the nature of infant memory. Throughout this chapter I have assumed that the infant, by acting differentially to novel and previously exposed stimuli, is acting *as if* he recognizes what he has seen. In other words I have, in agreement with the majority of students of infant cognition, adopted differential fixation to novel and previously exposed targets as a working definition of infant recognition memory (e.g., see Chapter 2). However, as the reader will learn in studying other chapters in this volume, not everyone is willing to accept differential attention to novel and previously exposed stimuli on the part of the infant as indicating "memory." Some (e.g., Ruff, Chapter 3) are reluctant to attribute memory to the infant because they are concerned with the legitimacy or theoretical utility of the construct of memory *per se*. Others (Lockhart, Chapter 6; Schacter and Moscovitch, Chapter 8) hesitate to impute memory to the infant because they would prefer to credit memory only to beings able to consciously reflect on their own past, that is, beings able to tell the experimenter that they have accomplished such reflection. Lockhart adopts such a position on the basis of historical convention and on philosophical grounds. Schacter and Moscovitch incorporate such a view into a more general theoretical formulation concerning early and later forms of memory and go on to summarize and integrate a great deal of literature pertaining to infant and adult memory into their framework.

My feeling is that a vigorous theoretical discussion about what infants' preferences for novelty actually represent (as raised by Lockhart, Ruff, and Schacter and Moscovitch) is both necessary and timely. Questions about the nature of infant memory serve a heuristic function by directing theoretical activity in the area of infant cognition and by leading us to explore commonalities and differences in the behavior of infants and adults. At the same time, we should not allow the debate over whether novelty preferences really reflect "memory" to obscure the many contributions that have come about from studying such preferences. In the present chapter I have sought to emphasize the fact that the infant's differential attention to novel and previously exposed stimuli has been used to tell us much about early perception and cognition. I have also noted that such findings with infants may be related to current concerns in the general areas of categorization and intelligence. I hope that questions about the nature of infant memory will be placed in a general perspective that recognizes that such questions constitute only one of the many important common issues facing students of infant and adult cognition.

References

Bornstein, M. H. Infants' recognition memory for hue. *Developmental Psychology*, 1976, *12*, 185–191.

Braine, L. G. A new slant on orientation perception. *American Psychologist*, 1978, *33*, 10–22.

Brown, A. L. Theories of memory and the problem of development: Activity, growth and knowledge. In L. S. Cermak & F. I. M. Craik (Eds.), *Levels of processing in human memory*. Hillsdale, N. J.: Erlbaum, 1979.

Caron, A. J. & Caron, R. F. Processing of relational information as an index of infant risk. In S. L. Friedman & M. Sigman (Eds.), *Preterm birth and psychological development*. New York: Academic Press, 1981.

Caron, A. J., Caron R. F., Caldwell, R. C., & Weiss, S. E. Infant perception of the structural properties of the face. *Developmental Psychology*, 1973, *9*, 385–399.

Caron R. F., & Caron A. J. The effects of repeated exposure and stimulus complexity on visual fixation in infants. *Psychonomic Science*, 1968, *10*, 207–208.

Cattell, R. B. Theory of fluid and crystallized intelligence: A critical experiment. *Journal of Educational Psychology*, 1963, *54*, 1–22.

Cohen, L. B. Lags in the cognitive competence of prematurely born infants. In S. L. Friedman & M. Sigman (Eds.), *Preterm birth and psychological development*. New York: Academic Press, 1981.

Cohen, L. B. & Strauss, M. S. Concept acquisition in the human infant. *Child Development*, 1979, *50*, 419–424.

Cohen, L. B., & Younger, B. A. *Perceptual categorization in the infant*. Paper presented at the Eleventh Annual Jean Piaget Symposium, Philadelphia, May 1981.

Cohen, L. B., Gelber, E. R., & Lazar, M. A. Infant habituation and generalization to repeated visual stimulation. *Journal of Experimental Child Psychology*, 1971, *11*, 379–389.

Cohen, L. B., DeLoache, J. S., & Pearl, R. A. An examination of interference effects in infants' memory for faces. *Child Development*, 1977, *48*, 88–96.

Cornell, E. H. Infant's discrimination of photographs of faces following redundant presentations. *Journal of Experimental Child Psychology*, 1974, *18*, 98–106.

Cornell, E. H. Infants' visual attention to pattern arrangement and orientation. *Child Development*, 1975, *46*, 229–232.

Cornell, E. H. Infants' recognition memory, forgetting and savings. *Journal of Experimental Child Psychology*, 1979, *28*, 359–374.

Cornell, E. H. Distributed study facilitates infants' delayed recognition memory. *Memory and Cognition*, 1980, *8*, 539–542.

Cornell, E. H. & Bergstrom, L. I. *Serial position effects in infants' recognition memory*. Paper presented at the Third International Conference on Infant Studies, Austin, March 1982.

Craik, F. I. M. & Lockhart, R. S. Levels of processing: A framework for memory research. *Journal of Verbal Learning and Verbal Behavior*, 1972, *11*, 671–684.

Craik, F. I. M. & Tulving, E. Depth of processing and the retention of words in episodic memory. *Journal of Experimental Psychology*, 1975, *104*, 268–294.

Deloache, J. S., Strauss, M. S., & Maynard, J. Picture perception in infancy. *Infant Behavior and Development*, 1979, *2*, 77–89.

Dirks, J. & Gibson, E. J. Infants' perception of similarity between live people and their photographs. *Child Development*, 1977, *48*, 124–130.

Fagan, J. F. Memory in the infant. *Journal of Experimental Child Psychology*, 1970, *9*, 217–226.

Fagan, J. F. Infants' recognition memory for a series of visual stimuli. *Journal of Experimental Child Psychology*, 1971, *11*, 244–250.

Fagan, J. F. Infants' recognition memory for faces. *Journal of Experimental Child Psychology*, 1972, *14*, 453–476.

Fagan, J. F. Infants' delayed recognition memory and forgetting. *Journal of Experimental Child Psychology*, 1973, *16*, 424–450.

Fagan, J. F. Infant recognition memory: The effects of length of familiarization and type of discrimination task. *Child Development*, 1974, *45*, 351–356.

Fagan, J. F. Infants' recognition of invariant features of faces. *Child Development*, 1976, *47*, 627–638.

Fagan, J. F. Infant recognition memory: Studies in forgetting. *Child Development*, 1977, *48*, 68–78. (a)

Fagan, J. F. An attention model of infant recognition. *Child Development*, 1977, *48*, 345–359. (b)

Fagan, J. F. Facilitation of infants' recognition memory. *Child Development*, 1978, *49*, 1066–1075.

Fagan, J. F. The origins of facial pattern recognition. In M. Bornstein & W. Kessen (Eds.), *Psychological development from infancy*. Hillsdale, N. J.: Erlbaum, 1979.

Fagan, J. F. *Infant memory and the prediction of intelligence*. Paper presented at the Society for Research in Child Development Meeting, Boston, April 4, 1981.

Fagan, J. F. & McGrath, S. K. Infant recognition memory and later intelligence. *Intelligence*, 1981, *5*, 121–130.

Fagan, J. F. & Shepherd, P. A. Infants' perception of face orientation. *Infant Behavior and Development*, 1979, *2*, 227–234.

Fagan, J. F. & Shepherd, P. A. Theoretical issues in the early development of visual perception. In M. Lewis & L. Taft (Eds.), *Developmental disabilities: Theory, assessment, and intervention*. New York: SP Medical and Scientific Books, 1982.

Fagan, J. F. & Singer, L. T. The role of simple feature differences in infants' recognition of faces. *Infant Behavior and Development*, 1979, *2*, 39–45.

Fagan, J. F. & Singer, L. T. Infant recognition memory as a measure of intelligence. In L. P. Lipsitt (Ed.), *Advances in infancy research* (Vol. 2). Norwood, N. J.: Ablex, 1983.

Fagan, J. F., Fantz, R. L., & Miranda, S. B. *Infants' attention to novel stimuli as a function of postnatal and conceptional age*. Paper presented at the Society for Research in Child Development Meeting, Boston, April 4, 1971.

Fantz, R. L. A method for studying early visual development. *Perceptual and Motor Skills*, 1956, *6*, 13–15.

Fantz, R. L. Visual experience in infants: Decreased attention to familiar patterns relative to novel ones. *Science*, 1964, *146*, 668–670.

Fantz, R. L. & Nevis, S. The predictive value of changes in visual preference in early infancy. In J. Hellmuth (Ed.), *The exceptional infant* (Vol. 1). Seattle: Special Child Publications, 1967.

Friedman, S. B. Habituation and recovery of visual response in the alert human newborn. *Journal of Experimental Child Psychology*, 1972, *13*, 339–349.

Friedman, S. B., Bruno, L. A., & Vietze, P. Newborn habituation to visual stimuli: A sex difference in novelty detection. *Journal of Experimental Child Psychology*, 1974, *18*, 242–251.

Gottfried, A. W., Rose, S. A., & Bridger, W. H. Cross-modal transfer in human infants. *Child Development*, 1977, *48*, 118–123.

Gottfried, A. W., Rose, S. A., & Bridger, W. H. Effects of visual, haptic, and manipulatory experiences on infants' visual recognition memory of objects. *Developmental Psychology*, 1978, *14*, 305–312.

Hebb, D. O. *Textbook of psychology* (3rd ed.). Philadelphia: W. B. Saunders, 1972.

Hyde, T. S. & Jenkins, J. J. Differential effects of incidental tasks on the organization of recall of a list of highly associated words. *Journal of Experimental Psychology*, 1969, *82*, 472–481.

Jensen, A. R. g: Outmoded theory or unconquered frontier? *Creative Science and Technology*, 1979, *2*, 16–29.

Lasky, R. E. Length of familiarization and preference for novel and familiar stimuli. *Infant Behavior and Development*, 1980, *3*, 15–28.

Lasky, R. E. & Spiro, D. The processing of tachistoscopically presented visual stimuli by five-month-old infants. *Child Development*, 1980, *51*, 1292–1294.

Lewis, M. & Brooks-Gunn, J. Visual attention at three months as a predictor of cognitive functioning at two years of age. *Intelligence*, 1981, *5*, 131–140.

Lewis, M., Fadel, D., Bartels, B, & Campbell, H. *Infant attention: The effect of familiar and novel visual stimuli as a function of age*. Paper presented at the meeting of the Eastern Psychological Association, New York, April 1966.

Martin, R. M. Effects of familiar and complex stimuli on infant attention. *Developmental Psychology*, 1975, *11*, 178–185.

McCall, R. B., Kennedy, C. B., & Dodds, C. The interfering effects of distracting stimuli on the infant's memory. *Child Development*, 1977, *48*, 79–87.

McGurk, H. The role of object orientation in infant perception. *Journal of Experimental Child Psychology*, 1970, *9*, 363–373.

McGurk, H. Infant discrimination of orientation. *Journal of Experimental Child Psychology*, 1972, *14*, 151–164.

Mervis, C. B. & Crisafi, M. A. Order of acquisition of subordinate-, basic-, and super-ordinate-level categories, *Child Development*, 1982, *53*, 258–266.
Mervis, C. B. & Rosch, E. Categorization of natural objects. *Annual Review of Psychology*, 1981, *32*, 89–115.
Milewski, A. E. Young infants' visual processing of internal and adjacent shapes. *Infant Behavior and Development*, 1978, *1*, 359–371.
Milewski, A. E., & Siqueland, E. R. Discrimination of color and pattern novelty in one-month infants. *Journal of Experimental Child Psychology*, 1975, *19*, 122–136.
Miranda, S. B. & Fantz, R. L. Recognition memory in Down's Syndrome and normal infants. *Child Development*, 1974, *45*, 651–660.
Mundy, P. C. *Encoding processes in infant recognition*. Paper presented at the Third International Conference on Infant Studies, Austin, March 1982.
Nelson, C. A., Morse, P. A., & Leavitt, L. A. Recognition of facial expressions by seven-month-old infants. *Child Development*, 1979, *50*, 1239–1242.
Olson, G. M. Infant recognition memory for briefly presented visual stimuli. *Infant Behavior and Development*, 1979, *2*, 123–134.
Pancratz, C. N. & Cohen, L. B. Recovery of habituation in infants. *Journal of Experimental Child Psychology*, 1970, *9*, 208–216.
Rolfe, S. A. & Day, R. H. Effects of the similarity and dissimilarity between familiarization and test objects on recognition memory in infants following unimodal and bimodal familiarization. *Child Development*, 1981, *52*, 1308–1312.
Rosch, R., Mervis, C. B., Gray, W. D., Johnson, D. M., & Boyes-Braem, P. Basic objects in natural categories. *Cognitive Psychology*, 1976, *8*, 382–439.
Rose, S. A. Enhancing visual recognition memory in preterm infants. *Developmental Psychology*, 1980, *16*, 85–92.
Rose, S. A. Developmental changes in infants' retention of visual stimuli. *Child Development*, 1981, *52*, 227–233.
Rose, S. A., Gottfried, A. W., & Bridger, W. H. Cross-modal transfer in infants: Relationship to prematurity and socioeconomic background. *Developmental Psychology*, 1978, *14*, 643–452.
Ruff, H. A. Infant recognition of the invariant form of objects. *Child Development*, 1978, *49*, 293–306.
Ruff, H. A. Effects of context on infants' responses to novel objects. *Developmental Psychology*, 1981, *17*, 87–89.
Saayman, G., Ames, E., & Moffett, A. Response to novelty as an indicator of visual discrimination in the human infant. *Journal of Experimental Child Psychology*, 1964, *1*, 189–198.
Shepp, B. E. From perceived similarity to dimensional structure: A new hypothesis about perceptual development. In E. Rosch & B. B. Lloyd (Eds.), *Cognition and categorization*. Hillsdale, N. J.: Erlbaum, 1978.
Shepp, B. E. & Swartz, K. B. Selective attention and the processing of integral and non-integral dimensions: A developmental study. *Journal of Experimental Child Psychology*, 1976, *22*, 73–85.
Sigman, M. & Parmalee, A. H. Visual preferences of four-month-old premature and fullterm infants. *Child Development*, 1974, *45*, 959–965.
Siqueland, E. R. & Delucia, C. A. Visual reinforcement of non-nutritive sucking in human infants. *Science*, 1969, *165*, 1144–1146.
Sternberg, R. Intelligence and nonentrenchment. *Journal of Educational Psychology*, 1981, *73*, 1–16.
Strauss, M. S. Abstraction of prototypical information by adults and 10-month-old infants. *Journal of Experimental Psychology: Human Learning and Memory*, 1979, *5*, 618–632.

Strauss, M. S. & Cohen, L. B. *Infant immediate and delayed memory for perceptual dimensions.* Paper presented at the International Conference on Infant Studies, New Haven, Conn., April 1980.

Thomson, D. M. & Tulving, G. Associative encoding and retrieval: Weak and strong cues. *Journal of Experimental Psychology*, 1970, *86*, 255–262.

Topinka, C. V. & Steinberg, B. *Visual recognition memory in 3½ and 7½ month-old infants.* Paper presented at the International Conference on Infant Studies, Providence, R. I., March 1978.

Tulving, E. & Osler, S. Effectiveness of retrieval cues in memory for words. *Journal of Experimental Psychology*, 1968, *77*, 593–601.

Watson, J. S. Perception of object orientation in infants. *Merrill-Palmer Quarterly*, 1966, *12*, 73–94.

Werner, J. S. & Siqueland, E. R. Visual recognition memory in the preterm infant. *Infant Behavior and Development*, 1978, *1*, 79–94.

Wetherford, M. J. & Cohen, L. B. Developmental changes in infant visual preferences for novelty and familiarity. *Child Development*, 1973, *44*, 416–424.

Yarrow, L. J., Klein, R. P., Lomoncao, S., & Morgan, G. A. Cognitive and motivational development in early childhood. In B. X. Friedlander, G. M. Sterritt, & G. E. Kirk (Eds.), *Exceptional infant* (Vol. 3). New York: Brunner/Mazel, 1975.

CHAPTER 2

The Development of Infant Memory

Gary M. Olson

Department of Psychology
University of Michigan
Ann Arbor, Michigan

and

Mark S. Strauss

Department of Psychology
University of Pittsburgh
Pittsburgh, Pennsylvania

The concept of memory has undergone a profound change in this century. In the late nineteenth century Ebbinghaus (1885/1964), the first experimentalist to study memory systematically, offered a view of memory that dominated research and theory until recently. His view had several components. First, he thought of memory as an isolable system, capable of being understood independent of other aspects of mind, such as perception, thought, and knowledge. This in part motivated his use of the nonsense syllable. He wanted an experimental unit that was devoid of meaning, which he clearly viewed as a complication for the study of memory. Second, he believed that memory could be understood in mechanistic terms. The formation of associations in memory resulted primarily from repeated experience of items in contiguity. This view reflected the atomistic view of mind that characterized the philosophical and physiological

Preparation of this chapter was supported by a Research Career Development Award (HD 00169) and a research grant (HD 10486) from the National Institute of Child Health and Human Development to Gary M. Olson, and a research grant from the Buhl Foundation to Mark S. Strauss.

roots from which modern experimental psychology originated (see Boring, 1950, for details). Third, his goal was to establish quantitative laws that described the regularities by which associations were acquired and forgotten. His pioneering research provided the first reports of such quantitative relationships, establishing a model for research on memory for much of the following century.

Little research on memory *per se* took place during the first half of the twentieth century. However, when its study revived in the 1950s and 1960s, it was Ebbinghaus's view that dominated, even though other important views had been offered by Bartlett (1932) and the Gestalt psychologists (e.g., Koffka, 1935; Kohler, 1940, 1947). The typical study of memory during this period had adult human subjects learn nonsense syllables in a paired associate task. Memory was viewed as a storehouse—maybe several storehouses—for "items," which accrued "strength" from frequency of experience and lost "strength" from competing "items" or from the passage of time. Theories of memory focused on the functional relations between independent variables like frequency, recency, and item similarity, and dependent variables like probability correct. One major achievement of this midcentury research was a series of mathematical and computer models of memory in the late 1960s (see Atkinson, Bower, & Crothers, 1965; Atkinson & Shiffrin, 1968; Feigenbaum, 1963; Hintzman, 1968) that provided the kinds of quantitative predictions that would have pleased Ebbinghaus.

The cognitive revolution that began in the late 1960s and proceeded throughout the 1970s produced a new modal view of memory, though it was quite similar to the earlier views of Bartlett, the Gestalt psychologists, and even Piaget. The study of the free recall of lists of words, of mental imagery and mnemonics, and of sentence memory suggested to researchers that Ebbinghaus's strategy of trying to "simplify" the study of memory through the use of nonsense syllables was misguided. A paper by Prytulak (1971) was symptomatic of the changed view. He studied how subjects actually learn nonsense syllables and documented in detail the effort subjects go through to give the syllables meaning. Basically, they make words or sentences out of them, even when they have been given instructions just to learn them. In the new view, memory was inextricably linked to the effort to create meaning. The learner attempts to construct something meaningful of his or her experiences. Memory was no longer viewed as a separate faculty but as one facet of cognition in general. The study of memory as a separate faculty virtually disappeared and was replaced by the study of organizational factors, imagery, comprehension, and knowledge structures.

Much research on infant memory has been carried out within the memory-as-a-separate-faculty tradition. Not surprisingly, this is beginning to change, in part because the changes within general cognitive psychology have begun to influence infant researchers. But part of the change has come from the increased study of infants in the 10- to 24-month-old range. The change in point of view is important. A much broader range of phenomena is now viewed as relevant to the early development of memory. Most of the early work focused on recognition memory as tapped by habituation tasks, but now investigators are examining object search, imitation, and a broad range of naturalistic behaviors that are indicative of memory. These studies are already enriching our view of the infant's capacities and should provide better continuity between infant data and data collected from preschool children.

A major thesis of this chapter, however, is that the contemporary, schema-based view of memory is appropriate only for the older infant. In essence, we agree with Piaget's argument that memory abilities develop gradually during infancy (Piaget, 1952, 1954; Piaget & Inhelder, 1973). The newborn has rudimentary adaptive skills and, lacking much knowledge of the world, can scarcely be said to engage in schema-driven processing of inputs. Those memory abilities that exist are highly constrained by neurological immaturity. During the first 6 months, there is substantial maturation of the nervous system, and the constraints on information processing become much less severe. Further, the infant begins to accumulate world knowledge that affects learning and memory. It makes sense to characterize the infant's abilities in terms of the modern view of memory during the second half-year of life, but not substantially earlier.

A major symptom of the transition is the emergence of categorization skills. Indeed, these skills may have a causal role, in that they make possible an economical and organized store of knowledge that in turn facilitates active, schema-based processing. Categorization is a complex skill, and infant researchers have only recently begun to investigate it. But, as we shall see later in this chapter, there is no doubt that these skills emerge during the second half of the first year.

Anyone who has followed the recent infant research literature knows that a variety of claims have been made about the information processing skills of very young infants that would appear to conflict with the view we have presented. However, it is important to examine the evidence closely. What exactly does the performance observed at different ages imply? We believe that a close examination of the data along with careful conceptual analysis supports our case. Since we are claiming that the emergence of categorization skills during the first year provides an important transitional link between the early, limited information-processing skills of the very young infant and the active, schema-based processing of the older one, we will discuss the emergence of categorization skills quite carefully to illustrate what we mean.

The Neonatal Period and the First Few Months

The central nervous system of the newborn infant is very immature. Considerable myelinization and dendritic branching of the cortex occur postnatally, and these developments have important consequences for perceptual and cognitive processing. Yet despite these physiological limitations, the newborn does process environmental information. Haith (1980) and others have documented the nature of newborn eye fixations, and there is little doubt that the newborn is examining the world in a systematic fashion. Although conditioning is very difficult to demonstrate in the newborn (e.g., Sameroff & Cavanagh, 1979), evidence of classical conditioning is apparent in even the 2- to 3-day-old infant who quickly learns to suck at the sight of a bottle (e.g., Piaget, 1954). Further evidence of memory comes from demonstrations of habituation in both experimental contexts (e.g., Friedman, 1972a, 1972b, 1975; Friedman, Bruno, & Vietze, 1974; Friedman & Carpenter, 1971; Friedman, Carpenter, & Nagy, 1970; Friedman, Nagy, & Carpenter, 1970; Slater, Morison, & Rose, in press) and in standard newborn tests like the Neonatal Behavioral Assessment Scale (Brazelton, 1973).

But what is the nature of these early information-processing skills? Are they at all comparable to the types of learning and memory abilities found in the older infant? The answers to these questions reflect one's conception of learning and memory. Broadly defined, memory is demonstrated when any type of past environmental information affects the organism's current behavior. By this definition, a single neuron that decreases its firing rate as a result of continued stimulation could be considered to possess a type of memory. This minimal definition of memory is clearly satisfied in the newborn.

However, there is a continuum of learning and memory abilities, ranging from adaptively modified reflexes to the active, schema-based systems that are characterized by contemporary theories of memory. Our claim is that the newborn is much closer to the former end of this continuum. As stated previously, the human central nervous system is not very mature at birth. Although most of the subcortical systems of the brain are fully developed, there are extensive immaturities in the sensory, motor, and especially nonspecific associational areas of the cortex (Conel, 1939). The rate of growth in brain size is maximal at birth (Conel, 1939), and considerable myelinization occurs in the major sensory and motor areas during the early months (Dodgson, 1962). The reflexes that characterize the newborn's behavior gradually disappear during this period and are replaced by more focused, organized, and voluntary behavior. Sleep cycles become more regular, and prolonged periods of alertness gradually emerge (Parmelee, 1974; Parmelee & Stern, 1972). Visual scanning matures and is no longer confined mainly to local contours (Salapatek, 1975). The infant tends to spend more time looking at complex as opposed to simple visual figures, mainly because such figures can now be seen clearly, due to maturation of the visual system (e.g., Banks & Salapatek, 1981). All studies of sensory and perceptual development show marked advances over the first few months (see reviews by Aslin, Pisoni, & Jusczyk, 1983; Salapatek & Banks, 1983). Motor skills are also more advanced: head and eye movements exhibit much better control, and reaching and grasping abilities emerge that are of enormous significance for information processing.

These early constraints must be given careful consideration when interpreting the behaviors of the newborn. For example, in the late 1950s and early 1960s, there were a number of studies by Fantz and others of infant preferences for visual patterns (see review by Olson & Sherman, 1983). These newborn "preferences" were originally interpreted as evidence that even the neonate could store a central representation of a stimulus and that these attentional biases were cognitive in nature, perhaps quite similar to the voluntary shifts of focal attention that are basic to adult processes. More recent research, however, has suggested a very different interpretation. Several researchers (e.g., Banks & Salapatek, 1981; Bronson, 1974, 1982; Fantz, Fagan, & Miranda, 1975; Haith, 1980; Karmel & Maisel, 1975) have shown that these early preferences are better interpreted as manifestations of the infant's developing sensory abilities and the degree of cortical excitation that is generated by an individual stimulus. Similar "lower order" explanations must also be considered when interpreting the newborn's learning and memory abilities.

Consider, for example the newborn's capacity to be conditioned. Although the neonate can be classically conditioned under some conditions (Fitzgerald & Brackbill, 1976; Sameroff & Cavanagh, 1979), there is no strong evidence of operant conditioning with neonates. Even though he did not use conditioning terminology, Piaget (1954) felt this represented an important distinction between the Stage 1 and Stage 2 infant. Viewing the newborn as a reflex-driven organism, Piaget believed that newborns are not capable of "true learning" and that true learning and accommodative behavior did not emerge until the second sensorimotor stage at around 3 months of age. Indeed, he used the term recognitory *assimilation* (not accommodation) to describe the newborn's ability to learn to suck in the presence of a bottle and not other irrelevant types of stimuli.

Piaget did not consider modifications of behaviors like sucking as evidence of true learning or accommodation. He felt this type of learning was always associated with an innate reflex and that the learning itself was innate and reflexive in nature. He believed that the types of learning that occur during the neonatal period are limited to modifications of preexisting innate reflexes. Thus, although these modifications can be labeled as a type of learning, they are very limited and neither voluntary nor very cognitive in nature.

Similarly, the processes that underlie the newborn's ability to habituate to a repeatedly presented visual or auditory stimulus must be carefully evaluated with respect to the known neural limitations of the newborn. Most current models of habituation (e.g., Cohen & Gelber, 1975, Lewis, 1971; Olson, 1976) assume that during the course of habituation the infant is gradually encoding a central representation of the stimulus. The infant's gradually decreasing looking times are assumed to result from "attentional boredom" of the old stimulus. The recovery in looking time to a novel stimulus is assumed to reflect the infant's ability to compare the novel stimulus to some centrally stored representation of the old stimulus.

Recently, Dannemiller and Banks (1983) have argued that though such a cognitive-oriented model may be appropriate for older infants (past 3–4 months of age), a sensory adaption model may be more appropriate for explaining habituation in the young, neurologically immature infant. Any stimulus that can be detected by the visual system will result in the stimulation of a selective set of feature detectors. Repeated presentations of a stimulus will result in a decrease in responsivity for the appropriately sensitive neurons (Hubel & Wiesel, 1959, 1962). Upon presentation of a novel pattern, other sensory channels will be stimulated and there will be an increase in visual fixation. Such a model could account for habituation in a cortically immature infant.

How does one separate a sensory adaption model from a more cognitively based model of habituation? Dannemiller and Banks (1983) list four types of findings that would tend to support a cognitive interpretation and disconfirm a more sensory based explanation: (1) generalization of habituation over long time periods, such as hours or days (e.g., Fagan, 1973); (2) generalization of habituation across stimuli whose invariant features are relatively abstract (e.g., Cohen & Strauss, 1979; Gibson, Owsley, & Johnston, 1978); (3) habituation or a novelty preference after a few brief presentations of a stimulus (e.g., Fagan, 1974; Olson, 1979); (4) recovery to a stimulus that is *less* intense than the familiar stimulus. Although the habituation studies that have been conducted with older infants tend to meet the above qualifications and thus tend to be inconsistent with a sensory adaption model, this is not true of the newborn habituation studies (see Olson & Sherman, 1983, for details). This suggests that a sensory adaption model is the more parsimonious explanation of newborn habituation.

Elaboration of Basic Perceptual and Memory Processes

The period from 3–7 months is characterized by elaboration of the infant's basic information-processing skills. This is the period for which the greatest amount of research exists, and since Olson and Sherman (1983) have recently reviewed this work in detail, we will present only a summary of the highlights of this transitional period here. The degree of physiological maturation that so limited the infant during the early months now provides the infant with the foundational skills to become an increasingly active information processor. The infant is curious about the world, is learning and remembering much about it, and is highly motivated to explore and learn. Attention is both controlled and actively exploratory. Acquisition is facile, and information can be retained over very long intervals. The knowledge base has become substantial enough for there to be effects of knowledge on the encoding and representation of new information. Motor skills have matured enough for the infant to be a much more active participant in the exploration of the world. Smiling and other facial expressions have emerged to make the infant an active social partner, a step of major significance for learning and memory. By the end of this period, the infant has in place the skills for a series of major achievements in cognitive and social development that will begin in the second half of the first year.

There is continuing physiological maturation during this period, but it is not nearly as dramatic as over the first few months. In many sensory and perceptual skills the infant of this period approaches adult levels of competence (see Aslin *et al.*, 1983; Salapatek & Banks, 1983). Learning and memory skills are robust and impressive. Infants show the ability to learn on the basis of only a few seconds of experience (Fagan, 1974; Olson, 1979), and readily show long-term retention of much that they have learned (Fagan, 1973). Although the younger infant can only readily show memory for bold patterns and sharp contrasts between test alternatives, the infant of 6–7 months shows a broad range of encoding skills that include recognition of details of patterns and subtle aspects of stimuli (Olson, 1976). Further, knowledge begins to have a role in learning and memory. It is well known from studies of adult cognition that knowledge has important effects on the perception and retention of experience. For example, highly skilled players of games like chess or go retain more information from a meaningful board pattern than do less skilled ones, even though level of skill does not affect memory performance from meaningless board configurations (Chase & Simon, 1973; Reitman, 1976). The superior knowledge of the expert leads to quicker and more effective encoding of meaningful patterns. Since the infant is learning an enormous amount about the world, it seems quite likely that the older infants would have an advantage relative to the younger infant similar to that enjoyed by the expert in these adult studies. Fagan's (1972) studies of infant face recognition suggest this is true. He presented 6-month-old infants with a right-side-up face and found they could discriminate this familiar face from a novel right-side-up face. However, when he presented the same face upside down for the same familiarization period, infants of the same age could not discriminate this from a novel upside-down face. Presumably the infant's knowledge of faces makes the encoding of the right-side-up stimulus easier than encoding the same stimulus when it is presented upside down. These effects have not been investigated developmentally, but since it is already clear that there are developmental shifts in infants' knowledge of faces (Olson, 1976, 1981), this seems like a rich domain in which to examine the effects of knowledge on recognition memory.

In sum, during these middle months of the first year the criteria suggested by Dannemiller and Banks (1983) to distinguish cognitive from sensory accounts of infant memory behavior come to be satisfied. These changes make possible the emergence of active, schema-based processing, which we trace in the next section.

The Emergence of Active, Schema-Driven Processing

The first 7 months produce enormous change in basic information-processing skills. Sensory and perceptual skills become much more refined. The disorganization of the newborn's states disappears, and by 7 months the infant has substantial periods of alertness. Exploration of the world and active acquisition of knowledge characterize the 7-month-old. Acquisition skills are excellent—information can be extracted and stored on the basis of limited experience. Retention is also good—information can readily be retained over periods of days and weeks, even on the basis of modest amounts of experience.

During the second half of the first year, these basic skills are put to use in several major developments. First, there is extensive growth of the knowledge base. The infant learns a large amount about his or her world and organizes this knowledge in systematic, even if still infantile, ways. The infant's current knowledge about the world will dominate new learning. Second, skills of abstraction and classification develop. The infant develops the ability to group and classify entities of his or her experience in useful ways. Classification skills play a major role in the emergence of the cognitive skill that will eventually signal the transition out of infancy: language. Further, they are central to the development of the schemata that will come to dominate memory processes. Third, the foundations of symbolic thought begin to appear in functional and symbolic play, imitation, and social interaction.

The most important development during this period is the emergence of categorization skills. The classic studies of learning and memory using shifts of attention focused on memory for specific items. Thus, in a typical infant habituation experiment, a single stimulus is presented repeatedly, and recovery of habituation is examined by presenting another specific stimulus. Although successful habituation–dishabituation behavior meant that the infant had recognized some commonality across a series of separate trials and thus had abstracted information from the temporally and contextually varying particulars of individual trials, the core experience— the to-be-remembered stimulus—was at least nominally the same. Therefore, these studies examined *recognition of recurrence,* that is, recognition that a specific pattern is one that was experienced before. A new type of study appeared during the late 1970s: studies that examined *recognition of class or category membership.* In these studies infants are presented with a variety of stimuli drawn from a class or category that is specified by the experimenter. The recognition test is a test for generalization: test trials consist of presenting novel instances from the class or category used during familiarization and novel instances from a different category. Assuming appropriate controls have been used, greater attention to the stimuli from the new category implies that the infants noticed the abstract properties shared by the category members during familiarization. Upon noticing this same property in the novel within-category item on the test, this "novel" item is regarded as less novel than the outside-category test item, leading to preferential looking toward the outside-category stimulus.

There are many important conceptual and methodological issues pertaining to experiments of this type. To facilitate our discussion, we will present an example of a categorization study so we can tie our points to a concrete case. In the subsequent discussion we will take up issues of design, control, and interpretation. Our example is a study by Cohen and Strauss (1979) on the ability of 18- to 30-week-old infants to abstract the features shared by different photographs of faces. In one experimental condition, infants received a photograph of a different female face on each habituation trial. In a second condition, infants saw varying poses of the same female on each trial. After the infants had decreased their looking, they were given two test trials, one with a familiar female and another with a totally novel female. The results indicated that the oldest infants had abstracted the relevant categorical information. In the first condition, they generalized their looking to both test stimuli. In contrast, infants in the second condition generalized their looking to the familiar female but dishabituated to the novel female. This ability to abstract categorical information was not demonstrated by any of the younger infants.

What are studies of this type about? The first issue is the definition of a class or category. A class or category is a mental representation of the common elements of a set of distinct experiences *that are known to be distinct by the infant*. Distinct events whose differences are not noticed because of sensory or perceptual limitations or incomplete encoding do not produce category knowledge. The differences among the items in a class or category must be *noticed but ignored* by the infant in the context of the experiment.

Second, does the typical categorization experiment teach the infants the category or provide an opportunity for the infants to manifest category knowledge they already bring to the experiment? It seems improbable that Cohen and Strauss (1979) taught the infants in their studies the characteristics of faces. More likely, the infants came to the experiment with knowledge of them and exhibited it under the conditions of the tasks. Category learning of this type is probably an extended process, based on long-term learning rather than a small number of trials in the laboratory. But nothing in this experiment or any others like it contain evidence to support this supposition. The distinction between category learning and category recognition is an important one, and it would be useful to see proposals for how to differentiate the two.

There is a special reason why this issue is so important. Essentially all the studies of infant categorization using natural categories have considered basic level categories (e.g., chairs) as opposed to superordinate level ones (e.g., furniture). This is logical, since Rosch, Mervis, Gray, Johnson and Boyes-Braem (1976) argued that basic level categories are learned first because they represent the level at which most members look like each other and have clusters of correlated attributes. This presents a dilemma for infant research, however. Because basic level exemplars are so similar to each other, infants in a habituation study *may* be able to abstract common perceptual features during the habituation trials and thus show appropriate generalization on test trials even though they have no prior knowledge of the category from the real world. In other words, it is not known if the infants are actually making these categorical judgments from their daily interactions with basic categories or whether they are learning these categories in the experimental session.

Third, the perceptual knowledge displayed in a typical categorization experiment should not be thought of as concept knowledge. Concepts embody many types of knowledge, of which perceptual knowledge is only one. For instance, the concept of a face, of person, or of number is not exhausted by the perceptual knowledge that underlies the abilities infants have to notice categorizations built into experimental designs in recent studies. The perceptual knowledge is an important constituent of *some* concepts. These studies should properly be thought of as studies on the use of knowledge about perceptual categories. Otherwise misleading claims about infant abilities can result when terms like *concept* are thrown around too loosely.

A good example of such loose usage from recent research is the concept of number. Strauss and Curtis (1981), and Starkey and Cooper (1980) have shown that preverbal infants can attend to the numerosity of perceptual displays, at least for small numbers. Consider the Strauss and Curtis (1981) study. The question they addressed was whether or not 10- to 12-month-old infants are able to discriminate stimuli that differ only in their numerosity. They presented infants with a series of familiarization trials in which each trial contained the same number of items. In one condition, the infants saw different items (e.g., dogs, houses) in different sizes and positions on each trial (heterogeneous condition). In another (homogeneous condition), the same item type (e.g., dogs) was presented on each trial, with the size and position varied. But in both conditions the *number* of items presented on each trial was constant. Different infants were familiarized with 2, 3, 4, or 5 items per trial. Following habituation, four test trials were presented, two with the same numerosity as in the familiarization trials and two with either $N + 1$ or $N - 1$ items. Different groups were tested on the 2 versus 3, 3 versus 4, and 4 versus 5 discriminations. For the 2 versus 3 discrimination, all infants were able to make the discrimination regardless of the familiarization condition (homogeneous vs. heterogeneous). In the 4 versus 5 discrimination, no infants showed differential attention on the test trials. An interaction of familiarization and sex occurred for the 3 versus 4 contrast. Females in the homogeneous and males in the heterogeneous conditions discriminated 3 from 4. The study by Starkey and Cooper (1980) reported similar results for younger infants (4–6 months).

What do these results mean? Although these studies, along with other more recent ones, show that infants can appreciate certain numerical properties of perceptual displays, this is not a demonstration that infants have a concept of number or of any particular number. It is unlikely that the infants understand the conceptual significance or meaning of a specific quantity. For example, they probably do not understand that a particular quantity (e.g., 2) is a concept in and of itself, and that there is a conceptual equivalence among pairs of any item. They probably do not understand the interval properties of a number like 2. For instance, the difference between 3 and 5 is the same as the difference between 2 and 4. Nor are they likely to understand that 2 lies between 1 and 3. In short, the perceptual classification skills demonstrated by infants in these studies are best thought of as "protonumerical" skills (see Strauss & Curtis, in press), which form a foundation upon which the formal counting system is later built. Put differently, the *concept* of number implies much more than the perceptual grouping skills demonstrated in the experiments, and thus it is misleading to attribute such a concept to the infant. The same holds true in other domains that have been investigated.

What are the implications of these issues for categorization experiments? First, the precise nature of the category being investigated must be explicated so the types of controls to be run are clear. In particular, the relevant and irrelevant perceptual features for any particular category must be explicitly defined. In the Strauss and Curtis (1981) and Starkey and Cooper (1980) studies, the investigators wanted to examine the infant's conception of numerosity. They wanted to have the numerosity of their displays constant across familiarization trials, but irrelevant features that might also attract the infant's attention had to be controlled. Item identity, item size, item orientation, and the configuration of items in the display are all irrelevant features. These irrelevant features were varied from trial to trial so that the infants' test behavior could not be based on these features. These issues are very tricky, and presumably there will be continuing debate among investigators interested in perceptual categorization about the proper definition and control of irrelevant and relevant features in particular experiments.

Second, there must be evidence that the infants can tell the different exemplars of the category apart. Few existing studies have coped with this issue satisfactorily. Some of the earliest studies that suggested infants were capable of displaying categorical knowledge in attentional experiments (e.g., Cornell, 1974; McGurk, 1972) did not address this issue at all. Some more recent studies (e.g., Cohen & Strauss, 1979; Fagan, 1976) showed that infants at the age tested could discriminate the stimuli used in the categorization experiment, but they did not assess whether they in fact could do so *under the condition of presentation used in the categorization experiment itself*. In a recent study, Sherman (1980) directly addressed this issue. She used a subset of the face stimuli from Strauss's (1979) study, but employed a familiarization procedure that required the infant to demonstrate discrimination between successive items as they were presented for familiarization. Her procedure guaranteed that the infants could discriminate all the category exemplars under the conditions used in the category study. She found evidence of categorization at 10 months, though the pattern of results regarding the infant's representation of the central tendency of the category was somewhat different than that reported by Strauss (1979). Although there were some other differences between these two studies, Sherman's findings suggest that the kinds of categorization behavior one finds in infants may be influenced by the extent to which one has guaranteed that the infants have discriminated the category exemplars *in the category experiment itself*. The criterion used in the Sherman (1980) study is quite stringent. In adult experiments, the subjects often know that the stimuli are different from trial to trial but cannot discriminate those they have seen from novel members of the same category (e.g., Posner & Keele, 1968, 1970). Knowing that the items are different is a more appropriate prerequisite for categorization in the sense we mean than remembering the specific instances. Yet testing for memory of specific instances is the most direct way of testing whether infants can tell the items apart. But requiring memory for specific instances may affect the way in which categorization occurs.

The infant's ability to recognize categories of perceptual stimuli has been investigated in a number of particular domains in the 6- to 12-month period: shape independent of specific orientation (McGurk, 1972), gender of pictures of faces (Cohen & Strauss, 1979; Cornell, 1974; Fagan, 1976), same face independent of pose (Cohen & Strauss, 1979; Fagan, 1976), the form of objects independent of size, color, and orientation (Ruff, 1978), faces generated from a common pool of features versus faces having totally novel features (Sherman, 1980; Strauss, 1979), types of motion (Gibson, Owsley, & Johnston, 1978), toys representing letters, men, animals, foods, furniture, and vehicles (Revelle, 1982; Ross, 1980), and numerosity (Starkey & Cooper, 1980; Strauss & Curtis, 1981). Strauss (1979) and Sherman (1980) investigated not just whether categorization occurs but also the nature of the representation of categories, focusing on the question of prototypes or the representation of the central tendency of a category. This is an important question that is at the heart of general issues of the nature of categorization (cf. Smith & Medin, 1981). Revelle (1982) studied a range of categories that varied in their perceptual similarity and found evidence in 9–11-month-old infants of categorization at the adult basic level and at a slightly more abstract level, but none at the most superordinate or the most subordinate levels she examined. The evidence that real-world categories like furniture, animals, and foods emerge toward the end of this period (Ross, 1980) is important. These are the kinds of categories that will be labeled by the words the child acquires in its native language. Indeed, there have been several recent experiments that have studied this link. Oviatt (1980) and Thomas, Campos, Shucard, Ramsay, and Shucard (1981) studied the tendency of infants to turn toward pictures of objects that were named. They found that infants were able to look longer at pictures or objects that are named, providing evidence of the emerging link between perceptual categories and the early stages of language acquisition.

Perceptual categorization clearly emerges during the 6- to 12-month period. Many results support this conclusion, including the most stringent tests (e.g., Sherman, 1980). So far the question of whether categorization occurs earlier than 6 months is indeterminate. Studies conducted with younger infants have not examined whether the familiarization stimuli could be discriminated (e.g., Cornell, 1974; Gibson et al., 1978). It seems probable that some form of categorization skill is present prior to 6 months, but so far this has not been identified in appropriately controlled experiments. More importantly, it is necessary to specify quite carefully exactly what kinds of categories infants at different ages can recognize and under what conditions they can do so. Merely finding any example of categorization behavior at a particular age is insufficient for studying development.

The ability to classify or categorize experiences is basic to intelligence. It provides the basis for an organizational framework for memory, important both for remembering and for language. Categorization also provides what Rosch (1978) called *cognitive economy*. The ability to form central representations, to represent information from a variety of stimuli in a summary fashion, significantly reduces memory load. This ability may be especially important to the infant, who is constantly being confronted with novel information. The ability to categorize provides the transitional skill that allows the infant to become the active, schema-driven information processor that is described by contemporary theories of memory.

There are other major developments in late infancy that constitute further evidence of the emergence of active, schema-based processing: the growth of symbolic representations, the development of recall abilities, and the development of imitation abilities. All of these are significantly related to the major overriding development that is occurring during the second year, the emergence of language. One of the things that makes the early months of infancy so interesting is that this important influence is missing. But starting late in the first year and continuing throughout the second year, language appears, signaling the end of infancy and marking a deep change in the nature of cognition.

Piaget's characterization of sensorimotor intelligence is a description of mental life without language or symbolic thought. Perceptions and actions are the dominant forms of internal processes. Piaget claimed strongly that in the absence of symbolic representations objects and events cannot be thought about or recalled. The transition from sensorimotor intelligence to preoperational thought at around 2 years is signaled by several significant achievements. One is the appearance of language. In addition, symbolic play, deferred or delayed imitation, and a fully elaborated object concept also mark the transition. The key feature among these latter phenomena is the ability to represent an absent object or event, which according to Piaget requires symbolic thought. Mandler (1983) recently provided an excellent discussion of the emergence of symbolic thought, and we will not duplicate her review here. As she summarizes, there is a growing body of research that indicates that symbolic thought develops earlier than Piaget had thought. He had put this achievement in the 18–24 month period, whereas the work Mandler reviews suggests symbolic thought may be present at around 12 months. However, regardless of the exact age, the appearance of symbolic thought is the dominant cognitive achievement of the second year.

Recognition and recall are two basic forms of memory performance. In recognition, the to-be-remembered item is presented to the person, and we look for some indication of familiarity in his or her behavior. In recall, however, the to-be-remembered item is to be produced by the person in response to the experimenter's cue. Unfortunately, these operational descriptions of recall and recognition are too narrow. By this characterization of recall, such tasks as classical, and operant conditioning would qualify as instances of recall. But these tasks require quite different cognitive skills than the act of recalling a word list or a prior experience. It is difficult to pin down what the difference is. Voluntariness is one candidate difference. A classically conditioned response occurs automatically, and the traditional view of operant conditioning is that it occurs without conscious awareness (Dulany, 1968). But these begin to be theoretical distinctions, and exactly how they are to be operationalized is difficult to specify (Dulany, 1968).

What might count as evidence of recall in the infant? Neither classical nor operant conditioning represent recall in the sense intended by Piaget or, more recently, by Mandler (1983). But there are other behaviors that seem more probable. Ashmead and Perlmutter (1980) had parents of infants keep diaries of events they observed that indicated memory for past events on the part of their children. There were ample indications of recall-like activities in the infants, all of whom were less than a year old. Most of the parents reported incidents in which their infant searched for a hidden object at a known location, including looking for objects in a location where the infant had seen it only once. Huttenlocher (1974) described children of roughly 1 year of age locating named objects when they were not in sight. Indeed, searching for hidden objects, especially in the typical Piagetian object search task, is a particularly good indicator of recall-like abilities. Sophian (1980) has reviewed a number of such studies from this perspective.

Another achievement that requires recall-like processes is imitation. It is scarcely surprising that Piaget linked the development of recall and of symbolic thought more generally with the appearance of deferred or delayed imitation. Piaget claimed in his studies of his own children that this ability did not appear until Stage 6, at roughly 18–24 months. Unfortunately, there is almost no research on deferred imitation. McCall,

Parke, and Kavanaugh (1977) studied the development of imitation in infants ranging from 12–36 months. A model performed actions with various objects, and the infant was given an opportunity to imitate the action. The youngest infants in their study showed little evidence of imitation when the test occurred 24 hours after the original modeling, but by 24 months of age deferred imitation was readily observed, consistent with Piaget. Interestingly, in one study the 24-month-olds showed just as much deferred imitation when their first opportunity to imitate occurred 24 hours after modeling as when they had had an immediate opportunity to model in addition to the 24-hour test. Thus, deferred imitation, to the extent that it counts as recall, is readily evident by the end of the second year. But this may be too conservative a test. McCall *et al.* gave their subjects a large number of actions to imitate, and they may have created a burdensome memory load for them. Tests of deferred imitation with simpler memory demands need to be conducted.

Of course, perhaps *the* major development throughout the second year is the acquisition of knowledge about the physical and social world. The infant's growing knowledge base has scarcely been investigated, but it is the key to the development of schema-based processing. The techniques that have been developed to study categorization and recall should allow investigators to provide a detailed portrait of the development of the knowledge base. This in turn can be related to the processes of acquisition and retention.

Conclusions

The contemporary, schema-based view of memory processes is applicable to infant memory, but only for the older infant of about 6 to 7 months. During the first half year, the infant's abilities to learn and remember are constrained by neurological immaturity and lack of world knowledge. The emergence of the ability to categorize perceptual experiences during the second half of the first year is a key symptom of the transition to an information processor more like the preschool child. Abstract, organized knowledge is the basis for the schemata that will come to dominate learning and memory. It is scarcely coincidental that concurrent with the ability to categorize, a host of memory-related cognitive skills should flourish: imitation, symbolic play, attachments, and recall. We do not mean to downplay the importance of the learning and memory skills present in the first six months. They are real and substantial (see Olson & Sherman, 1983). Our main point is that they are *different* from the skills of the older infant, and that the conceptual portrait of learning and memory contained in contemporary cognitive psychology is inappropriate for the earliest months of infancy. We would not want to go so far as to say the Ebbinghaus faculty view of memory is correct for the young infant. But the neurological and cognitive limitations of the early months make learning and memory quite different from what they will be by the end of the first year.

References

Ashmead, D. H., & Perlmutter, J. Infant memory in everyday life. In M. Perlmutter (Ed.), *New directions for child development: Children's memory* (Vol. 10). San Francisco: Jossey-Bass, 1980.

Aslin, R. N., Pisoni, D. B., & Jusczyk, P. W. Auditory development and speech perception in infancy. In M. M. Haith & J. J. Campos (Eds.), *Manual of child psychology: Vol. 2. Infancy and developmental psychobiology*. New York: Wiley, 1983.

Atkinson, R. C., & Shiffrin, R. M. Human memory: A proposed system and its control processes. In G. H. Bower & J. T. Spence (Eds.), *The psychology of learning and motivation* (Vol. 2). New York: Academic Press, 1968.

Atkinson, R. C., Bower, G. H., & Crothers, E. J. *An introduction to mathematical learning theory*. New York: Wiley, 1965.

Banks, M. S., & Salapatek, P. Infant pattern vision: A new approach based on the contrast sensitivity function. *Journal of Experimental Child Psychology*, 1981, *31*, 1–45.

Bartlett, F. C. *Remembering*. New York: Cambridge University Press, 1932.

Boring, E. G. *A history of experimental psychology*. New York: Appleton-Century-Crofts, 1950.

Brazelton, T. B. *Neonatal behavioral assessment scale*. Philadelphia: J. B. Lippincott, 1973.

Bronson, G. The postnatal growth of visual capacity. *Child Development*, 1974, *45*, 873–890.

Bronson, G. *The scanning patterns of human infants: Implications for visual learning*. Norwood, N.J.: Ablex, 1982.

Chase, W. G., & Simon, H. A. Perception in chess. *Cognitive Psychology*, 1973, *4*, 55–81.

Cohen, L. B., & Gelber, E. R. Infant visual memory. In L. B. Cohen & P. Salapatek (Eds.), *Infant perception: From sensation to cognition* (Vol. 1). New York: Academic Press, 1975.

Cohen, L. B., & Strauss, M. S. Concept acquisition in the human infant. *Child Development*, 1979, *50*, 419–424.

Conel, J. L. *The postnatal development of the human cerebral cortex: Vol. 1. The cortex of the newborn*. Cambridge: Harvard University Press, 1939.

Cornell, E. H. Infants' discrimination of photographs of faces following redundant presentations. *Journal of Experimental Child Psychology*, 1974, *18*, 98–106.

Dannemiller, J. L., & Banks, M. S. Can selective adaptation account for early infant habituation? *Merrill-Palmer Quarterly*, 1983, *29*, 151–158.

Dodgson, M. C. H. *The growing brain: An essay in developmental neurology*. Baltimore: Williams & Wilkins, 1962.

Dulany, D. E. Awareness, rules, and propositional control: A confrontation with S-R behavior theory. In T. R. Dixon & D. L. Horton (Eds.), *Verbal behavior and general behavior theory*. Englewood Cliffs, N.J.: Prentice-Hall, 1968.

Ebbinghaus, H. *Memory*. New York: Dover, 1964. (Originally published, 1885)

Fagan, J. F., III. Infants' recognition memory for faces. *Journal of Experimental Child Psychology*, 1972, *14*, 453–476.

Fagan, J. F., III. Infants' delayed recognition memory and forgetting. *Journal of Experimental Child Psychology*, 1973, *16*, 424–450.

Fagan, J. F., III. Infant recognition memory: The effects of length of familiarization and type of discrimination task. *Child Development*, 1974, *45*, 351–356.

Fagan, J. F., III. Infants' recognition of invariant features of faces. *Child Development*, 1976, *47*, 627–638.

Fantz, R. L., Fagan, J. F., III, & Miranda, S. B. Early visual selectivity as a function of pattern variables, previous exposure, age from birth and conception, and expected cognitive deficit. In L. B. Cohen & P. Salapatek (Eds.), *Infant perception: From sensation to cognition* (Vol. 1). New York: Academic Press, 1975.

Feigenbaum, E. A. Simulation of verbal learning behavior. In E. A. Feigenbaum & J. Feldman (Eds.), *Computers and thought*. New York: McGraw-Hill, 1963.

Fitzgerald, H. E., & Brackbill, Y. Classical conditioning in infancy: Development and constraints. *Psychological Bulletin*, 1976, *83*, 353–376.

Friedman, S. Habituation and recovery of visual response in the alert human newborn. *Journal of Experimental Child Psychology*, 1972, *13*, 339–349. (a)

Friedman, S. Newborn visual attention to repeated exposure of redundant versus "novel" targets. *Perception and Psychophysics*, 1972, *12*, 291–294. (b)

Friedman, S. Infant habituation: Process, problems and possibilities. In N. Ellis (Ed.), *Aberrant development in infancy*. Potomac, Md.: Erlbaum, 1975.

Friedman, S., & Carpenter, G. C. Visual response decrement as a function of age of human newborn. *Child Development*, 1971, *42*, 1967–1973.

Friedman, S., Bruno, L. A., & Vietze, P. Newborn habituation to visual stimuli: A sex difference in novelty detection. *Journal of Experimental Child Psychology*, 1974, *18*, 242–251.

Friedman, S., Carpenter, G. C., & Nagy, A. N. Decrement and recovery of response to visual stimuli in the newborn infant. *Proceedings of the 78th Annual Convention, APA*, 1970, *5*, 273–274.

Friedman, S., Nagy, A. N., & Carpenter, G. C. Newborn attention: Differential response decrement to visual stimuli. *Journal of Experimental Child Psychology*, 1970, *10*, 44–51.

Gibson, E., Owsley, C., & Johnston, J. Perception of invariants by five-month-old infants: Differentiation of two types of motion. *Developmental Psychology*, 1978, *14*, 407–415.

Haith, M. M. *Rules that babies look by: The organization of newborn visual activity*. Hillsdale, N.J.: Erlbaum, 1980.

Hintzman, D. L. Explorations with a discrimination net model for paired-associate learning. *Journal of Mathematical Psychology*, 1968, *5*, 123–162.

Hubel, D. H., & Wiesel, T. N. Receptive fields of single neurones in the cat's striate cortex. *Journal of Physiology*, 1959, *148*, 574–591.

Hubel, D. H., & Wiesel, T. N. Receptive fields, binocular interaction and functional architecture in the cat's visual cortex. *Journal of Physiology*, 1962, *160*, 106–154.

Huttenlocher, J. The origins of language comprehension. In R. L. Solso (Ed.), *Theories in cognitive psychology: The Loyola symposium*. Hillsdale, N.J.: Erlbaum, 1974.

Karmel, B. Z., & Maisel, E. B. A neuronal activity model for infant visual attention. In L. B. Cohen & P. Salapatek (Eds.), *Infant perception: From sensation to cognition* (Vol. 1). New York: Academic Press, 1975.

Koffka, K. *Principles of Gestalt psychology*. New York: Harcourt, Brace & World, 1935.

Kohler, W. *Dynamics in psychology*. New York: Grove Press, 1940.

Kohler, W. *Gestalt psychology*. New York: Liveright, 1947.

Lewis, M. Individual differences in the measurement of early cognitive growth. In J. Hellmuth (Ed.), *Exceptional infant: Vol. 2. Studies in abnormalities*. New York: Brunner/Mazel, 1971.

Mandler, J. M. Representation. In J. H. Flavell & E. M. Markman (Eds.), *Manual of child psychology: Vol. 3. Cognitive development*. New York: Wiley, 1983.

McCall, R. B., Parke, R. D., & Kavanaugh, R. D. Imitation of live and televised models by children one to three years of age. *Monographs of the Society for Child Development*, 1977, *42*, Whole No. 173.

McGurk, H. Infant discrimination of orientation. *Journal of Experimental Child Psychology*, 1972, *14*, 151–164.

Olson, G. M. An information processing analysis of visual memory and habituation in infants. In T. J. Tighe & R. N. Leaton (Eds.), *Habituation: Perspectives from child development, animal behavior, and neurophysiology*. Hillsdale, N.J.: Erlbaum, 1976.

Olson, G. M. Infant recognition memory for briefly presented visual stimuli. *Infant Behavior and Development*, 1979, *2*, 123–134.

Olson, G. M. The recognition of specific persons. In M. E. Lamb & L. R. Sherrod (Eds.), *Infant social cognition: Empirical and theoretical considerations*. Hillsdale, N.J.: Lawrence Erlbaum Associates, 1981.

Olson, G. M., & Sherman, T. Attention, learning and memory in infants. In M. Haith & J. Campos (Eds.), *Manual of child psychology: Vol. 2. Infancy and developmental psychobiology*. New York: Wiley, 1983.

Oviatt, S. L. The emerging ability to comprehend language: An experimental approach. *Child Development*, 1980, *51*, 97–106.

Parmelee, A. H., Jr. Ontogeny of sleep patterns and associated periodicities in infants. In F. Falkner, N. Kretchmer, & E. Rossi (Eds.), *Modern problems in paediatrics* (Vol. 13). Basel: S. Karger, 1974.

Parmelee, A. H., Jr., & Stern, E. Development of states in infants. In C. D. Clemente, D. P. Purpura, & F. E. Mayer (Eds.), *Sleep and the maturing nervous system*. New York: Academic Press, 1972.

Piaget, J. *The origins of intelligence in children*. New York: W. W. Norton, 1952.

Piaget, J. *The construction of reality in the child*. New York: Basic Books, 1954.

Piaget, J., & Inhelder, B. *Memory and intelligence*. New York: Basic Books, 1973.

Posner, M. I., & Keele, S. W. On the genesis of abstract ideas. *Journal of Experimental Psychology*, 1968, *77*, 353–363.

Posner, M. I., & Keele, S. W. Retention of abstract ideas. *Journal of Experimental Psychology*, 1970, *83*, 304–308.

Prytulak, L. S. Natural language mediation. *Cognitive Psychology*, 1971, *2*, 1–56.

Reitman, J. S. Skilled perception in go: Deducing memory structures from inter-response times. *Cognitive Psychology*, 1976, *8*, 336–356.

Revelle, G. L. *Categorization abilities in preverbal infants*. Unpublished doctoral dissertation, University of Michigan, 1982.

Rosch, E. Principles of categorization. In E. Rosch & B. B. Lloyd (Eds.), *Cognition and categorization*. Hillsdale, N.J.: Erlbaum, 1978.

Rosch, E., Mervis, C. B., Gray, W. D., Johnson, D. M., & Boyes-Braem, P. Basic objects in natural categories. *Cognitive Psychology*, 1976, *8*, 382–439.

Ross, G. S. Categorization in 1- to 2-year-olds. *Developmental Psychology*, 1980, *16*, 391–396.

Ruff, H. A. Infant recognition of the invariant form of objects. *Child Development*, 1978, *49*, 293–306.

Salapatek, P. Pattern perception in early infancy. In L. B. Cohen & P. Salapatek (Eds.),

Infant perception: From sensation to cognition (Vol. 1). New York: Academic Press, 1975.

Salapatek, P., & Banks, M. S. Infant visual perception. In M. Haith & J. Campos (Eds.), *Manual of child psychology: Vol. 2. Infancy and developmental psychobiology.* New York: Wiley, 1983.

Sameroff, A. J., & Cavanagh, P. J. Learning in infancy: A developmental perspective. In J. D. Osofsky (Ed.), *Handbook of infant development.* New York: Wiley, 1979.

Sherman, T. L. *Categorization skills in infants.* Unpublished doctoral dissertation, University of Michigan, 1980.

Slater, A., Morison, V., & Rose, D. Visual memory at birth. *British Journal of Psychology,* in press.

Smith, E. E., & Medin, D. L. *Categories and concepts.* Cambridge: Harvard University Press, 1981.

Sophian, C. Habituation is not enough: Novelty preferences, search, and memory in infancy. *Merrill-Palmer Quarterly,* 1980, *26,* 239–257.

Starkey, P., & Cooper, R. G. Perception of number by human infants. *Science,* 1980, *210,* 1033–1035.

Strauss, M. S. Abstraction of prototypical information by adults and 10-month-old infants. *Journal of Experimental Psychology: Human Learning and Memory,* 1979, *5,* 618–632.

Strauss, M. S., & Curtis, L. E. Infant perception of numerosity. *Child Development,* 1981, *52,* 1146–1152.

Strauss, M. S., & Curtis, L. E. Development of numerical concepts in infancy. In C. Sophian (Ed.), *The origin of cognitive skills.* Hillsdale, N.J.: Erlbaum, in press.

Thomas, D. G., Campos, J. J., Shucard, D. W., Ramsay, D. S., & Shucard, J. Semantic comprehension in infancy: A signal detection analysis. *Child Development,* 1981, *52,* 798–803.

CHAPTER 3

An Ecological Approach to Infant Memory

Holly A. Ruff

Department of Pediatrics
Albert Einstein College of Medicine
The Bronx, New York

There are many ways to approach the problem of memory in infancy. I was asked to examine the problem from a Gibsonian point of view. This is no easy task given Gibson's (1966, 1979) rejection of the need for memory in perception. His rejection is based on his view that perception is a process that continues over time; therefore, it becomes very difficult to separate past from present, and the attempts to do so lead to what Gibson (1966) called the "muddle of memory." This chapter represents my attempt to apply Gibson's ecological approach to perception to topics that are generally included under the rubric of infant memory. The chapter may not, in the end, be as radical as Gibson's view, but it will reflect the Gibsonian emphasis on events, that is, changes that occur over time, and actions. The initial portions of the chapter will be a discussion of what is perceived and recognized in the context of events. The last part will approach the definition of memory more directly.

This chapter is based on a paper presented at the Erindale Symposium on Infant Memory in Toronto, May, 1982. The writing of the chapter was supported by Grant 80-13064 from the National Science Foundation and Grant HD 11916 from the National Institutes of Health.

The Ecological Approach

Let me outline what I think are the most important aspects of an ecological approach. Gibson (1979) considered the information that specifies the environment to be rich and, for the active observer, unambiguous. Starting with this premise, Gibson focused on how the observer picks up information about reality and not how the observer interprets or constructs reality. Mace (1977) summarized Gibson's view as "Ask not what's inside your head but what your head's inside of." This aphorism reflects the view that the perceptual systems are provided with highly structured information, but it also refers to a strategy of study in which analysis of stimulus information plays a major role. Use of such a strategy does not mean that the brain is considered to have no function or that there is no need to study the mechanisms underlying perception. But the kind of mechanisms considered necessary must be related to the information that is considered to be available to the observer. According to Gibson, that information has been underestimated, insufficiently analyzed, and sometimes misconceived. The burden that falls upon anyone working in the Gibsonian tradition is to analyze and specify that information in an attempt to show that the information is adequate for much of normal activity.

The information available to the observer can only be considered adequate and rich if perception is considered to be an active process of picking up information from a continuous flow of stimulation. The flow arises from the motions of objects, animate and inanimate, and from the motion of the observer in relation to the objects. Perception, therefore, does not involve momentary sensations or retinal images nor does it involve a passive receiver, and activity does not refer so much to internal mental activity as it does to the observer's bodily motion: moving around, turning the head, looking, listening, and touching in order to increase the amount of information about the event that is of interest or concern. The Gibsonian approach, therefore, focuses on the events in the environment of the observer—happenings that occur in time and require time to apprehend—and on the observer as an active seeker of information.

From an evolutionary point of view, Gibson considered all species to be sensitive to nonchange or invariance in events. That which remains the same over the flow of continually changing stimulation specifies the structure of the environment and the structure of the objects that make up the environment. Invariant patterns of change specify the activities or events in which the objects and the observer participate. The invariants can, therefore, specify with a high degree of precision what is happening outside the observer.

It is much easier to discuss the general concept of invariance than it is to analyze specific stimulus situations and to determine what information is actually being used by the subject. A careful series of studies by Cutting, Proffitt, and Kozlowski (1978) provides an example. They took a paradigm introduced by Johannson (1973) in which lights are attached to the joints of a person who then walks while being filmed. The film can then be presented to subjects in a way that the moving pattern of lights is the only stimulus. Adults can identify the display as a human being walking in less than a second. Cutting and his colleagues found that subjects could identify known individuals (Cutting & Kozlowski, 1977) and the sex of unknown people (Cutting, *et al.* 1978) on the basis of these displays of moving lights. In a series of studies, these investigators isolated the important invariant in the perception of the sex of the walker. They labeled this invariant "the center of moment" and provided a mathematical description. Describing and analyzing invariants in this manner is only beginning, but the important point is that such experiments address the problem of how the observer detects structural and transformational invariants as he observes moving objects or as he moves around static ones. Such analyses have clear implications for what is remembered from participating in events or observing them.

Information, as the term is used in this framework, is not something that needs to be processed so much as picked up because it is available in the structure of stimulation. Furthermore, the form or nature of the specific sensations involved is less important than the object or event that is being specified. We easily recognize, for example, still photographs of the faces of people that we know, suggesting that we use some features, or more likely, configurations of features (Baddely, 1979) to recognize people. But, as Cutting and Kozlowski have shown, it is also possible to recognize people from a moving display of lights attached to the joints of that person (Cutting & Kozlowski, 1977). Some invariant characteristics of movement must be used for recognition in that case rather than a static configuration as in the photo. The point of the illustration is that both the photograph of the face and the moving display of lights specifies the *same* individual.

In summary, the ecological approach to perception emphasizes the gathering of information by an active observer about the structure of the world and the events within it. Perception is the detection of change and nonchange in the flow of stimulation over time. It is a continuing process. An analysis of the information available in different situations is basic to our understanding of behavior, including behavior that reflects what we call "memory." Where does this approach lead in a discussion of infant behavior?

Infants' Recognition of Objects and Events

When we consider the problem of recognition, the ecological approach suggests the following kinds of questions: What information is available that allows us to recognize an object when it is seen from a different perspective? How do we recognize an object or event from only part of it? How do we recognize particular motions of objects regardless of the object that is making the motion? How do we recognize particular behaviors regardless of whether we are performing them or someone else is? Gibson's theory of the detection of invariants provides a good starting point for answering such questions.

A discussion of recognition in infants depends on the inferences we make from behavior. There are two widely used methods of studying visual recognition in infants, both of which follow the same logic. One is the habituation–recovery paradigm and the other is the familiarization-and-response-to-novelty paradigm (see Chapters 1 and 2). In the case of habituation, the infant responds less to an object after being exposed to it for a period of time. The necessary length of time varies with the nature of the stimulus display. If the infant's looking continues at the reduced level when the same stimulus is presented but recovers when a novel stimulus is presented, the inference is that the infant not only discriminates between the two stimuli but also recognizes or remembers the old one. We could also consider that the object is being explored during the habituation period; the infant is perceiving that particular object, and the process requires time. Each time the object is presented, the infant is better able to pick up information about the properties of the object; that is, he detects the invariants specifying those properties more quickly. When a new object is presented, the process of exploration begins again. The very information that is used to perceive the object is the information used to recognize it, and the processes may be the same. The usefulness of such an interpretation can be judged by the following discussion.

Dynamic Events

What have we learned through these two techniques about the infant's ability to detect invariance within dynamic events? The evidence, I think, indicates considerable sensitivity to various kinds of nonchange, though most of the data suggests that the information picked up is very general. When an infant or an adult observes an event, he detects two kinds of invariants—structural and transformational. The first deals with the layout of the environment or the relationship of surfaces in the object (its form), and the second refers to the motions of the object or the observer within the environment. Several studies will serve as illustrations.

Let me start with one of my own studies that deals with transformational invariants (Ruff, in press). The purpose of this study was to determine whether the young infant can detect patterns of stimulation that specify a particular motion so that he would recognize the motion if he observed an object of another shape making the same objective motion. I used an habituation–recovery paradigm, and I presented 5-month-old infants with 30-sec trials in which one of five different objects was moved in a particular way. Trials were presented until the infant was looking 50% or less of his initial level of looking. During this habituation period the infant was presented with five different objects making the same motion. The infant was then presented with a *new* object for two trials. On one trial, the object made the same motion made during habituation. On the other trial, the object made a novel motion. In one study, the two motions were translation, that is, lateral motion without rotation, and translation plus rotation. Familiar and novel motions were counterbalanced. In another study rotation and an oscillating motion were compared. In both studies the infants' looking recovered to the novel motion but not to the familiar one (see Figure 1 for results of first study). I concluded

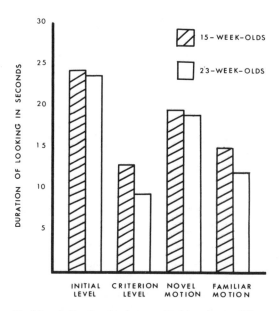

Fig. 1. Duration of looking, indicating the degree of habituation to different objects making the same motion, and the degree of recovery to a novel object making the familiar motion and a novel one.

that infants of 5 months are able to detect some patterns of change in these particular motions regardless of the object making the motions.

In a more general sense, I would say that the infants in such studies are exposed to an event, that is, a series of trials on which something is repeated. Assuming that the infant is sensitive to nonchange, the detection of the pattern of change means that he automatically responds to the sameness in the pattern of change over trials. On the basis of other work, I think the sameness in my studies involves what happens to texture elements and to the projective contour when the object moves. The degree of projective change, the pattern of appearance and disappearance of texture elements, and the frequency with which the elements change direction are the same regardless of the shape of the object being presented on a particular trial. When I present the *new* object making the *same* motion, the infant continues to detect the same pattern. When a new object is presented making a *different* motion, the infant must now begin to detect the invariants specifying the new motion. Figure 1 shows that the infants' looking recovered to the novel motion, but not completely to the initial level. Because certain invariants are shared by the two motions (e.g., the amount of background texture covered), the infants would have already detected some of the invariants specifying the second motion from their experience with the first motion. In summary, the infant responds to the whole series of trials; his looking continues to decline as long as the invariant aspects of the situation continue to be present and detected; when something novel interrupts the series, he responds appropriately.

Using these particular motions, I found some change with age. Infants of 3½ months performed in much the same way as the 5-month-olds in some conditions (see Figure 1) but showed no differential response in others. In the cases where they did differentiate between familiar and novel motions, they took longer than the 5-month-olds to reach criterion, a finding which suggests that the younger infants took longer to detect the same patterns of change. In the cases where they did not differentiate, they still reached criterion during habituation; this finding suggests that they were picking up some invariants during habituation. This last is an important point. The test that follows habituation only tests for the particular aspects of the situation in which the experimenter is interested. If the infant makes no differentiation, he may indeed have failed to pick up the information being tested for, but we must be cautious about negative results. They do not mean that he has not learned or perceived something about the event which he could recognize given another kind of test.

Since many of the events that are important to infants do not involve rigid objects, it is important to consider the infant's ability to detect and recognize the motions of elastic and jointed objects. Gibson and her colleagues (Gibson, Owsley, & Johnston, 1978; Gibson, Owsley, Walker, &

Megaw-Nyce, 1979; Walker, Owsley, Megaw-Nyce, Gibson, & Bahrick, 1980) have addressed the problem of the infant's ability to detect invariants specifying rigid and elastic motions. They habituated 3- and 5-month-old infants to an object making several kinds of rigid motions (rotations around several axes). When criterion was reached, the infants were presented with a new rigid motion and an elastic deformation. The infants showed no recovery to the new rigid motion and significant recovery to the deformation. When elastic motions were used during habituation, the infants showed no recovery to the new deformation and significant recovery to a rigid motion. These results suggest that infants detect invariants in the patterns of change specifying the two kinds of motion. Gibson and her colleagues suggest that the basis may be that cross-ratios of texture elements are maintained during rigid motion whereas they are disturbed during a deformation. These invariants that specify the motions also provide information about the substance of the objects making the motions. In general, observers of an event are likely to pick up information simultaneously about both structure and action. Accordingly, Gibson and her colleagues provide evidence that 3-month-olds pick up information about shape across motion; that is, infants generalize habituation to the same shape even when it is making a new motion.

Other investigators (Bertenthal, Proffitt, & Cutting, 1984; Fox & McDaniel, 1982) have recently begun to explore the stimulus information involved in recognizing biological motion, particularly the jointed motion of human beings. So far, the studies have concentrated on walking and the infant's ability to detect the coherence of a pattern in a display of moving spots of light. Coherence refers to the fact that the motions of the lights are generated by an organized whole—a requirement for the adult identification of the displays as a human being moving. The results suggest that 4- to 6-month-old infants are sensitive to the coherence of such events. The results do not tell us whether infants can recognize the display as the motion of a human being, but studies could be designed to test that possibility. It would be interesting, for example, to know how infants would respond to a display of lights generated by an individual walking after their experience with a videotape of that person walking; the question is whether infants pick up the same kind of differentiated information as adults from such events.

The investigation of infants' responsiveness to and recognition of motions is an exciting enterprise. The studies cited above demonstrate the variety of methodological approaches to the problem, but they are all concerned with the rich information available in change over time. Infants in the first 6 months seem quite able to pick up at least some of that information from observation of events.

The gathering of information is, of course, not limited to the visual system. The recent interest is cross-modal transfer has advanced our understanding of the interaction of the tactual and visual systems in gathering information about objects. Considerable evidence now exists that infants, at least by 12 months, are able, after tactual familiarization, to recognize forms and substances visually (Bryant, Jones, Claxton, & Perkins, 1972; Gibson & Walker, 1982; Gottfried, Rose, & Bridger, 1978; Ruff & Kohler, 1978). Rose, Gottfried, and Bridger (1981) have also shown that 12-month-olds tactually recognize a form after visual familiarization. These studies involve the paradigm that introduces a paired comparison test after a period of familiarization so that recognition is indexed, in general, by relatively greater attention to the novel object.

Positive results in cross-modal studies are impressive because there seems to be such a dramatic change in the form of the information from the familiarization to the test period. A study by Rose, Gottfried, & Bridger (1983) serves as a particularly good illustration. It showed that 12-month-old infants, after tactual familiarization with an object, will respond more not only to an object of novel shape but also more to pictures and to line drawings of an object of novel shape. Their conclusion is that infants are able to pick up information about contour from their tactual exploration and transfer that information to another modality. The infants' recognition of that contour also transfers to abstract contour, as shown in the response to the line drawings. In correlation with the previous interpretation, we could say that the infants are capable of detecting the particulars of that contour faster during the test as a result of their prior tactual experience. Faster detection would be reflected in the lower level of responsiveness to the familiar contour. I have phrased the conclusion in this way in order to emphasize again that the *form* of the information may be less important than *what* is being specified by the information. Tactual exploration of an object involves considerable transformation in the stimulation over time. These changes or the flow allow the infant to detect the nonchange specifying the contour. The ability to generalize to pictures and line drawings reflects mainly the general and amodal nature of those invariants.

The ability to detect amodal properties of objects does not exclude learning arbitrary associations between properties that can be picked up in only one modality—the association of color with shape, for example. It seems to me, however, that the ability to feel an object and know its color is based on experience of highly probable combinations, whereas the ability to feel an object and know how it looks is based on the detection of invariants. As Bushnell (1982) has indicated, this distinction between amodal properties and arbitrary multimodal compounds is important. Spelke (in press) has demonstrated, for example, that infants spontaneously associate certain kinds of sounds with certain visual events—a face in motion and a voice or a percussive sound and a drumstick hitting a drum—presumably on the basis of a common property between the visual and auditory stimulation. On the other hand, 6-month-old infants seem to learn completely arbitrary associations between an object and its sound given certain constraints on spatial and temporal congruence (Lawson, 1980). The relationship between the tactual and visual aspects of an object, however, is far less likely to be arbitrary, because both modalities pick up the same structural properties of objects. Infants of 6 months may have more difficulty making arbitrary connections between the tactual and visual experiences with an object than they do between the auditory and visual aspects. Bushnell (1982), for example, found it difficult to demonstrate associations between color and temperature in 6-month-olds.

The manipulation of objects by the infant leads to a complex experience involving visual, auditory, tactual, and kinesthetic stimulation. Out of that dynamic event emerges the recognition of objects and their properties because the different systems are picking up information about the external world. The infant is also acquiring information about his own actions and their consequences, a topic that will be discussed in detail later.

The Pickup of Information from Static Instances

The detection of invariance refers to the ability to pick up nonchange from a flow of stimulation generated by a dynamic event. The infant is obviously able in some cases to pick up information for nonchange from discrete and static instances. There are many examples of studies in which the infant is habituated to a group of different objects or pictures that have something in common (See Chapter 2). Infants show generalization to a novel member of the group and recovery to an object that is outside the group. There is some evidence for such responding in infants as young as 3 months of age (Milewski, 1979).

Even a series of discrete instances can usefully be considered an event. There is evidence in the adult literature that subjects respond to the coherence of events (as represented by discrete samples) and not to particular instances within the event. Jenkins, Wald, and Pittenger (1978) have studied the recognition of pictures that sample a particular activity, such as getting a cup of tea. The observers apparently pick up information about the overall event and have difficulty remembering whether they have previously seen a particular picture, providing that the picture is consistent with the pictured event. In these cases, pictures were taken from the same point of view so that station point was an invariant aspect of the event as it was originally presented. The fact that the subjects readily responded to a picture taken from a different station point (different camera position) emphasizes the perceptual nature of the task. The fact that adults are not sensitive to particular instances within the event and "recognize" pictures that were never shown to them suggests that instances are responded to only in terms of whether they fit the invariants extracted from the whole event.

This point is relevant to some of the studies of infants in which the infant, during habituation, is presented with different stimuli that are the same in some respects but different in others. If the infants are responding to a sequence of pictures or displays as an event, then a sequence with varying instances is a very different event from a sequence of identical instances; each has different invariants to be detected. Infants discriminate among the various instances of sequence, a fact that can be demonstrated by presenting an instance repeatedly to an infant and then showing that infants respond to a novel instance with recovery of looking. Infants can discriminate, for example, between slides of different stuffed animals (Cohen & Caputo, 1978). However, after seeing a series of slides of different stuffed animals, infants show no recovery of looking to a novel instance of stuffed animal but do recover to another kind of toy. The lack of recovery to the novel instance, in the case where the infant is habituated to a class of objects, is taken as evidence for concept formation; that is, the infants perceive the differences among instances but they respond on the basis of class membership. My interpretation of what is happening in such cases is somewhat different. When the infant sees the series of stuffed animals, he may pick up visually the roundedness of the objects' surfaces because this is the information that is repeated. Although the infant can discriminate on the basis of color and shape in the case where only one object is shown during the habituation period, he may be able to pick up only the more general information when shape and color change from trial to trial. Habituation to both multiple examples and single examples involves a response to nonchange; because what remains unchanged is different, the perceptual response to the novel exemplar is different.

Although the work with multiple instances is frequently referred to as the study of concept formation (Caron & Caron, 1982; Cohen, 1979), the responses of infants are still very much tied to perceptual processes and physical properties of objects. The infant generalizes his response to physically different instances, but these instances are different in only some respects; they are identical to others. The physical identity is specified by the information picked up perceptually. Later on in development, of course, we can and do assign the same label to perceptually unrelated instances, but such a process seems to call for considerably more than the detection of invariance—symbolic function, for example.

Whether or not the detection of invariance over a group of separate instances is referred to as concept formation or perception, it is important to note that the invariants are very general. Under normal circumstances in which related events are spaced over time and embedded in larger events, the infant probably picks up general invariants when the information is sufficient for his needs or activities. On the other hand, when necessary and with time, the infant detects the invariants that specify unique objects. This is obvious with the recognition of parents. In this case, the infant's needs are closely tied to those particular objects, and the perceptual experience is varied and rich. What is recognized, therefore, will be general in some cases and highly specific in others. Brooks (1978) has argued that a nonanalytic formation of concepts, a process based on analogy from highly familiar instances, occurs along with the more familiar analytic process that involves little memory for specific instances. The development of the earliest concepts, those that form the basis for naming (MacNamara, 1972; K. Nelson, 1974), may be based on either process and depend on the nature of the prior perceptual experience.

Events Involving the Subject's Motor Activity

Most of the studies in the previous section allowed the infant to pick up information about objects and events by looking and touching. Under normal circumstances, the observer is frequently a more active participant and learns as much about himself as about the external world. There are two other techniques used in the study of infant memory that examine what the infant learns about his own actions and the consequences of those actions.

Operant Conditioning

Rovee-Collier and her colleagues (e.g., Rovee-Collier & Gekoski, 1979; Rovee-Collier & Sullivan, 1980) have been looking at memory in the context of operant conditioning. They have successfully conditioned footkicking in 3-month-olds with conjugate reinforcement, that is, reinforcement that increases in frequency with the increasing strength or frequency of the conditioned response. Their method is to attach a mobile to the infant's crib. After a baseline period in which the spontaneous level of kicking the foot is measured, a ribbon attached to the mobile is tied to the infant's ankle. Now the infant's kicking moves the mobile. The harder and more frequently he kicks, the more the mobile moves. An increase in kicking over the baseline is taken as evidence that the infant has learned the contingency. Retention can be tested by later presenting the mobile without the connecting ribbon to the infant and observing the level of kicking. Rovee-Collier, Enright, Lucas, Fagen, and Gekowski (1981) have suggested that the conditioning technique allows for the learning of a specific response within a distinctive context and that the effect of contextual cues on the retrieval of the response can be studied in a way that is impossible with the habituation paradigm. The paradigm does avoid confounding preferences (or lack of them) with memory; the conditioning technique also has the advantage of studying something that involves high motivation in the infant and of forcing us to view the situation as an event. The following analysis of the event and the perception of it are not intended to contradict other explanations but to emphasize the nature of the information picked up.

Since the technique involves learning a motor response, the infant must pick up information about his own bodily movement as well as information about environmental events. What is perceived and learned initially are the invariants specifying the total event, which includes the appropriate behavior and the contingent relationship between behavior and reinforcement. It is clear that some invariants must specify the mobile and its physical characteristics, because a completely novel mobile does not lead to generalization of increased kicking. But the response and its consequences must also be specified by invariants; there would be kinesthetic invariants, for example, to specify the kicking. The infant kicks intially without intending to move the mobile but gradually detects the relationship between the kinesthetic invariants and the invariants specifying the mobile and its motion. On the retention test, the mobile is basically stationary. The infant does respond, for a short time after training, to the stationary mobile with increased kicking, but after 2 weeks, the stationary mobile is insufficient to elicit the conditioned response. At this point the moving mobile (even though its motion is noncontingent) seems to be a powerful stimulus, because conditioned response is reactivated. This is not surprising, given the general expectation that moving objects carry more information, especially in this case where movement of the mobile is at the heart of the event.

Spear (1973), who has inspired much of the current work with infants, emphasizes the multiplicity of cues (internal and external) that are part of the context in which the learning takes place. The question then is whether there are enough cues during the retention test to arouse the conditioned response. As more cues are involved, the conditioned response is more likely to be activated. Spear argues that arousal or retrieval takes time and does not seem to be a matter of increasing motivation.

Although Spear doesn't characterize it as such, part of what is taking time may be the pick up of information in the retention situation.

The infant perceives the contingency between his own motions and the motion of the mobile because of the temporal relationship between the two. He needs to attend only to the kinesthetic information from his kicking and to the visual information from the mobile. Visual information is, however, available for the infant's motion; that is, the infant could look at his feet and observe the connection between the action, his foot, and the ribbon. Unless the infant attends to the visual information about his kicking and the events that occur between himself and the mobile, he may not be able to learn about the specific and causal nature of the contingency.

The operant-conditioning paradigm offers a valuable tool for the investigation of the infant's learning about the effect of his actions on the world. That learning requires the infant's attention for many aspects of the event. If the required action is in the infant's repertoire, he or she readily learns to apply it in the appropriate situation. Whether an account of this learning necessitates the concept of memory is a question that will be taken up later (see also Chapter 6). A full account seems to call for a considered analysis of the information that is available in the events and that makes such learning possible.

Search for Objects

Another activity that has considerable relevance to the infant's ordinary life is the ability to search for objects that are out of sight. A number of studies have investigated the factors that affect either turning the head to look at events or manual search for hidden objects. The infant in these studies is demonstrating what he has learned about the persistence and location of objects, either in the context of the experiment or beforehand. As with the other topics in this chapter, the current concern is the information that enables the infants to respond appropriately.

The infant's ability to search for objects at the location where the object was seen to be hidden develops gradually in the first 2 years. At first, infants fail to search for an object that is completely hidden, though they will search when it is only partially hidden. Then they will search but make the much discussed $A\overline{B}$ error; that is, after the experience of seeing and/or finding an object hidden at A, the infant later searches at A even though he has seen the object hidden at B. Piaget (1952) interprets the failure to search and the $A\overline{B}$ error as infants' not knowing that an object that goes out of sight must continue to exist and that it can be in only one place at a time. In order to illustrate how an analysis of stimulus

information may lead to a somewhat different interpretation, let me start
with the task of manually searching for an object that has been covered.
It seems obvious on the face of it that the infant must remember the object
if he is going to search for it, but one might ask what information specifies
the persistence of objects and how does the infant pick up this information.
One of the aspects of our perceptual experience is the frequency with
which we observe partially hidden objects and the frequency with which
we experience covering and uncovering. One object (A) is occluded by
another that is in front of it (B), but we pick up information for the
continuation of A behind B because, when we move our heads or bodies
while looking at the partially hidden A, part of A that was previously
covered becomes gradually uncovered. If we move in the opposite direction, the uncovered portion of A becomes covered again. This occluding
of one surface by another happens all the time as we move and provides
information for the continuation of hidden surfaces. The information for
objects going out of existence (burning up, for example) is very different
in that the event is not reversible with a change in point of view. It takes
time for the infant to pick up the information for persistence or continuation, and it is possible that the child of 8 or 9 months has just begun
to perceive something that he had not previously perceived about the
relationship of objects in space. In spite of the fact that manual search
involves more than head movement, the task is still a matter of covering
and uncovering, a reversible operation.

If the repeated experience with reversible occlusions serves as at
least one determinant for the simple task of finding an object that has
been hidden, then we can make two predictions. First, the manner of
hiding should influence the infant's performance: Something that is slowly
occluded should be searched for more readily than something that is
abruptly occluded. The only directly relevant data that I know of is in a
report by Bower (1967), in which he used some ingenious techniques to
study the problem in 1- to 2-month-old infants. He found that infants
responded differently to abrupt than to gradual occlusion of objects and
differently to objects that were occluded than to objects that disappeared
by other means. The interpretation of these findings is not clear-cut, but
the data do suggest that infants are sensitive to the relevant variables
early on. The second prediction is that it should be possible to facilitate
the infant's performance with experience that will highlight the important
information. There is some evidence to support this prediction. K. E.
Nelson (1974) gave 6- to 7-month-olds repeated trials of an object moving
on a trajectory that took it behind a screen and out again. After the
experience, the infants showed more visual anticipation of an object reap-
pearing from behind the screen than before, even when the object or the
trajectory was different from the "training" trials. Cornell (1977) has also

facilitated manual search by using procedures that emphasize certain features of the hiding event.

Within this context, the infant's successful uncovering of an object that was covered while he watched depends, in part, on his adequate perception of the entire event. The event in this case is "covering" and contains information to specify persistence as well as location. What is the role of the infant's activity in this event? It has been assumed that, to some extent, the infant comes to the task having already learned that his own actions are efficacious in such situations. An interesting study by Harris (1971) suggests, however, that manipulation of the object before hiding leads to more persistent search in 8-month-olds than only looking at the object beforehand. The length of manipulation was not important, suggesting that just having the object in hand may help the infant to perceive more readily the role of the manual system in the event.

In the Piagetian test for the $\overline{AB}$ error, the infant is allowed to search for an object in one place (A) and then watches the object hidden at another place (B). Before 9 months, the infant is more likely to search at A than at B. This error has been interpreted in various ways. Piaget (1952) interprets it as the infant's failure to conceive of the object as independent of his own action. Cornell (1977) suggests that the infant has not yet learned the behaviors appropriate to successful search. Both of these interpretations suggest a lack of coordination between visual information for location of the object and information about the infant's response and its consequences. Other investigators (Acredelo, 1978; Acredelo & Evans, 1980; Bremner & Bryant, 1977; Butterworth, Jarrett, & Hicks, 1982; Cornell & Heth, 1979) have considered the problem in terms of a conflict between egocentric and objective spatial reference systems or, in other words, response vesus place learning. That is, in one case, the infant locates the object in terms of himself, and in the other, he locates it in reference to the objective layout. The experimenter can determine which system is being used by training the infant to respond in a particular direction to a particular event and then turing the infant around to see whether he continues to respond to the same direction relative to himself (left or right) or to the objective location of the event. There is clear evidence that infants respond more to objective locations as they get older. A study by Cornell and Heth (1979) illustrates this developmental change nicely. Groups of 4-, 8-, 12-, and 16-month-old infants learned to turn 90° either right or left to view a novel slide. The location of the novel slide was the same in every trial; on the opposite side, one slide was repeated on every trial. The environment was cluttered in order to provide many landmarks. There were 20 acquisition trials: by the last block of 5 trials all age groups were turning to the novel slide in 80% of the trials. After these 20 trials, the infants were rotated 180°; the objective location of the novel slide remained the same, so that the infants could view the novel slide only by turning their heads in the opposite direction. In the first 5 trials after rotation, all age groups dropped in the percentage of turns to the novel slide; the 4-month-olds were down to 27%, significantly lower than the other age groups. The low percentage reflects the fact that they continued to turn their heads in the same direction relative to their own bodies, that is, they demonstrated response learning instead of place learning. They either failed to take into account their own movement within the environment or they failed to note initially the objective location of the novel slide. The older infants were apparently more attentive to the objective spatial layout.

Studies such as these have clear implications for what is remembered. In response learning, the subject seems to be depending on kinesthetic information from the particular response. In place learning he is remembering or responding to objective spatial information. In a second study by Cornell and Heth (1979), infants were tested under two conditions. In one, the response was kept constant while objective location varied; this was accomplished by turning the infant around for some of the trials and varying location of the novel slide. In the other condition, location was kept constant while response varied; the infant was turned around for some of the trials, but the objective location stayed the same. When the two conditions were compared, infants of all ages learned faster in the constant response condition than in the constant place condition. These results suggest the possiblity that kinesthetic information is perceived and remembered more easily than information about the layout.

Although it is clear that egocentric responding becomes less dominant over responding to objective spatial location as development proceeds, it is of value to consider the conditions under which one or the other is more likely. For example, it is possible that egocentric responding is used when the information for objective spatial location is not adequate, either because of an impoverished layout or because the subject is not very good yet at picking up the information that is there. A study by Reiser (1979) shows that 6-month-olds in a situation that offered four choices could, in some cases, respond on the basis of landmarks as well as egocentrically. "Geocentric" responding, as Reiser calls it, was clearest when the doors that could be chosen were painted with bright, distinctive patterns. Acredelo (1978), and Acredelo and Evans (1980) found an increasing effect of landmarks from 6–12 months with even 6-month-olds tending toward more objective responding when the landmark was highly distinctive. The same generalization applies to manual search, where distinctive covers will reduce the incidence of the $A\overline{B}$ error (Bremner, 1978; Butterworth et al., 1982). But just how much is the infant learning about spatial location with the use of landmarks? The infant may be learning only that reinforcement is associated with a certain color or pattern. To respond to an object's location within the layout means to perceive the relative spatial relationship of many objects including the target object, but the perception of any complex layout takes time. In studies that involved tests in a reasonably complex environment, the infants may not have had adequate time to perceive the relationship of the objects within that space. A study by Acredelo (1979) supports this contention. She found significantly more objective responding in 9-month-olds when they were tested at home than when they were tested in an object-filled office. Interestingly, performance was no different in the object-filled office than in the empty lab, a fact which strengthens the assumption that the young infant may require considerable time to perceive the environment in a differentiated way. When he does not have time to do so, he falls back on egocentric responding.

The trouble with egocentric responding is that it is successful only as long as the subject maintains a fixed position in the layout. Objective location, on the other hand, is useful no matter how much the subject changes position. The design of the studies cited so far involved moving the infant into the new position. If the infant has a very clear and differentiated perception of the layout, it should not matter whether he moves himself or is moved passively, but, in other cases, the extent to which the infant attends to the actual motion of his body through space and to the layout as he moves may affect his performance. A study by Benson and Uzgiris (1981) showed that 10-month-olds who moved to the other side of the table by themselves made more correct choices in a two-choice task than infants who were carried to the other side. Moving under their own steam, infants may be more aware of the motion itself but may also be forced to pay attention to the location of all the objects around them in a way that is not necessary during passive movement.

Searching successfully for objects requires that several kinds of information be picked up. The infant must attend both to the location of objects relative to other objects and to his own motion through the layout. In complex situations, he must also attend to the motion of other objects, sometimes moving at the same time he does. The tasks designed to tap the later stages in the development of the object concept involve invisible displacements. For example, the object is put into a box, the box is put under a cloth, and the object is dumped from the box while both are covered by the cloth; the empty box is then brought out from under the cloth. Here the infant must make elementary inferences to determine the location of the object and cannot do so on the basis of direct perception. The inferences, however, must be grounded in the infant's previous perceptual experience with visible displacements. He would not infer that the object was dumped from the box while under the cloth unless he had previously picked up information specifying the event of one object leaving the inside of another object.

The tasks involving the object concept have provided a rich source of data about the infant's growing ability to perceive and know about objects. The implications for infant's perception of location is only one aspect. LeCompte and Gratch (1972) investigated the extent to which the infants have an expectation that a *specific* object was hidden. They gave 9-, 12-, and 16-month-old infants eight trials in which an object was hidden and the infant searched for it. On the first three trials the infant found the same object that had been hidden. On the fourth trial, the experimenter surreptitiously switched the object, and the infant found a different object. On the next three trials the infant again found the object that had been hidden, and on the eighth trial there was another switch. LeCompte and Gratch found that oldest infants reacted to the toy switch with high puzzlement, whereas the youngest ones reacted with only mild puzzlement. The older infants also actively searched the whole situation, whereas the younger infants attended mainly to the novel object. Object recognition is clearly a prerequisite for this task, but the oldest infants were responding to more than the novelty of the toy. It could be argued that the infant's recall or recollection of the particular object underlies his active search, but I think we can understand the behavior better if we consider the entire event. The situation involves a switch of the toy, something that happens only in experiments; not only is the toy novel, the entire event has changed as a result of the switch. If there is information to specify the persistence of an object and invariants to specify the particular object, then the switch signals the infant that his information is somehow inadequate and search ensues. Active exploration of a whole situation will be different and involve more of the entire situation—the apparatus, for example—than exploration of a particular object. The search in this case does suggest that the older infant has an expectation that is based on the probabilities of occurrence in his previous experience—part of what is referred to as the infant's world knowledge. Such knowledge could be said to involve memory, but the expectation is so general that it takes on the characteristic of a principle.

By 16 months, the infant has developed a considerable body of knowledge. Practical knowledge enables him to behave appropriately in many different situations. The knowledge is based on the common and repeated events in the infant's life and depends on his differentiated perception of those events. How much does it depend on memory? That is the question I would like to deal with next.

What Is Memory?

Up to this point, the chapter has been concerned with what stimulus information is picked up in different circumstances, but not directly with the issue of memory. Let me, in summary, try to be explicit. For Gibson (1966), recognition is the detection of "same-as-before," and its opposite is response to novelty, the detection of "different-from-before." That is, according to Gibson, recognition and response to novelty fall into the arena of direct perception. In evaluating the usefulness of such a view, I think it is important to note that it is consistent with some alteration in the organism as a result of experience but not with psychological constructs such as comparison of past with present.

I would like to return briefly to the topic of habituation to illustrate my point. It has been widely assumed that during habituation the subject is building up or constructing a model of the object and that the model is then used to match incoming stimuli. When there is a match, looking continues to decline, and when there is a mismatch, looking time recovers. Some process in the brain underlies the decrement in looking, but this process may be the temporary or more permanent facilitation of particular pathways, with the response taking less time on later trials. Such a process would be akin to the strengthening of muscles with exercise, which has the consequence of making it easier to lift a heavy object. This facilitation might be referred to as memory, but there would be no need to talk about a comparison of present input with past input. As Posner and Warren (1972) observed, the results of experience may be "habitual structures that are contacted automatically by input" (p. 26).

All of the behaviors discussed are subject to the effects of delay. In the habituation and familiarization procedures, certainly something happens over time that reduces the differentiation between novel and familiar (see Werner & Perlmutter, 1979, for extended discussion). Conditioned footkicking is harder to elicit after delays of 2 weeks (Rovee-Collier et al., 1981). Searching for a covered object is also vulnerable to delay; infants are more likely to search successfully right away than after even a few seconds delay (Gratch, Appel, Evans, LeCompte, & Wright, 1974; Harris, 1973). All of these results imply a trace that fades with time. By the same token the trace, however it is defined physiologically, may strengthen and even become permanent, given sufficient experience with an event. The important point is that later experience may rearouse connections made earlier in an automatic way. In the conditioning paradigm, for example, the original learning must lead to permanent or semipermanent connections in the brain, resulting in a pathway having both sensory and motor components. If one part of this pathway is stimulated by the mobile at a later time, why not the rest of the pathway? The infant clearly does not engage in random behavior until he recognizes the correct action; in some sense, the action is initiated automatically given the stimulus. Although the infant's current behavior is clearly affected by his past experience, there may be nothing gained by bringing in the concepts of retrieval or even memory (see Chapters 5, 6, & 8).

One of the difficulties is that we wish to compare infants with adults. Adults demonstrate by verbal means that something is familiar; that is, they are sometimes aware of whether something is the "same-as-before" and can say so. However, we have to beware of assuming that something less automatic is happening just because we can put our awareness into words. Although we could not do so if there were no consciousness of the experience, the consciousness could easily be a by-product rather than a necessary part of the process.

The object permanence tasks are of interest because, in the later stages, the infant's behavior seems to demand more than can be explained on the basis of direct or automatic processes. There is a need to bring in expectations and, possibly, internal representations of objects and events, but caution seems worthwhile. Do expectations imply more than a preparation to act in a certain way (Neisser, 1976)? When an event occurs with regularity it is not surprising that the infant begins to prepare himself for the end of the event when he sees the beginning of it. If the event unfolds rigidly in a particular sequence with particular objects, the preparation will be specific. If the event involves a general sequence but with many different objects, the preparation will be more general. If the child did not detect the regularities in the events of his life, no expectations would develop. Given this, infancy might be seen as a period during which the infant is learning to recognize many events. He may in some sense be developing schemas and expectations that will later be determinants of perception and attention (see Chapter 4), but in most cases, expectations are elicited by a particular context, and, in that sense, have no existence independent of current perception. In the LeCompte and Gratch study, for example, the infants could not experience specific expectations before the experiment began. Once the objects were covered, expectations were present for the 16-month-olds; at least, we infer so from the infant's subsequent surprise and search. An adult may initiate his own expectations; if so, the development from perceptually elicited to independently initiated expectations would be interesting to explore.

The focus on the information outside the observer should not be taken as an empty organism approach. A recent article by Wilcox and Katz

(1981) discusses the virtues of the ecological over the cognitive approach. One virtue they see is that the ecological approach does not have to concern itself with the "state" variable between input and output. In their terms, "state" refers to memory and cognitive organization. Although the cognitive approach emphasizes the internal changes, the ecological approach emphasizes the organization in the environment. To the extent that the organization is "out there," that is, to the extent that the environment is specified by information in the light, encounters with the world will be determined in part by the amount of information that has been picked up. Experience, however, does lead to an altered state of the organism. When invariants have been detected, there must be some change (permanent or semipermanent) in the brain that makes those invariants more easily detected at another time and allows for the perception of "same-as-before." There is also some predictability in the order in which information is picked up; a process of differentiation ensures such sequences because finer distinctions can be made only after grosser ones. An experienced organism, therefore, perceives more and different things than an inexperienced one.

A second role of the organism depends not on perceptual learning but on motivational factors. Our perception is determined in part by our needs and our intentions. We are usually not just "looking," for example, but "looking for." If someone is walking on a rocky beach looking for a stone to throw at a seagull, he will pick up information that is different from the information he would pick up if he were looking for stones to skip in the water. An infant who is satisfied may be looking for friendliness in any adult around him, but a hungry infant is more likely to detect the invariants specifying the unique characteristics of his mother. Intention must be generated internally, but our recognition of familiar objects will be somewhat different (i.e., we will detect different invariants) depending on the extent and way in which those objects can serve our particular needs and intentions at the time.

This difference in the cognitive and ecological approaches is one of emphasis, in the sense that not all of our knowledge of the world can be acquired by perception alone. In general, however, the more carefully we analyze the information available outside the observer, the more likely we are to explain some aspects of behavior and development without recourse to cognitive structures. Although development involves the growth of knowledge, the manipulation of symbols, or processes like inference and memory, it seems parsimonious to consider first the possiblity that observed behavioral changes over age stem from an increasing ability to pick up information about the world as a result of differentiation and changes in motivation.

Everything I have said suggests that the perceiver frequently has all the information he needs, but there are situations in which we must act and make decisions without adequate information. One form of action, of course, is to obtain more information by moving around or by repeating some movement, and I think that is exactly what happens in many cases where the situation is ambiguous. When further exploration is not possible and where there is a need for judgment—being an eyewitness at a car accident, for example—then we do rely on processes other than perception. In general, we are helped tremendously by learning the probabilities of co-occurence of different events, so that when we see one we assume the presence of the other even though we do not perceive it. These are all very important aspects of behavior to study. It is useful, however, to balance these endeavors with a consideration of how we behave in situations in which the information is adequate and in which there is a very precise analysis of that information.

The thrust of my comments is clearly that memory may not be a necessary or useful concept in the explanation of much of infant behavior, including that which indexes recognition and expectations. We all have a commonsense notion of what the term means, but scientific inquiry demands more precision. My opinion is that we would be better served by reserving the term memory for "recollection," the evocation of images or words representing absent objects and events. Are infants capable of recollection? There are several chapters in this volume that address that intriguing question (see Chapters 4, 5, & 8), and I will leave the topic to them. For the behaviors I have discussed, there seems to be little reason to distinguish between perception and memory. This assertion leaves me in a somewhat paradoxical position in a discussion of infant memory, but the position is a necessary outcome of the view that perception occurs over time and is continuous.

References

Acredelo, L. P. Development of spatial orientation in infancy. *Developmental Psychology*, 1978, *14*, 224–234.

Acredelo, L. P. Laboratory versus home: The effect of environment on the 9-month-old infant's choice of spatial reference system. *Developmental Psychology*, 1979, *15*, 666–667.

Acredelo, L. P., & Evans, D. Developmental changes in the effects of landmarks on infant spatial behavior. *Developmental Psychology*, 1980, *4*, 312–318.

Baddely, A. Applied cognitive and cognitive applied psychology: The case of face recognition. In L. G. Nilsson (Ed.), *Perspectives on memory research*. Hillsdale, N.J.: Erlbaum, 1979.

Benson, J. B., & Uzgiris, I. C. *The role of self produced movement in spatial understanding.* Paper presented at the Society for Research in Child Development, Boston, April 1981.

Bertenthal, B. I., Proffitt, D. R., & Cutting, J. E. Infant sensitivity to figural coherence in biomechanical motions. *Journal of Experimental Child Psychology*, 1984, in press.

Bower, T. G. R. The development of object permanence: Some studies of existence constancy. *Perception and Psychophysics*, 1967, *2*, 411–418.

Bremner, J. G. Egocentric versus allocentric spatial coding in nine-month-old infants: Factors influencing the choice of code. *Developmental Psychology*, 1978, *14*, 346–355.

Bremner, J. G., & Bryant, P. E. Place versus response as the basis of spatial errors made by young infants. *Journal of Experimental Child Psychology*, 1977, *23*, 162–171.

Brooks, L. Nonanalytic concept formation and memory for instances. In E. Rosch & B. B. Lloyd (Eds.), *Cognition and categorization*. Hillsdale, N.J.: Erlbaum, 1978.

Bryant, P. E., Jones, P., Claxton, V., & Perkins, G. M. Recognition of shapes across modalities. *Nature*, 1972, *240*, 303–304.

Bushnell, E. W. *The basis of infant visual-tactual functioning—amodal dimensions or multimodal compounds?* Paper presented at the International Conference on Infant Studies, Austin, Texas, March 1982.

Butterworth, G., Jarrett, N., & Hicks, L. Spatiotemporal identity in infancy: Perceptual competence or conceptual deficit? *Developmental Psychology*, 1982, *18*, 435–449.

Caron, A. J., & Caron, R. F. Cognitive development in early infancy. In T. Field, A. Huston, H. C. Quay, L. Troll, & G. E. Finley (Eds.), *Review of human development*. New York: Wiley, 1982.

Cohen, L., & Caputo, N. *Instructing infants to respond to perceptual categories.* Paper presented at the International Conference on Infancy Studies, Providence, R.I., March 1978.

Cohen, L. B. Our developing knowledge of infant perception and cognition. *American Psychologist*, 1979, *34*, 894–899.

Cornell, E. H. Learning to find things: A reinterpretation of object permanence studies. In L. S. Siegel & C. J. Brainerd (Eds.), *Alternatives to Piaget: Critical essays on theory*. New York: Academic Press, 1977.

Cornell, E. H., & Heth, C. D. Response versus place learning by human infants. *Journal of Experimental Psychology: Human Learning and Memory*, 1979, *5*, 188–196.

Cutting, J. E., & Kozlowski, L. T. Recognizing friends by their walk: Gait perception without familiarity cues. *Bulletin of the Psychonomic Society*, 1977, *9*, 353–356.

Cutting, J. E., Proffitt, D., & Kozlowski, L. T. A biomechanical invariant for gait perception. *Journal of Experimental Psychology: Human Perception and Performance*, 1978, *4*, 357–372.

Fox, R., & McDaniel, C. The perception of biological motion by human infants. *Science*, 1982, *218*, 486–487.

Gibson, E. J., & Walker, A. S. *Intermodal perception of substance.* Paper presented at the Third International Conference on Infant Studies, Austin, Texas, April 1982.

Gibson, E. J., Owsley, C. J., & Johnston, J. Perception of invariants by 5 month old infants: Differentiation of two types of motion. *Developmental Psychology*, 1978, *14*, 407–415.

Gibson, E. J., Owsley, C. J., Walker, A., & Megaw-Nyce, J. Development of the perception of infants: Substance and shape. *Perception*, 1979, *8*, 609–619.

Gibson, J. J. The problem of temporal order in stimulation and perception. *The Journal of Psychology*, 1966, *62*, 141–149.

Gibson, J. J. *An ecological approach to visual perception.* Boston: Houghton Mifflin, 1979.

Gottfried, A., Rose, S., & Bridger, W. Effects of visual, haptic, and manipulatory experiences on infants' visual recognition memory of objects. *Developmental Psychology*, 1978, *14*, 305–312.

Gratch, G., Appel, K. J., Evan, W. F., LeCompte, G. K., & Wright, N. A. Piaget's Stage IV object concept error: Evidence of forgetting or object conception? *Child Development*, 1974, *45*, 71–77.

Harris, P. L. Examination and search by young infants. *British Journal of Psychology*, 1971, *62*, 469–473.

Harris, P. L. Perseverative errors in search by young infants. *Child Development*, 1973, *44*, 28–33.

Jenkins, J. J., Wald, J., & Pittenger, J. B. Apprehending pictorial events: An instance of psychological cohesion. In C. W. Savage (Ed.), *Minnesota studies in the philosophy of science* (Vol. 9), Minneapolis: University of Minnesota Press, 1978.

Johannson, G. Visual perception of biological motion and a model for its analysis. *Perception and Psychophysics*, 1973, *14*, 201–211.

Lawson, K. R. Spatial and temporal congruity and auditory-visual integration in infants. *Developmental Psychology*, 1980, *16*, 185–192.

LeCompte, G. K., & Gratch, G. Violation of a rule as a method of diagnosing infants' levels of object concept. *Child Development*, 1972, *43*, 385–396.

Mace, W. James J. Gibson's strategy for perceiving: Ask not what's inside your head but what your head's inside of. In R. Shaw & J. Bransford (Eds.), *Perceiving, acting, and knowing*. Hillsdale, N.J.: Erlbaum, 1977.

MacNamara, J. Cognitive basis of language learning in infants. *Psychological Review*, 1972, *79*, 1–13.

Milewski, A. Visual discrimination and detection of configurational invariance in 3-month-old infants. *Developmental Psychology*, 1979, *15*, 357–363.

Neisser, U. *Cognition and reality*. San Francisco: W. H. Freeman, 1976.

Nelson, K. Concept, word and sentence: Interrelations in acquisition and development. *Psychological Review*, 1974, *81*, 267–285.

Nelson, K. E. Infants' short-term progress toward one component of object permanence. *Merrill-Palmer Quarterly*, 1974, *20*, 3–8.

Piaget, J. *The origin of intelligence in children*. New York: International Universities Press, 1952.

Posner, M. I., & Warren, R. E. Traces, concepts, and conscious constructions. In A. W. Melton & E Martin (Eds.), *Coding processes in human memory*. Washington, D.C.: Winston & Sons, 1972.

Reiser, J. J. Spatial orientation of six-month-old infants. *Child Development*, 1979, *50*, 1078–1087.

Rose, S. A., Gottfried, A. W., & Bridger, W. H. Cross-modal transfer and information processing by the sense of touch in infancy. *Developmental Psychology*, 1981, *17*, 90–98.

Rose, S. A., Gottfried, A. W., & Bridger, W. H. Infants' cross-modal transfer from solid objects to their graphic representations. *Child Development*, 1983, *54*, 686–695.

Rovee-Collier, C. K., & Gekoski, M. J. The economics of infancy: A review of conjugate reinforcement. *Advances in Child Development and Behavior*, 1979, *13*, 195–255.

Rovee-Collier, C. K., & Sullivan, M. W. Organization of infant memory. *Journal of Experimental Psychology: Human Learning and Memory*, 1980, *6*, 798–807.

Rovee-Collier, C. K., Enright, M., Lucas, D., Fagen, J. W., & Gekoski, M. J. The forgetting of newly acquired and reactivated memories of 3-month-old infants. *Infant Behavior and Development*, 1981, *4*, 317–331.

Ruff, H. A. *Detection of information specifying the motion of objects by infants of three and five months. Developmental Psychology*, in press.

Ruff, H. A., & Kohler, C. J. Tactual-visual transfer in six-month-old infants. *Infant Behavior and Development*, 1978, *1*, 259–264.

Spear, N. E. Retrieval of memory in animals. *Psychological Review*, 1973, *80*, 163–194.

Spelke, E. S. The development of intermodal perception. In L. B. Cohen & P. Salapatek (Eds.), *Handbook of infant perception*. New York: Academic Press, in press.

Walker, S., Owsley, C. J., Megaw-Nyce, J., Gibson, E. J., & Bahrick, L. E. Detection of elasticity by young infants as an invariant property of objects. *Perception*, 1980, *9*, 713–718.

Werner, J. S., & Perlmutter, M. Development of visual memory in infants. *Advances in Child Behavior and Development*, 1979, *14*, 1–56.

Wilcox, S., & Katz, S. The ecological approach to development: An alternative to cognitivism. *Journal of Experimental Child Psychology*, 1981, *32*, 247–263.

CHAPTER 4

Representation and Recall in Infancy

Jean M. Mandler

Department of Psychology
University of California at San Diego
La Jolla, California

Introduction

A pervasive part of the Piagetian legacy is the belief that fundamental changes in the representation of knowledge occur over the course of development. The most dramatic shift in the representational system is said to take place at the end of infancy (the sensorimotor period). This shift can be understood as a change from merely *knowing how* to also *knowing that*. In other words, it is a shift from a procedural to a declarative form of representation (J. Mandler, 1983). As conceived by Piaget, the infant has no representation of the world other than sets of motor and perceptual procedures, that is, mechanisms for acting and for recognizing things. Altogether lacking, in this view, are sets of concepts about the world, gathered together into categories or other abstract formats and accessible to thought independently of familiar recognitory or motor routines.

What are the implications of this view for memory? As I have described it elsewhere,

> it is a most un-Proustian life, not thought, only lived. Sensorimotor schemata . . . enable a child to walk a straight line but not to think about a line in its absence, to recognize his or her mother but not to think about her when she is gone. It is a world difficult for us to conceive, accustomed as we are to spend much of our time ruminating about the past and anticipating the future. Nevertheless, this is the state that Piaget posits for the child before 1½, that

Preparation of this chapter was supported in part by NSF research grant BNS-8109657.

is, an ability to recognize objects and events but an inability to recall them in
their absence. Because of this inability . . . the child cannot even remember
what he or she did a few minutes ago, what his room looks like or what she
had for lunch, except accidentally in the course of carrying out actions relevant
to these past perceptions and activities. (J. Mandler, 1983, pp. 424–425)

This is indeed a primitive human, with a representational system akin
to that of any garden variety mammal. It can recognize that which has
been experienced before, so it can be said to have a functioning memory
system. But it cannot remember its past without external support, and
even with such support (for example, in the context of repeating a familiar
activity), retrieval is severely restricted. At best, after about a year of
life, the infant is said to be capable of "prevision," in which the early
portion of a familiar sequence gives rise to a kind of imageless (contentless)
anticipation of something further to come (Piaget, 1952).

The transition from the sensorimotor period of infancy to the preoperational period of early childhood is, according to Piaget, marked by
the onset of a new type of process—the ability to recall, or, as Piaget
defined it, the ability to evoke absent objects. The emergence of this
fundamental human ability is associated, for Piaget, with two other new
and qualitatively distinct characteristics: the development of a conceptual
system and the formation of symbols to refer to those concepts. Indeed,
it is only at this stage that Piaget was willing to ascribe any representational
system to the child. He was unwilling to admit the prior sensorimotor,
procedural knowledge to the realm of representation, because for him
representation meant concepts, and concepts in turn had to be, if not
context-free, at least accessible out of context. Early concepts might be
primitive (unanalyzed images, for example), but for recall (or thinking)
to occur, there must be some mechanism to query them independently
of perceptual or motor procedures. For Piaget that mechanism was a
symbol system.

Piaget believed that many processes commonly found in older children and adults are absent before about 1½ years. He stated that infants
do not use symbols either in play or as a communicative device. They do
not solve problems through thought alone, only through the procedurally
guided trial and error he called "intelligent groping." Infants do not recall
(although it may be noted that recall unaccompanied by language is difficult to document). Even early language he found to be tied to specific
sensorimotor procedures, to be used as an accompaniment to a routine,
not for symbolic purposes.

These observations have been made by others as well, but more
recently there have been occasional suggestions that recall may occur
considerably earlier than Piaget believed, perhaps in the second 6 months
of life. Would such a finding mean that a declarative system of conceptual

knowledge is being formed earlier than Piaget thought? Or is it possible for a purely procedural organism to engage in recall? It appears that to consider the question of memory in infancy is to raise fundamental questions about the architecture of the infant's representational system.

In the first part of this chapter, I will reexamine Piaget's formulation. To begin, I will try to clarify the terminology, because *recall* and *recognition* carry different implications for psychologists who work with infants than for those who work with adults. I will then raise the issue of the conditions in any organism that are required for recall to take place. In the second part of the chapter, I will turn to the charge given to me at the conference on which this book was based, to relate infant memory to memory in older children and adults. My search will be for continuity, to see if we can find mechanisms whose roots lie in infancy that will help us to understand the retrieval processes that underlie recall.

The Ontogenesis of Recall

Because the terms *recall* and *recognition* often go undefined in the literature, there are serious problems in trying to trace the continuity of memory from infancy to adulthood. Let us first consider studies of recognition, because most research on infant memory has involved this concept. I believe that in all adult studies the term *recognition* implies consciousness or awareness of prior occurrence. It is assumed that the adult is aware that the item in question has been experienced in his or her personal past. In adults, such recognition is thought to have two components (G. Mandler, 1980). One of these is a familiarity component, caused by repeated exposures during which perceptual integration and organization take place. The other is a retrieval component that involves the search for contextual information, typically concerning when or where the item was experienced in the past. We meet someone who seems familiar, whom we cannot identify; a retrieval search is required to find the person's name or the place where we met. We read a word which seems familliar but whose meaning we cannot recover without examining the context in which it occurs. The retrieval process in these examples is thought to be the same process that occurs in recall (G. Mandler, 1980).

Recognition is usually studied in adults by requiring them to make some sort of yes/no judgment as to whether or not they have experienced the item before. They can do this on the basis of sheer familiarity and/or by engaging in a retrieval process such that they can recall the item. Whether one or both components are involved, the ability to make a yes/

no judgment requires *awareness* of prior occurrence or "pastness"; its loss is one of the hallmarks of amnesia (see Chapter 8). A number of studies have shown that amnesics retain the ability to be influenced by past experience and to learn at least certain kinds of new skills, but they have lost the awareness that these experiences are familiar to them (e.g., Cohen & Squire, 1980; Graf, Squire, & Mandler, 1984; Warrington & Weiskrantz, 1974, 1982).

The literature on infant recognition has been concerned almost exclusively with the familiarity component. It has not concerned itself by and large with the retrieval component and, to my knowledge, has not even raised the issue of whether or not the infant who demonstrates familiarity with a stimulus has any awareness of "having seen that before." Familiarity with a stimulus is typically measured by habituation (e.g., a decrease in looking time); lack, or relative lack, of familiarity is measured by dishabituation (e.g., an increase in looking time). The issue here is not that these measures are fallible (which they are because of the interaction of familiarity with interest or other factors). The point is that measures of habituation and dishabituation do not tap the same process as a yes/no recognition task in which the subject is asked specifically about awareness of the past.

Let us call the ability to recognize, in the sense of showing the effects of past experience on behavior, *primitive recognition.*[1] This kind of recognition is due to a modification of the perceptual apparatus itself and does not require retrieval of information from elsewhere in the system. This very basic process is present in the neonate, as it is in all animal species, but it need not be accompanied by an awareness of familiarity. Great caution will be needed when relating the large infant recognition literature to most studies of recognition in adults, since with the exception of the amnesic literature (and related studies of normals inspired by the findings from amnesics), the adult literature assumes awareness of familiarity as part of the tasks being used. The infant literature does not.

Turning to the concept of *recall*, we find a slightly different set of problems. Here we often find the terms *recall* and *retrieval* being used synonymously. Although recall is sometimes defined as that which results from retrieval, frequently it is not defined at all, and a commonsense meaning for the term is assumed. In fact, Piaget's definition of recall as the evocation of absent objects is probably close to what most of us have in mind when we use the term. We probably also have in mind that the evocation should be conscious, but we may disagree as to whether or not this consciousness must include awareness of prior occurrence. I will

---

[1]The term refers to the process that in the adult literature is sometimes called *perceptual learning* or *perceptual identification* (Jacoby, 1983; Jacoby & Dallas, 1981).

define recall as accessing (bringing to awareness) a cognitive structure pertaining to a past experience not currently available to perception. Thus, the definition includes a component of conscious awareness. It does not, however, include the necessity of the person's being aware that the item or event in question comes from past experience. That has to do with the person's belief system and is probably not vital for distinguishing the types of processes involved in recall. We sometimes recall things that we have not experienced, as when we remember default values (i.e., the most likely things to have happened) in an incompletely experienced situation, and we often know something without knowing how we know it or even being sure that we knew it before.

Although conscious recognition can sometimes occur on the basis of familiarity alone without the necessity of a retrieval component, recall always involves retrieval. Information about an absent experience must be retrieved from the memory (representational) system on the basis of an external or internal cue; that is, retrieval is the mechanism by which recall takes place. Retrieval itself is not available to consciousness, only its products, and its products must reach consciousness for recall to occur. It is possible for information to be retrieved from the memory system and acted on, as in expectancy learning, without this information becoming conscious. Hence, retrieval is a necessary, but not sufficient, condition for recall.

The recalled information need not be of a particular type; it can be verbal or imaginal, visual or auditory, a motor act or an emotional state. The only criterion is that it be all or part of a cognitive structure relevant to a prior experience that is not currently being perceived. I cannot think of a reason to restrict recall to any subset of the attributes of a past experience. Yet when it is stated explicitly that recall can involve retrieval of an action or an emotional state as well as an image or a thought and that it need not include awareness of its "pastness," it becomes apparent that in principle it might be an early developing phenomenon.

Another distinction we must make concerns intentional and incidental remembering. Recall can occur as a result of a query to the representational system; that is, some cue instigates a deliberate search process. This is the common laboratory situation. We ask people to remember; we give them a task and they set about it with deliberate intent to remember. We also set ourselves queries, as when we try to recall what we ate for dinner last Sunday or where we left the car keys. Retrieval in these cases is directed and controlled (to some extent) by the query.

Recall, however, can also occur incidentally through a process of being reminded. We are not trying to retrieve a piece of information, but an external or internal cue automatically brings it to our awareness. We see a bearded gentleman and are reminded of our father. We find ourselves murmuring the next line of a familiar play before it is spoken. We are reminded of many things in the reverie that comes before sleep, when thought skips idly from topic to topic. In none of these cases is a deliberate search taking place; information is being automatically retrieved. The retrieval process may have different characteristics in reminding than in deliberate recall (perhaps a broader spread of activation); but it would unduly restrict our definition of recall if these kinds of reminding were excluded.

With these definitions in place we come to several choice points as to the capabilities we are willing to ascribe to the infant. First, can infants retrieve information but not recall it (i.e., bring it to awareness)? Second, if infants can recall, can they only be reminded or can they engage in deliberate memory search? Third, if infants can engage in either kind of recall, can they do so only on the basis of external cues or also on the basis of self-generated ones?

Let us assume that infants do *not* engage in deliberate memory search. Certainly they are not asked to do so before the age at which parents play "Can you do it?" games with them, and we have no evidence they set themselves this task. Nevertheless, there *is* evidence that infants have the capacity to be reminded. In contrast to the Piagetian position that recall is not possible until Stage VI (roughly 1½ years), Ashmead and Perlmutter (1980) have presented data indicating this type of recall in children as young as 7 months. Some of Piaget's observations of his own children in Stage III can be interpreted (although he did not) as instances of reminding. For example, he describes one of his Stage III children reaching behind her to recover a toy with which she had been playing a minute before (Piaget, 1954). She might have been engaged in a deliberate retrieval search or more likely was merely being reminded, but it appears that some sort of recall was taking place. For purposes of demonstrating reminding, it would not matter if an action schema or an external cue were the only kinds of retrieval cue the infant could use; what does matter and remains unanswered is whether the retrieval process results in awareness.

As long as reminding by an external cue is included in our definition of recall, the necessary retrieval mechanism is in place very early. At the simplest level, the earliest type of retrieval occurs in simple conditioning. We know that S-S expectancy learning and operant conditioning occur in the neonate, and classical conditioning begins shortly thereafter (Sameroff & Cavanaugh, 1979). Piaget used examples of conditioning to chart the earliest precursors of later symbolic functioning. The 3-week-old infant who begins sucking movements at the sight of bottle or breast is responding to a signal, according to Piaget, or to a discriminative stimulus, to use the terminology of another literature. Piaget described the course of attaching an unconditioned response to a conditioned stimulus as reciprocal assimilation, as for example, when the innate response of sucking to buccal stimulation becomes aroused by, or integrated with, a visual schema. Although he explicitly rejected the terminology of learning theory, Piaget let assimilation and reciprocal assimilation in particular function as his principle of association (Piaget, 1952).

Whatever terminology we use, the formation of an expectancy involves retrieval of information about an absent object; that is, something beyond primitive recognition has taken place. The expectation of milk in the mouth may be context-bound and limited to occasions when an external cue is present, but the activation of one schema by another involves retention of and retrieval of information. Indeed, the infant conditioning literature is sometimes interpreted in terms of cued retrieval or recall (e.g., Rovee-Collier & Fagen, 1981; Spear, 1976). However, conditioning experiments ignore the component of consciousness, so given the definition of recall as requiring awareness, such terminological usage may be misleading. To reiterate, retrieval of information is a necessary, but not sufficient, condition for recall to occur.

It is clear why Piaget did not consider early conditioned signals or their more sophisticated sisters, the "indications" of Stage IV, to have symbolic status (Piaget, 1952). Such signals do not have the mobility and flexibility that he required symbols to have; they are limited to cueing highly specific schemas that have been previously associated with them. It is less clear why he maintained that the information retrieved by a signaling cue is so limited in extent. Even in the case of a cue enabling a year-old child to have prevision of some object or event to come, Piaget claimed that the child cannot imagine the object or event. For example,

> when Jacqueline expects to see a person where a door is opening, or fruit juice in a spoon coming out of a certain receptacle, it is not necessary, in order that there be understanding of these signs and consequently prevision, that she picture these objects to herself in their absence. It is enough that the sign set in motion a certain attitude of expectation and a certain schema of recognition of persons or food. (Piaget, 1952, p. 252)

Hence in Piagetian theory the child has no explicit (conscious) information in this situation. She expects something but does not have the capacity to be aware of what it is that she expects. We should note, however, that in terms of the available evidence, there are two other possibilities; either the child can explicitly recall what she expects or, upon encountering it in the surround, can then be aware (in contrast to the primitive recognition that Piaget seems to have assumed) that that was what she expected. The latter phenomenon is a common experience of adults. Sometimes when we are searching for an item, we realize that we do not remember what we are looking for; we may continue to search

in the hope that when our eyes alight on the object we will be aware that
that was it! (As an absent-minded professor, I can verify that the technique
often works.)

If it is possible for the child to realize that the something seen is the
something expected, why cannot he or she recall the expected object in
its absence? The ability to be aware that something was the object of
one's expectation or search seems to be closely related to the ability to
bring the information to mind in the first place. We cannot answer this
question about infants at the present time and may have to rely on both
new techniques and a theory of the growth of consciousness, which have
yet to be worked out. Nevertheless, I see no evidence in the observations
of Piaget or others militating against the notion that an infant can recall
(be reminded of) explicit information by means of a cue associated with
it. It may be that such cues are effective only if they are external or part
of an action schema. Even if an infant cannot recall her mother, for
example, when waking alone and hungry in the night, she may be able to
recall her mother at the sound of footsteps coming down the hall.

Indeed, some of the recently collected examples of recall in 7- and
9-month olds are easier to explain if we posit some form of explicit conceptualization.[2] Take an example from Ashmead and Perlmutter (1979).
A 9-month-old girl is accustomed to play with ribbons kept in the bottom
drawer of a bureau. One day she crawls to the bureau, opens the bottom
drawer, and finds no ribbons. She proceeds to open all the drawers until
she finds the ribbons, which have been removed to the top drawer. The
next day she crawls to the bureau and immediately opens the top drawer
and removes the ribbons. It is easier to explain such performance by
assuming that the information retrieved by the cue of the bureau was an
explicit conceptualization of the location of the ribbons and not merely
an attitude of expectation followed by recognition, conscious or otherwise. At the least, Piaget's hypothesis would require an explanation of
how the child had updated her usual procedure so easily, a finding not
easy to reconcile with his notion of a still incomplete concept of the object
and the likelihood of an $A\overline{B}$ error in this type of situation.

The Ashmead and Perlmutter observations are anecdotal (as, of course,
were Piaget's) but should be amenable to test in more formal fashion. It
would seem an important route of research to follow, since at present we
have little notion as to just how early we will find recall of a past experience. The data just described suggest such processing by 9 months of
age, but it might well occur earlier. It should also be noted that the data

---

[2]The conceptualization need not be an image; the present formulation is neutral with respect
to a propositional or imaginal format.

are neutral with respect to the issue of deliberate retrieval versus reminding. What little evidence we have about recall in infancy is consistent with retrieval through reminding alone rather than through externally or self-instigated search of memory. Although Piaget did not discuss this issue, his statements about recall as a relatively late acquisition probably referred to deliberate recall—an active attempt to remember, rather than an automatic by-product of certain cues. Deliberate recall is indeed likely to be a later acquisition than reminding, but if we restrict our studies of recall, as has typically been done in the laboratory, to deliberate remembering, we are apt to miss important information about the mechanisms underlying the process.[3]

We must still consider the relationship between various forms of representation and the ability to recall, whether that be of the reminding variety or the result of deliberate search through memory. The *sine qua non* for recall is the ability to access stored information, that is, to bring it to awareness. As stated earlier, one may not have to know that it is from the past (as one must be *aware* of familiarity to meet the criterion for conscious recognition), but one must be able to represent the information to oneself. Such accessibility may or may not require the ability to image or to form some kind of symbol to represent the information, as Piaget suggested, but in either case, accessibility is the crucial question when we ask about the ontogenesis of recall. Accessibility is more than the ability to retrieve information; as discussed earlier, retrieval mechanisms are operative from birth, but in themselves they may not be sufficient to bring information to consciousness.

It may be that consciousness does not exist at birth but requires some maturation or accumulated experience to develop. Alternatively, awareness may be present and reminding processes in place, but we merely lack the techniques to measure them. A third possibility is that even reminding requires information to be stored in an accessible knowledge system.

Piaget (1952) and others (e.g., Bruner, 1966) have given a convincing account of the procedural nature of infant representation. To the extent that the infant's representational system is solely procedural in nature, knowledge may be organized in such a way that conscious access to it is quite restricted. Further, the procedures that have been described in infancy are of a relatively limited character, in that they all involve sensory or motor routines. The infant's knowledge of how to do things, such as to execute motor programs or to recognize familiar things (in the primitive

---

[3]Deliberate recall refers, of course, to the processes occurring at the time of retrieval and not to the conditions (deliberate or incidental learning) under which the to-be-recalled material was encoded.

sense of the term), may simply not permit the accessibility associated with a declarative system of concepts and facts.

In general, information from sensorimotor procedures remains inaccessible. Piaget and others have documented the lack of knowledge, even in adults, of how we walk and crawl and of many physical principles that we use in our actions (e.g., diSessa, 1982; Piaget, 1976). We also have relatively little conscious knowledge about what people's faces and other complex stimuli look like in spite of our great accuracy in recognizing them. For example, complex information about the proportions of the human face is used during the process of recognition, but without artistic training few people can say what the proportions are. Similarly, skilled typists frequently cannot say or reconstruct exactly where the letters appear on the keyboard (Grudin, 1983). Furthermore, our descriptions of the information we use in our perceptual and action procedures are often mistaken (e.g., McCloskey, Caramazza, & Green, 1980; Shannon, 1976). Of course, we may simply not have analyzed a given procedure, but even when we have, the information that has been extracted is partial at best and often incorrect. It seems that it is the *descriptions* that we access when we try to recall procedural information. The descriptions are influenced by our beliefs about our bodies and the world and are not the same as the procedures themselves; that is, when we recall, we are accessing the products of our procedures or conclusions we have drawn about their workings (see Nisbett & Wilson, 1977 for related arguments).

If information encoded in sensory and motor procedures is not accessible to consciousness and if an organism has only such a representational system, then recall, which requires accessibility, may not be possible. How then could such an organism ever acquire the ability to recall? I believe the traditional view is that procedures are initially opaque to consciousness, but with development the organism gradually learns how to become aware of them. This seems to be the assumption underlying most theories of metacognitive awareness (e.g., Flavell, 1978), but the problem of recall is broader than this. We need to understand how the infant comes to recall anything—not just procedures, but their results as well.

An alternative view would be that recall can occur only when analysis of the results of a procedure (a perception or a state produced by an action) has been carried out and the results of the analysis transferred to a declarative system. On this view, the infant could not be aware of, or recall, information *unless* it had been stored declaratively. The infant could learn to modify its procedures, just as do lower species, without storing the modifications in an accessible form.

Piaget's description of the development of recall is, I believe, of this type, although I admit to some free interpretation of his theory of symbol development (Piaget, 1952). I understand him to mean that one must form symbols for various pieces of information in order to call the information to mind. Symbols are formed initially through analysis of perceived information (a process he calls interiorized imitation). The symbols refer to concepts that are stored in a new kind of representational system, which I have referred to as a declarative knowledge base (J. Mandler, 1983). In other words, concepts derived from procedures are not themselves procedures; they have a format of their own.

In addition, verbally encoded information is entered directly into the declarative system. In general, the view that recall is only possible from such a system makes the following claim. Recallable (accessible) information is either stored in a symbolic form in the first place (presumably chiefly through language) or has been entered into the declarative system by analysis of perceptual information. Thus, when one is asked whether an acquaintance wears glasses, one can access this information only if the relevant perceptual analysis has been carried out (and it often has not) or if one has verbal information about the question.[4]

Although a view in which recall is possible only through one representational system may sound radical, it has a number of attractive characteristics. It allows a way of accounting for both continuities and discontinuities across species (for example, see Chapter 7). Motor and perceptual learning processes may be similar across most species, yet few species may be able to recall information in the sense in which the term is used in this chapter. The view also allows a way of characterizing a human infant, who may not be able to recall in the early days of life but within some months develops such a capacity. It is also consistent with the amnesic data referred to earlier, in which adults with certain types of brain injury retain procedural information and procedural learning abilities but have lost access to various types of information. In Chapter 8, Schacter and Moscovitch discuss a similar point of view with their description of early and late memory systems.

It remains to be said that this view of the requirements for recall is neutral with respect to the age at which a declarative system is formed. I have suggested elsewhere (J. Mandler, 1983) that the foundations of such a knowledge system may begin quite early. Since information can

[4]One can sometimes find the answer through a process of imagery (Kosslyn, 1980). If Kosslyn's formulation is correct, imagery requires two components: one is accessing a propositional store of facts, the other is carrying out a procedure based on stored perceptual information. However, unless the relevant information is in one of these stores, forming an image will not help answer the question. It is worth noting that the sensorimotor procedures described here as the earliest form of representation should not be taken to mean that there are no other kinds of procedure. Retrieval procedures are needed to access declarative information; imagery involves still other procedures.

enter the declarative system through perceptual analysis as well as verbally, there is no need to restrict recall to the verbal organism, even though
the rate at which knowledge enters a declarative system must vastly
increase with the onset of language. In the rest of the chapter, then, I
will not assume any particular stage of onset of the ability to recall,
although on the basis of data discussed earlier and elsewhere (J. Mandler,
1983), it may be much earlier than previously thought. Based on somewhat
similar reasoning, Schacter and Moscovitch (Chapter 8) suggest it may
occur around 8 months of age, which seems like a fair guess given the
small amount of available evidence.

If correct, it would place the onset of recall in Piaget's Stage IV. It
would be consistent with many of Piaget's observations during this stage
of development. He documented the onset of the "examining schema,"
which might indicate an upsurge in the tendency to engage in perceptual
analysis (Piaget, 1952). He also observed the coordination of secondary
schemata that allow means–end analyses (i.e., planning), the beginning
of search for vanished objects, the ability to imitate actions of invisible
body parts, the appearance of one-word speech, and even prevision. All
these observations suggest that the infant has become capable of accessing
information about absent objects.

Schema Formation and Recall

We can now turn to the complex issue of how the growing declarative
knowledge system controls the time course and nature of the retrieval
processes that result in recall. We have little information about this aspect
of infant memory. The best that I can do is to summarize some of what
we know about these matters in early and later childhood and to speculate
about what we might expect to find when they are investigated in infants.

In what follows, I will emphasize the schematic forms of representation that organize our knowledge of familiar events and places and hence
are based on temporal and spatial relations. This type of representation
differs in organization and in its effects on retrieval from taxonomic, or
classificatory, systems (J. Mandler, 1979; Rabinowitz & Mandler, 1983).
Although both forms of organization are found in the declarative system,
there is some evidence that taxonomic systems are an ontogenetically
later development than schematic forms. It is worth noting in passing,
however, that infants must be as responsive to similarity relations, on
which taxonomic systems are based, as they are to spatiotemporal rela-

tions. Certainly as early as 2 years (which is about the earliest age for which we have deliberate recall data), children recall lists of objects on the basis of similarity. They recall more from lists of related (similar) objects and show at least some clustering of their output into similar groups (Goldberg, Perlmutter, & Myers, 1974; Perlmutter & Myers, 1979).

In this section, however, I will consider the schematic representations of events, how they are formed, what their organization is like, and how they control retrieval. These are important questions for developmental studies of memory because one should expect major differences in recall between a situation in which a well-organized schema is available and one in which a schema is still primitive or as yet unformed. In fact, differences in recall in the two cases should provide an excellent source of information about the details of the underlying representations.

Event schemas are generalized knowledge structures formed through experiencing regularities in the environment. They are subject to largely unknown constraints on the kinds of things that will be segregated as units, the size of those units, and so forth. The constraints themselves are an interesting developmental question. Some units must occur because of procedural constraints on perception—for example, seeing objects *qua* objects or relating visual to auditory patterning (see Gibson & Spelke, 1983). Infants probably schematize events from an early age, in the sense of forming units from the ongoing stream of behavior and encoding them as sequences. Indeed, the conditioning of expectancies in neonates suggests an onset near birth. Expectations about event sequences may develop fairly rapidly. For example, Charlesworth (1966) and Greenfield (1972) found that by at least 4 months infants have learned to expect regular sequences in games such as peekaboo. Recently, Smith (in press) has demonstrated that 5 month olds are capable of accurate anticipations of a familiar sequence of events, if the sequence conforms to a well-organized, hierarchical structure.

The principles guiding the breakdown of activities, the coding of one sequence as having ended and the next begun, are for the most part unknown. It must be added that the extent to which the initial "parsing" of an event stream is a purely procedural issue and the conditions under which sufficient analysis of events is carried out to store information about them in a declarative system are also unknown. We do know from Nelson's work, however (e.g., Nelson, 1978; Nelson & Gruendel, 1981) that by at least age three such analyses have taken place and unified representations of some event sequences have been formed of sufficient stability to enable recall and verbal reports about them.

What are some possible principles that organize these early declarative representations? One way to organize knowledge about an event sequence would be to isolate some of the elements and to weight them or give them special prominence. The units in the representation might all be at the same level of generality, but some might be encoded as central, or even obligatory, to the sequence, whereas others might be given lesser weight. Such an analysis suggests a network or heterarchical representation, in which the number of connections or distance among nodes varies. It might also be cast into a quasi-hierarchical structure (e.g., Galambos & Rips, 1982), but it is important to bear in mind that "more central" is not the same thing as "more general." A hierarchical analysis of an event sequence typically aggregates basic units into more general ones to form higher level units, as in the analysis of scripts into scenes (Schank & Abelson, 1977) or the analysis of stories into episodes (J. Mandler & Johnson, 1977; Rumelhart, 1975). This form of analysis is a part–whole analysis, in which higher level units within a given branch of a tree are more general; they may or may not be more central or important (see Johnson & Mandler, 1980; J. Mandler, 1984).

Although relatively little work has been done on the structure of event sequences, the most common assumption in the adult literature on scripts has been that the organization of our knowledge about events is based on goals (Lichtenstein & Brewer, 1980; Schank & Abelson, 1977). According to this view, people break activities down into units on the basis of the goals and subgoals of each of the acts making up the sequence. This kind of analysis leads to a hierarchical format, with main goals near the top of the hierarchy and the subgoals nested beneath them. Hence, it amalgamates the two kinds of analysis described above; higher levels are both more important (or central) and more general.

Such a view seems appropriate for many kinds of human activities, but it is not obvious that it will account for the formation of event schemas in infancy and early childhood. The younger the infant the less likely that regularities in activities will be encoded in terms of the goals that structure them for adults. In addition, infants' own goals are often irrelevant to many of the activities they experience. This is not to deny that a great many infant schemas are goal based from their inception; many of the infant's sensorimotor procedures surely are. Here, however, I am considering those daily routines that the infant is involved in or observes, but that are arbitrary with respect to the child's goals. That is, I am not considering here procedural knowledge, such as that involved in grasping or feeding, but the formation of recallable, and eventually reportable, knowledge about the structure of daily activities.

It may also be noted that not all adult event schemas are goal based (G. Mandler, 1975). For example, the goals of some ritualized activities (not to mention many aspects of our daily routines) may be obscure even to adult participants. There are also abstract schemas, such as our knowledge of musical forms and the forms of traditional stories. Goals are also unlikely to form the basis of the schematic representation of places, although in this case the basis of unit formation might be expected to be different.

These considerations suggest that the initial basis for forming units in an event schema may be more primitive than a goal-based analysis, perhaps involving instead analysis in terms of objects, their locations, and changes in their locations over time. There is at least some evidence that the boundaries of units in the perception of simple action sequences are determined by distinctive changes in movement rather than by the achievement of goal states (Newtson, Engquist, & Bois, 1977). If this kind of analysis is the initial basis for forming units in event sequences, then goal-based analyses of events may be higher order analyses of simpler forms. Such higher order analyses are achieved at least by the preschool years. By this age many children's scripts for common event sequences are goal based in the same fashion as those of adults (Nelson, Fivush, Hudson, & Lucariello, 1983) and appear to influence recall in the same way as well. However, this may be a development that occurs after the initial stages of schema formation.

This discussion suggests one possible basis for differences in memory for event sequences between infancy and later childhood. To the extent that an event schema is organized around goal-based plans, that is, in terms of "in-order-to" relations, it will have a different structure from one based on a simple succession of acts, no matter what principle is involved in segregating the acts themselves. As discussed above, a goal-based script provides a basis for a hierarchical format in terms of important and unimportant acts, that is, for acts that are central or peripheral to the main goal. It also allows a different organization to be imposed on simultaneously occurring episodes from different schemas. For example, the mother's representation of cooking four courses for dinner at the same time may be quite different from that of the young child watching her. Little, if any, of the mother's complex structure of goals and subgoals is apt to be represented in the child's conception of the activity.

The present analysis is not concerned with differences in *content* between an infant's and an adult's schema. It seems obvious that an infant's representation will lack many aspects that an adult's possesses. Rather, I am concerned with the possibility that there may be different structural bases for earlier and later developing schemas. To the extent that a schema is formed without respect to the goal of the activity, it may not have the same hierarchical structure that a goal-based schema does. Non-goal-related aspects of the situation might be more heavily weighted, or each of the elements might be given roughly equal weight.

One basis for organization of a representational structure might be invariance of occurrence. In a mature schema, invariance is rare and few units can be said to be obligatory. This might not be true in the early stages of schema formation. If some element always occurs and others are variable when the schema is being developed, the former might be more heavily weighted in the representation. For example, it might be impossible for an infant to realize that a room is a bedroom if it is missing a bed or, to take an example of Nelson (1974), to understand that bedtime has arrived in the absence of a goodnight kiss. Another basis of structuring might be end-point anchoring. Primacy and recency effects might emphasize the end points of an event sequence, even though that is no longer true of a mature event schema (J. Mandler, 1979). Finally, an event sequence might be encoded as a linear string with all units given equal weight.

To the extent that a representation of an event sequence does not weight some units more than others or does not have a hierarchical structure in which more general units are subdivided into subsidiary parts, we might expect its linear sequential character to loom larger in processing. One can even speculate that, if there are only links between each event and the next, retrieval might be restricted to a linear search in a forward direction and that an irretrievable link might block further search. (Young children playing a piano piece from memory comes to mind—when memory fails they have no other recourse than to start over again.) Once a representation attains varying levels or branches, it should be possible to retrieve information either horizontally (sequentially) or vertically through the hierarchy.

Although recall of scripted activities typically proceeds in a sequential fashion and therefore has a strong horizontal component, Galambos and Rips (1982) have provided data indicating that there are some tasks in which adults access information in a primarily vertical fashion. They found that adults judged a central action to be part of a routine faster and more accurately than a peripheral one, but were no faster in judging actions early in the sequence than late ones. When required to confirm that two actions belonged to the same routine, again they were no faster or more accurate if the two actions were close together in the sequence than if they were far apart. Finally, when asked to say which of two actions occurs first in a routine, subjects were faster and more accurate when the actions were far apart rather than close together. These data, which involve judgments of category membership and in the last case judgments about sequential structure, can be contrasted with recall, in which members of the same unit are retrieved faster than items that cross a unit boundary (J. Mandler & Goodman, 1982; see Bower, Black, & Turner, 1979, for related data). Apparently a mature script has a number of access routes to and within it, which can be called on for different tasks.

When the task is recall, a schema provides a specific retrieval plan.

(This characteristic has mainly been studied for events but could plausibly be demonstrated for scenes as well.) An event schema, whether of scripted activities such as eating in a restaurant or getting up in the morning, or a schema for traditional stories, provides a known starting point, a temporally organized series of units or slots that narrow the search space considerably, and a clear-cut stop rule (J. Mandler, 1979). There have been a number of studies documenting the role that a schema plays in ordering recall in both children and adults. Some of the most convincing of these are studies in which misordered material is presented. During recall, the material tends to be output in canonical form, rather than in the sequence in which it was presented (J. Mandler, 1978; Stein & Nezworski, 1978). We have found this phenomenon from second grade to adulthood, using stories as materials, and Nelson and Gruendel (1981) have found the same thing for scripts in preschool children. The same result occurs even when children and adults are specifically instructed to recall the material in the order in which it was presented (J. Mandler and DeForest, 1979).

A related finding is that more is recalled when the material is presented in correct sequence than when it is misordered. Similarly, more is remembered from pictures of scenes when they are presented in organized form than when they are disorganized (e.g., J. Mandler & Ritchey, 1977; J. Mandler & Robinson, 1978). These phenomena, for both events and scenes, have been found at all ages tested, but they tend to be more pronounced in children. I have previously suggested that young children may be more dependent on familiar schemas for retrieval than adults, who are more flexible and have more options for retrieval (J. Mandler, 1979; 1983; see also Johnson, 1983, for similar arguments about children's summarization skills). Nelson et al. (1983) have also suggested that the younger the child, the more likely that memory will be affected by canonical script form.

The studies just described tell us that by age 3 or 4, declarative representations of familiar event sequences have a canonical order that controls recall. They do not tell us, however, whether the linear ordering has a hierarchical structure imposed on it. Further, it is possible that before age 3 the declarative representation of event sequences merely involves associations among a series of actions or individual events without any temporal structure at all. We are currently investigating these questions in 20-, 24-, 28-, and 36-month-old children, by having them imitate brief event sequences. This work is being conducted primarily by Tony Gerard and Barbara O'Connell. We devised a series of three-action sequences that should be familiar to children in this age range. For example, one sequence consists of putting a teddy bear in a tub, washing him, and drying him off. Another is putting food in a pan, stirring it, and then putting it on a plate. These sequences are presented in correct order, or in reversed order, or one action is taken from each of three different sequences, thus making an unrelated collection. After the child watches a given sequence, he or she is asked to do the same thing. The procedure is essentially a nonverbal version of a recall test.

In the two studies that have been carried out so far (O'Connell, Gerard, & Leong, 1983; Gerard, in preparation), the data indicate that even the youngest children show some rudimentary sequencing ability in their recall. The youngest children have higher sequencing scores on forward than on reversed sequences; they also recall more from related than from unrelated sequences. Slightly older children have higher sequencing scores and they are more successful in recalling the reversed sequences in backward order. By around 28 months, children begin to recall both forward and reversed sequences in the canonical forward order. By 36 months they do the sequencing well but once again tend to produce the reversed sequences in backward order. These data are reminiscent of the story and script data for older children and adults. As an event sequence is learned, it is easier to recall in its canonical order, even when it has been presented in some other manner. When a sequence is either very easy or very well known, it eventually becomes possible to recall in an unusual order if one is asked to do so. It is tempting to speculate that a tendency to recall a reversed sequence in a canonical forward order is a sign of a schema having been organized to the extent that it now plays a major role in retrieval of information.

Recent data by Haake and Somerville (in press) suggest that even younger children can recall sequential information. They studied 9- to 18-month-old children's ability to find an object that was hidden during the course of an event sequence. Fifteen- and 18-month-old children were able to use ordering information in the sequence to select the appropriate place to search for the object, although the 9- and 12-month-old children could not.

These data suggest that early representations of common event sequences contain ordering information, insofar as accessible versions of them are concerned. It remains to be seen if ordering information is accessible in the earliest declarative representations (that is, those developed before 15 months). In any case, the onset of this ability seems to be a later development than the acquisition of procedural knowledge about event sequences. The data of Smith (in press), discussed earlier, indicate that anticipation of familiar sequences can be demonstrated at 5 months. Anecdotal reports of parents about infants' distress when ordinary routines are changed also suggest that expectancies about event sequences influence encoding procedures at a relatively early age, as do the conditioning data discussed above; however, such information may not be accessible for purposes of recall as it has been defined in this chapter.

Another way in which a mature schema controls memory is by providing a source for reconstructing material that is not well remembered. A fully formed schema consists of slots or variables that guide attention toward a particular level of generality and away from the details embedded within them. The accuracy with which the main aspects of a situation or scene are encoded is a function of the values of the variables that fill these slots. If a given instantiation of the schema provides values for the variables that are near the ends of or outside the acceptable range of expectations, extra attention is drawn to them. If however, the values are within a normal range, the mature processor does not need to expend much attention on their details; it can rely on default processing, in which the most likely value is assumed to have occurred. Hence, when one cannot remember exactly what happened or exactly what some place looked like (perhaps because of not having attended to the information in the first place), the default value is the most likely to be recalled. It is worth noting that these reconstructed memories are often accompanied by a feeling of certainty and even imagery. We tend to assume that, if we can image something from the past, we must have seen it. Unfortunately for accuracy, we often confuse images from different occasions or construct an image to match a description.

Schematically based reconstruction in recall of stories has been reported for both children and adults (Mandler & Johnson, 1977; Stein & Glenn, 1979). In these studies, when subjects produced intrusions in recall, they tended to maintain the structural role of the forgotten material. Thus, the intrusions were correct in spirit, even though wrong in detail. I know of no comparable recall data earlier than age 5. However, we have found a similar phenomenon in the imitation experiments just described; many of the children intrude typical actions from the event sequences even though these were not modeled.

The final aspect of schematic representation to be discussed, one with far reaching implications for the study of infant memory and for schema formation itself, is the relationship between expectation and memory. This relationship is negative; the more expected something is, the less likely it is to be remembered. As discussed above, people tend to devote their attention to unusual values of variables and consequently to remember them better.

In one of the most detailed studies of this phenomenon, Friedman (1979) examined recognition of scenes of common places. She had subjects rate the probability of occurrence of each of the objects in the scenes. Other subjects studied the scenes and then took a recognition test. In each of the distractors, one object in a scene was either deleted or transformed in some way. Recognition was a strictly decreasing function of an object's probability of occurrence. Using the same technique, Goodman (1980) found that 7- to 9-year-old children responded in the same fashion as adults.

During encoding, subjects' first fixations on high-probability (expected) objects are shorter than on low-probability (unexpected) objects, suggesting that the scene schema, by specifying higher order properties, speeds the primitive recognition process. Even when asked to remember all the objects in a scene, subjects devote more attention to low-probability objects, which indicates the deep-seated control that schemas have on encoding (Friedman & Liebelt, 1981). Similar findings for verification time and accuracy of recognition have been reported for pictures of typical and atypical members of basic-level categories (Thompkins, 1981). In addition, recognition of atypical objects retains its advantage over time.

Exactly the same phenomena are found in memory for texts describing scripted activities (Graesser, 1981). Unexpected events are better recognized than expected ones and remain so over time. Similarly, low-probability events are better recalled than high-probability events. In the case of recall, however, the function changes over time, with low-probability events rapidly losing their advantage, eventually lagging behind recall of high-probability events (Graesser, 1981).[5] We have found related results in our laboratory; with delay, recall of irregular stories becomes more canonical in form. These findings suggest that recall, as opposed to recognition, becomes more dependent on the generic schema with the passage of time (see also Graesser & Nakamura, 1982).

The frequency effects described here are ubiquitous; they are even found in recognition of high- and low-frequency words (Kinsbourne & George, 1974; G. Mandler, Goodman, & Wilkes-Gibbs, 1982). For purposes of this chapter, however, the point emphasized is that the negative relationship between probability of occurrence and memory is surely one that develops. To the neonate, all objects and events are new, and the probabilities of their occurrence in various contexts have to be learned. Therefore, one would not expect in early infancy to find the effects of probability on encoding and memory that have been clearly established in adulthood. My understanding of the literature on infant (primitive) recognition literature is that this may be the case. Apparently, until about 2 months of age, there is no consistent preference for looking at the old

---

[5]Graesser's studies are unique in that careful correction was carried out in the recall tasks. When such corrections are not used, recall appears to be better for expected items (Brewer & Treyens, 1981; Goodman, 1980). High recall of expected items is usually accompanied by high rates of intrusion of schema-relevant, but unpresented, items.

or at the new. After about 2 months, however, infants typically prefer to look at novel (i.e., unusual) things.[6]

Although it is something of a leap to go from data on infant looking times to the duration of adult fixations on contextually familiar versus contextually unfamiliar objects, the comparison may have merit. In studies of infants' looking preferences, familiarity is built up during the course of an experimental session. During the first days of life, when visual schemas are few and encoding still primitive, infants tend to distribute their attention inconsistently across the stimuli with which they are presented. Once schema formation becomes more rapid and objects in general more easily encodable, infants begin to pay attention to novelty. The remarkable thing about this course of events is not that it occurs but that it develops so rapidly. When an infant reliably begins to gaze longer at new objects than at familiar ones suggests that the encoding process is beginning to be determined by mechanisms similar to those found in older children and adults. Whether longer gaze implies the transfer of information to the declarative knowledge system or whether these probability effects will be found in early recall are questions that remain to be answered.

Conclusions

This account of representation and recall in infancy has been speculative, hampered as we are by lack of both data and theory. I have suggested, however, that scene and event schemas begin to be formed early in life and that when formed they provide a set of retrieval mechanisms that in principle are the same as those used by adults. I also speculated on some possible differences that might obtain in the early stages of schema development. Enough data have accumulated by now to suggest that a representational system sufficient to mediate recall is established before the end of the first year. Further, at least one of the processes—expectancy learning—that will eventually lead to recall is operative during early infancy.

The mechanisms underlying the formation of expectancies are present at birth, and it seems plausible that they form the basis for the development

---

[6]The literature on this point is complex and varied. Under conditions of high uncertainty or inconsistent inputs (as in some cross-modal studies), familiarity may be preferred. On the other hand, preference for novelty may occur even earlier, depending on the saliency of the stimuli (see Chapter 1).

of later, more complex types of retrieval. Infants encode regularities in the environment and use them to anticipate what is to come: the baby is picked up and cradled, and milk follows; the diaper is removed and the bottom soothed. One might assume that in ontogenetical terms the infant becomes aware of the past before beginning to anticipate the future, but, if expectancy learning forms the first basis of retrieval, it seems likely that recall of an expected event (i.e., anticipation) would occur earlier than recall of a specific event from the past. Kessen and Nelson (1978) have suggested that, by the second 6 months of life, infants may be able to represent an absent object when a normal part of a familiar routine is missing. The tendency of a schema to run off automatically would provide the default value for the missing variable. An infant's fussing or searching may indicate an awareness of the absent portion, and hence, that recall has occurred.

This assumption is obviously speculative, and it is not clear how the issue of determining awareness in a preverbal organism will be solved. Persistent search is not in itself a clear indication of the presence of explicit information about the absent object (J. Mandler, 1983). Surpise might be a candidate measure if we could develop a sensitive system for measuring it. The problem with surpise (above and beyond its indirect nature) is in distinguishing it from a response to novelty *per se* since the latter is found in primitive recognition. However, it might be possible to develop scales of facial expression and other bodily responses as indicators of the violation of explicit knowledge.

The other major speculative issue discussed in this chapter concerns the notion of a dual representation system. The idea of more than one type of memory system is not in itself new, nor that some representations are procedural in nature and others declarative (e.g., Winograd, 1975). The particular problem raised by the present conception is how to relate the information used in perception to that which is recallable. The same information and sets of expectancies seem to be involved in both processes, and we typically speak about *a* schema in both cases.

Although in this sense the notion of two representational systems seems to be redundant, it might not be. When new information enters the declarative system, either by verbal means or by perceptual analysis, it is directly accessible in a way that it was not before. The information may have been contained in the procedure and used in the past, but it was not available to awareness. I used the example of face recognition to illustrate this point. The new, and now explicit, information must be stored in some format, and the speed and ease with which we can access it suggest that the format is not the same as that of the original procedure. That is, the explicit information is no longer buried in the recognitory procedure; there are other ways to get to it. This accessible information is what the organism is able to use productively for purposes of recall and a host of other functions, such as imitation, play, and language. Both the procedural and declarative forms of the information in question can be considered part of a single overall system, but if one wishes to speak of *a* schema for something that can be both primitively recognized and also recalled, one must still distinguish its procedural and declarative, or inaccessible and accessible, components.

I began by assuming very simple procedures in the infant, essentially the set of sensorimotor procedures discussed by Piaget. As infants experience regularities in the world, their perceptual procedures are modified to incorporate this information, and sets of expectancies (schemas) are set up. These expectancies determine which aspects of the environment are encoded. They presumably also determine which pieces of information receive the analysis that is required to transfer them to the declarative system. For example, they focus the infant's attention on the novel or unusual. In any case, only a subset of the information that is encoded becomes available for later recall.

This new type of information, which I have described as resulting from perceptual analysis or existing in already analyzed form by virtue of being prepackaged in language, presumably is also used to modify the perceptual procedures still further. That is, declarative knowledge influences procedural knowledge, and the entire system is probably highly interactive (see McCloskey & Kohl, 1983). Even if recall is only possible when a declarative system has been established, the retrieval processes presumably make use of the schemas that guided encoding in the first place. The retrieval processes involved in recall are themselves procedures and are also inaccessible. The present proposal, however, is that they output information that has been stored declaratively and that specific requirements must be met for such storage to take place. An organism can function relatively efficiently without the ability to recall. Even in its absence, learning can take place, and recognitory and motor procedures can be modified by experience.

As indicated throughout this chapter, accessibility of information is the most crucial issue in recall. Increasing ability to access information has been described by a number of psychologists as one of the major changes with development (e.g., Brown & Campione, 1980; J. Mandler, 1983). The stress has usually been placed on an increasing ability to reflect on or think about one's procedures (metacognition). The present conception forms an alternative way of describing the same phenomena: Information *about* one's procedures and derived *from* one's procedures must go through a process of analysis (which is not itself a conscious process) to be transferred to a declarative memory system. It is the latter system that allows conscious access to the information within it and upon whose contents we are able to reflect.

ACKNOWLEDGMENTS

   I am grateful to Nancy Johnson and George Mandler for their many insightful comments on the issues discussed.

References

Ashmead, D. H., & Perlmutter, M. *Infant memory in everyday life*. Paper presented at the American Psychological Association meetings, New York, 1979.
Ashmead, D. H., & Perlmutter, M. Infant memory in everyday life. In M. Perlmutter (Ed.), *New directions for child development: Children's memory* (Vol. 10). San Francisco: Jossey-Bass, 1980.
Bower, G. H., Black, J. B., & Turner, T. J. Scripts in memory for text. *Cognitive Psychology*, 1979, *11*, 177–120.
Brewer, W. F., & Treyens, J. C. Role of schemata in memory for places. *Cognitive Psychology*, 1981, *13*, 207–230.
Brown, A. L., & Campione, J. Inducing flexible thinking: The problem of access. In M. P. Friedman, J. P. Das, & N. O'Connor (Eds.), *Intelligence and learning*. New York: Plenum Press, 1980.
Bruner, J. S. On cognitive growth. In J. S. Bruner, R. R. Olver, & P. M. Greenfield (Eds.), *Studies in cognitive growth*. New York: Wiley, 1966.
Charlesworth, W. R. Persistence of orienting and attending behavior in infants as a function of stimulus-locus uncertainty. *Child Development*, 1966, *37*, 473–491.
Cohen, N. J., & Squire, L. R. Preserved learning and retention of pattern-analyzing skills in amnesia: Dissociation of knowing how and knowing that. *Science*, 1980, *210*, 207–210.
diSessa, A. A. Unlearning Aristotelian physics: A study of knowledge-based learning. *Cognitive Science*, 1982, *6*, 37–75.
Flavell, J. H. Metacognitive development. In J. M. Scandura & C. J. Brainerd (Eds.), *Structural-process theories of complex human behavior*. Leyden, The Netherlands: Sitjhoff, 1978.
Friedman, A. Framing pictures: The role of knowledge in automatized encoding and memory for gist. *Journal of Experimental Psychology: General*, 1979, *108*, 316–355.
Friedman, A., & Liebelt, L. S. On the time course of viewing pictures with a view toward remembering. In D. F. Fisher, R. A. Monty, & J. W. Senders (Eds.), *Eye movements: Cognition and perception*. Hillsdale, N.J.: Erlbaum, 1981.
Galambos, J. A., & Rips, L. J. Memory for routines. *Journal of Verbal Learning and Verbal Behavior*, 1982, *21*, 260–281.
Gerard, A. B. *Imitation and sequencing in early childhood*. Doctoral dissertation, University of California, San Diego, in preparation.

Gibson, E. J., & Spelke, E. S. The development of perception. In J. H. Flavell & E. M. Markman (Eds.), *Cognitive development: Vol. 3. Manual of child psychology.* New York: Wiley, 1983.

Goldberg S., Perlmutter, M., & Myers, N. Recall of related and unrelated lists by 2-year-olds. *Journal of Experimental Child Psychology,* 1974, *17,* 1–8.

Goodman, G. S. Picture memory: How the action schema affects retention. *Cognitive Psychology,* 1980, *12,* 473–495.

Graesser, A. C. *Prose comprehension beyond the word.* New York: Springer-Verlag, 1981.

Graesser, A. C., & Nakamura, G. V. The impact of a schema on comprehension and memory. In G. H. Bower (Ed.), *The psychology of learning and motivation* (Vol. 16). New York: Academic Press, 1982.

Graf, P., Squire, L. R., & Mandler, G. The information that amnesic patients do not forget. *Journal of Experimental Psychology: Learning, Memory and Cognition,* 1984, *10,* 164–178.

Greenfield, P. M. Playing peekaboo with a four-month-old: A study of the role of speech and non-speech sounds in the formation of a visual schema. *Journal of Psychology,* 1972, *82,* 287–298.

Grudin, J. Personal communication, 1983.

Haake, R. J., & Somerville, S. C. The development of logical search skills in infancy. *Developmental Psychology,* in press.

Jacoby, L. L. Perceptual enhancement: Persistent effects of an experience. *Journal of Experimental Psychology: Learning, Memory, and Cognition,* 1983, *9,* 21–38.

Jacoby, L. L., & Dallas, M. On the relationship between autobiographical memory and perceptual learning. *Journal of Experimental Psychology: General,* 1981, *110,* 306–340.

Johnson, N. S. What do you do if you can't tell the whole story? The development of summarization skills. In K. E. Nelson (Ed.), *Children's language* (Vol. 4). Hillsdale, N.J.: Erlbaum, 1983.

Johnson, N. S., & Mandler, J. M. A tale of two structures: Underlying and surface forms in stories. *Poetics,* 1980, *9,* 51–86.

Kessen, W., & Nelson, K. What the child brings to language. In B. Z. Presseisen, D. Goldstein, & M. H. Appel (Eds.), *Topics in cognitive development: Vol. 2. Language and operational thought.* New York: Plenum Press, 1978.

Kinsbourne, M., & George, J. The mechanism of the word-frequency effect on recognition memory. *Journal of Verbal Learning and Verbal Behavior,* 1974, *13,* 63–69.

Kosslyn, S. M. *Image and mind.* Cambridge, Mass.: Harvard University Press, 1980.

Lichtenstein, E. H., & Brewer, W. F. Memory for goal-directed events. *Cognitive Psychology,* 1980, *12,* 412–445.

Mandler, G. *Mind and emotion.* New York: Wiley, 1975.

Mandler, G. Recognizing: The judgment of previous occurrence. *Psychological Review,* 1980, *87,* 252–271.

Mandler, G., Goodman, G. O., & Wilkes-Gibbs, D. L. The word frequency paradox in recognition. *Memory & Cognition,* 1982, *10,* 33–42.

Mandler, J. M. A code in the node: The use of a story schema in retrieval. *Discourse Processes,* 1978, *1,* 14–35.

Mandler, J. M. Categorical and schematic organization in memory. In C. R. Puff (Ed.), *Memory organization and structure.* New York: Academic Press, 1979.

Mandler, J. M. Representation. In J. H. Flavell & E. M. Markman (Eds.), *Cognitive development: Vol. 3. Manual of child psychology.* New York: Wiley, 1983.

Mandler, J. M. *Stories, scripts, and scenes: Aspects of schema theory.* Hillsdale, N.J.: Erlbaum, 1984.

Mandler J. M., & DeForest, M. Is there more than one way to recall a story? *Child Development,* 1979, *50,* 886–889.

Mandler, J. M., & Goodman, M. S. On the psychological validity of story structure. *Journal of Verbal Learning and Verbal Behavior*, 1982, *21*, 507–523.

Mandler, J. M., & Johnson, N. S. Remembrance of things parsed: Story structure and recall. *Cognitive Psychology*, 1977, *9*, 111–115.

Mandler, J. M., & Ritchey, G. H. Long-term memory for pictures. *Journal of Experimental Psychology: Human Learning and Memory*, 1977, *3*, 386–396.

Mandler, J. M., & Robinson, C. A. Developmental changes in picture recognition. *Journal of Experimental Child Psychology*, 1978, *26*, 122–136.

McCloskey, M., & Kohl, D. Naive physics: The curvilinear impetus principle and its interactions with moving objects. *Journal of Experimental Psychology: Learning, Memory, and Cognition*, 1983, *9*, 146–156.

McCloskey, M., Caramazza, A., & Green, B. Curvilinear motion in the absence of external forces: Naive beliefs about the motion of objects. *Science*, 1980, *210*, 1139–1141.

Nelson, K. Concept, word, and sentence: Interrelations in acquisition and development. *Psychological Review*, 1974, *81*, 267–285.

Nelson, K. How young children represent knowledge of their world in and out of language: A preliminary report. In R. Siegler (Ed.), *Children's thinking: What develops?* Hillsdale, N.J.: Erlbaum, 1978.

Nelson, K., & Gruendel, J. Generalized event representations: Basic building blocks of cognitive development. In M. E. Lamp & A. L. Brown (Eds.), *Advances in developmental psychology* (Vol. 1). Hillsdale, N.J.: Erlbaum, 1981.

Nelson, K., Fivush, R., Hudson, J., & Lucariello, J. Scripts and the development of memory. In M. T. H. Chi (Ed.), *Trends in memory development research*. Contributions to Human Development Monograph Series. Basel, Switzerland: S. Korgor, 1983.

Newtson, D., Engquist, G., & Bois, J. The objective basis of behavior units. *Journal of Personality and Social Psychology*, 1977, *35*, 847–862.

Nisbett, R. E., & Wilson, T. D. Telling more than we can know: Verbal reports on mental processes. *Psychological Review*, 1977, *84*, 231–259.

O'Connell, B., Gerard, A. B., & Leong, K. *The development of sequential understanding*. Paper presented to the Society for Research in Child Development, Detroit, April, 1983.

Perlmutter, M., & Myers, N. A. Development of recall in 2- to 4-year-old children. *Developmental Psychology*, 1979, *15*, 73–83.

Piaget, J. *The origins of intelligence in children*, New York: International Universities Press, 1952.

Piaget, J. *The construction of reality in the child*. New York: Basic Books, 1954.

Piaget, J. *The grasp of consciousness: Action and concept in the young child*. Cambridge, Mass.: Harvard University Press, 1976.

Rabinowitz, M., & Mandler, J. M. Organization and information retrieval. *Journal of Experimental Psychology: Learning, Memory, and Cognition*, 1983, *9*, 430–439.

Rovee-Collier, C. J., & Fagen, J. W. The retrieval of memory in early infancy. In L. P. Lipsitt (Ed.), *Advances in infancy research* (Vol. 1). Norwood, N.J.: Ablex, 1981.

Rumelhart, D. E. Notes on a schema for stories. In D. G. Bobrow & A. Collins (Eds.), *Representation and understanding: Studies in cognitive science*. New York: Wiley, 1975.

Sameroff, A. J., & Cavanaugh, P. J. Learning in infancy: A developmental perspective. In J. D. Osovsky (Ed.), *Handbook of infant development*. New York: Wiley, 1979.

Schank, R. C., & Abelson, R. *Scripts, plans, goals, and understanding*. Hillsdale, N.J.: Erlbaum, 1977.

Shanon, B. Aristotelianism, Newtonianism and the physics of the layman. *Perception*, 1976, *5*, 241–243.

Smith, P. H. Five-month-old recall of temporal order and utilization of temporal organization. *Journal of Experimental Child Psychology,* in press.

Spear, N. E. Retrieval of memories: A psychobiological approach. In W. K. Estes (Ed.), *Handbook of memory and cognitive processes* (Vol. 4). Hillsdale, N.J.: Erlbaum, 1976.

Stein, N. L., & Glenn, C. G. An analysis of story comprehension in elementary school children. In R. Freedle (Ed.), *New directions in discourse processing* (Vol. 2). Norwood, N.J.: Ablex, 1979.

Stein, N. L., & Nezworski, T. The effects of organization and instructional set on story memory. *Discourse Processes,* 1978, *1,* 177–194.

Thompkins, B. A. *The effect of typicality on pictured object perception and memory.* Paper presented at the American Psychological Association meetings, Los Angeles, 1981.

Warrington, E. K., & Weiskrantz, L. The effects of prior learning on subsequent retention in amnesic patients. *Neuropsychologia,* 1974, *12,* 419–428.

Warrington, E. K., & Weiskrantz, L. Amnesia: A disconnection syndrome. *Neuropsychologia,* 1982, *20,* 233–248.

Winograd, T. Frame representations and the declarative-procedural controversy. In D. G. Bobrow & A. Collins (Ed.), *Representation and understanding: Studies in cognitive science.* New York: Academic Press, 1975.

CHAPTER 5

The Transition from Infant to Child Memory

Katherine Nelson

Graduate School and University Center
City University of New York
New York, New York

There are many factors that make the study of infant memory incomparable with the study of memory in children and adults. The impossibility of using verbal instructions, verbal materials, or verbal response systems stands as a primary barrier to establishing comparability and thereby to assessing the continuity of systems. Infant memory studies have mainly relied on controlled stimulus presentations and attentional responses to stimulus change or repetition. Fagan's research (Chapter 1) is an excellent example. Much has been learned in this way about recognition memory in the nonverbal infant, both short-term and longer-term. However, limitations of the method leave open a number of issues that are of interest to memory theorists in general and developmentalists in particular. In addition, we are probably missing memory phenomena of interest because we are not able to tap the baby's own spontaneous internal organization of encounters in the world but are confined to our own guesses as to what interests her and how she represents and organizes her understanding of those encounters.

This chapter concentrates on the development of a long-term memory system. Development is conceived of within a constructive memory framework, broadly defined. I will outline a few central issues first to

Preparation of this paper was supported in part by a grant from the National Science Foundation BNS 79-14006.

provide some perspective on the problems that I think must be considered in dealing with the development of knowledge representation in infancy and early childhood and then present some new data that suggest an interesting hypothesis about memory development in the transition from infancy to childhood.

Central Issues in the Transition

The important issues to be resolved if we are to understand the relation between memory in infancy and later memory are basically issues of representation: How is knowledge represented in infancy? How is it organized? To what extent is it generalized or transformed over time? When is a representation activated?

Recall and Recognition Memory

The issue of whether there is recall memory in infancy is integrally related to the representation issue. If infants can recognize perceptual patterns but not recall images in the absence of an external stimulus, then the ability to represent knowledge of the world is in serious doubt. This is in fact Piaget's (e.g., Piaget, 1962) view; he claims that representation itself develops during the second year when evidence that the child can use representations of absent objects becomes available. It is, however, difficult to demonstrate convincingly that recall memory is *not* present in the infant.

Virtually all laboratory studies done with infants rely on recognition paradigms, but recognition, however interpreted, differs from recall in specifiable ways. The closest thing to recall assessments are the object hiding studies carried out in the Piagetian paradigm of object permanence development. These studies show that, before 8 or 9 months of age, infants give virtually no evidence that they can recall the location of an object when it is out of sight, even for a brief moment. This failure is interpreted in the Piagetian paradigm as a lack of mental representation. In the memory literature it is interpreted as an inability to recall an object even in the presence of a salient cue (the cover that hides the object). Gradually over the next 12 months the child acquires the ability to solve increasingly difficult representational problems involving hidden objects. Thus, short-term recall memory appears reasonably well-developed by 18 months to 2 years.

But do these studies truly indicate that younger infants can recognize old objects, states, or events but cannot recall them? To interpret the data in such a way is shaky on a number of grounds. First, evidence from the naturalistic study of infants' memory by Ashmead and Perlmutter (1980) using parental diary accounts showed that, before the age of 1 year, children gave considerable evidence of recall. For example, they initiated games such as peek-a-boo and recalled both permanent and temporary locations of objects. Ashmead and Perlmutter emphasized the social orientation of infants' memory and the dependence of their search patterns on general knowledge of patterns of behavior. They provided many examples of memory for people, places, and objects beginning as early as 7 months.

An example from my own observations is a striking case in point. At 11 months, HS was given an object hiding test using small toys and failed to search, thus demonstrating Stage III object concept behavior, typical of children of 8 months or younger. However, during the same visit he was able to find mother or a visitor behind one of five different doors on command after a 30 sec delay without error over six trials. Thus, by this standard, we would have to attribute to him very good recall memory for locations of objects, but by the standard test, he would be judged very poor. These observations are consistent with the study by Bell (1970) finding earlier object permanence when mother was the object than when a small toy was. These inconsistencies may reflect the effects of size, familiarity, the role of affect, or other factors. They have not yet been sufficiently explored, but do question the general conclusion that infants cannot represent—and therefore recall—absent objects.

The question of recall versus recognition in infancy is complicated by consideration of the problem of cuing. Gail Ross and I (Nelson & Ross, 1980) carried out a study with children of 21–27 months, in which parents kept diary records of their children's memories. Our analysis of these records showed that children were able to remember episodes that had happened several months previously, even in some cases from a time prior to when they had learned to talk. In almost half (48%) of the cases studied, the memory was cued by a spatial locative cue. For example, one child remembered a friend whom he had not seen for 4½ months when they passed the house in which the friend had lived. In no case was a memory reported that could not be related to an external cue of some sort. Unfortunately this result is confounded by the fact that mothers reported memories of the children, raising the question: Would they have been able to recognize memories in the absence of an external cue of some sort?

On reflection, however, it appears that *all* memories are cued in some way. From this perspective, the distinction between recall and recognition is not a hard and fast one but rather represents two points along a continuum of more or less salient cuing possibilities. When a subject is asked to recall a list of words, for example, the request itself is the cue as to what to bring out from memory. More direct cuing is involved when category members are requested or when paired associates are learned and later recalled. In a recognition test, a matching item is given as a cue for the memory. When reminiscing, an internal cue presumably calls up the memory; something in the present train of thought cues a related memory. Thus, the dependence of memory on cuing appears to run from exact external to distantly related internal. This range of dependence may conceivably be a dimension of developmental interest in the progression from infancy to childhood memory. In other words, rather than presuming a progression from recognition to recall memory, it may be more fruitful to attempt to trace a finer grained progression along the joint cuing dimensions of external to internal and from exact match to remote associate. Because what may be an effective cue for the infant is not known *a priori*, more studies employing observations in natural settings will be necessary for this investigation. (See Chapter 6, for a similar point of view and Chapter 8 for a somewhat different view of the development of recognition and recall.)

Specific and General Memory

Another dimension requiring intensive study is that of specific and general memory. I prefer the terms *specific* and *general* to Tulving's (1972) *episodic* and *semantic* because they lack the mode and structure connotations of the latter terms (Nelson & Brown, 1979). General memory, like semantic, is not dated; it is part of the knowledge base rather than part of the autobiographical, temporally organized system. Specific memory includes all those bits that can be tied to some specific past experience—those that form the basis for recounting and reminiscing. These are not independent systems: the general must derive from experience as does the specific; moreover, the specific is influenced by the general. Nor is it the case that a particular type of content is stored in one and not the other. For example, the concept "hamburger" may enter into the general system organized around fast food chains and around types of meat; it may also enter into a specific autobiographical memory for a teenage date or a backyard barbecue (see Kintsch, 1974 on this point). Moreover, it is not the case that general memory is categorically organized while specific memory is organized around episodes. Although specific memory is frequently so organized, it may also be oreganized spatially (e.g., one's memory for where things are located in a kitchen) or procedurally in list form (e.g., specific telephone numbers, recipes, formulas). Unlike episodes, these specific memory types are not dated. Moreover, general knowledge is often formulated in script form, (i.e., as generalized episodes), and these scripts may subsume lists of specific details appropriate to them.

These different facets of memory have been treated in various ways in recent years. The present distinctions grow out of our work with young children and reflect a supposition that the general-specific dimension is also an important one in the early development of memory. For example, it has sometimes been held (e.g., Anglin, 1977) that young children's knowledge is episodic and idiosyncratic, becoming general and abstract with development. On the other hand, our research has indicated that young children generalize their representations very easily.

Short-Term and Long-Term Memory

How much and *how long* are, of course, also questions of interest in early development, since it is generally assumed that older children will remember more of an experience than will younger children and they will remember it for a longer period of time. Like most other claims about children's real world knowledge, the evidence for this assumption is actually not very strong. As Fagan has shown (Chapter 1), infants have much longer term recognition memory than had been previously thought. Although young children typically remember little and for short delays in experimental tests, when the situation is made ecologically significant, their memory spans are increased considerably (e.g., Istomina, 1948/1975; de Loache & Brown, 1979). The child's theory of the task and motivation to perform are of central importance in attempting to get veridical measures of their competence in basic skills such as memory. If the child's theory is not consonant with the experimenters', the assessment is useless. The best way around this problem is to study what children remember naturally from their experience rather than what we present to them.

Verbal and Nonverbal Memory

A final developmental issue to consider is the possible role of verbalization to self or to others in establishing memory or transforming it. Because infants do not talk and therefore do not rehearse episodes to themselves or recount them to others, infant memory is by definition independent of rehearsal. Of course an analogue of verbal rehearsal might be found in the re-presentation to self of an imaginal representation of an experience. Such rehearsal cannot, at least at the present time, be evaluated. Young children, however, often do talk to themselves about their experiences, and their parents talk to them about plans for the future and what happened in the past. Thus, an important factor in the transition from infant to child memory may well be the ability to talk about experience.

Evidence from Scripts

In our recent work with preschool children, we have studied evidence for the establishment and usefulness of scriptlike organizations of experience (Nelson & Gruendel, 1981; Nelson, Fivush, Hudson, & Lucariello, 1983). Three- and four-year-old children, when asked, produce well-formed and sequenced general narratives describing what they know about familiar activities that are remarkable in a number of ways that relate to the issues just raised.

First, they are general accounts, using general tenseless verb forms and general activity verbs (such as *eat, food, play games*). They have temporal sequential structure. They provide an open framework into which specific elements can be placed and, indeed, are sometimes offered as alternatives. Three-year-olds will often say, "We put on clothes," whereas older 4- and 5-year-olds will say, "We could put on a dress *or* pants and a skirt *or* shorts." Thus, specific possibilities are offered as candidates for fitting the open slots of the script.

A remarkable finding, however, is that children of 3 and 4 years who can produce a reasonably good general account of, say, dinner at home have difficulty producing a specific account of one time when they had dinner. The general script appears to block or override the specific experience (Nelson *et al.,* 1983). In effect, specific experiences appear to be fused with the general script, whereas possible slot fillers are filtered out and are available as optional entries but do not remain tied to a particular experience of the event.

This finding has been replicated in a study of school scripts by Fivush (1982) who found that 5-year-old children have great difficulty remembering anything that happened "yesterday" at school, although they are perfectly capable of telling what happens in general. (Parents often complain that young children reply "nothing" when asked what happened at school today. It appears to be a very real possibility that they do not know—they cannot remember.)

Taken by itself, this observation seems to put a very severe limitation on the young child's specific memory system while establishing a high degree of competence in the general system. At first glance, it also appears that such a finding would serve nicely to explain the establishment of an autobiographical memory system during the preschool years and thereby incidentally explain the lack of such a system, the phenomenon underlying infantile amnesia, prior to that time. Indeed, we initially hypothesized that all experience was at first generalized and that general scripts needed to be established and elaborated in such a way that the child had well-defined expectations about what happens in the course of daily life before variations from those expectations could become notable and be entered as a different kind of memory—one that was memorable in its own right and not as an optional path in a general framework (see Chapters 3 & 4).

However, the data we have subsequently encountered do not all fit this proposal so neatly. First, it is clear from the studies that Hudson has carried out (Hudson & Nelson, 1983) that children can remember details of novel events, such as going to the circus, over a period of many months. The evidence from children under 2 years of age and even before 1 year (Nelson & Ross, 1980) shows that specific knowledge is available from episodes that have taken place months earlier. Memory for spatial locations, procedures, and scripts have all been documented for children between 1 and 2 years and even (although less certainly) below 1 year (Perlmutter, 1980).

An alternate possibility modifies the hypothesis only slightly by suggesting that a new experience tends to be remembered in quite specific terms, and it is only with repetition that the general script gets built up and takes over. If unrepeated experiences tend to fade, drop out, or become inaccessible with time, one could adequately account for all the data. (Similar views are set forth by Spear, 1979, Campbell & Jaynes, 1966, and Rovee-Collier & Fagen, 1981). Although these possibilities remain open, still a third factor that may play a role is the impact on specific memory of verbalizing one's experience either to oneself or to others.

Memories from the Crib

I have recently had the opportunity to obtain evidence relevant to some of these issues that sheds new light on them and suggests some new hypotheses about the transition from infancy to childhood. This evidence is based on tapes of a child talking to herself before falling asleep at nap or nighttime. As many parents are aware, it is quite common for children of two or three years to talk themselves to sleep on these occasions. A few prior studies (Black, 1979; Keenan, 1974; Weir, 1962) have attempted to characterize such talk, where the focus has been on the language forms used and particularly on the practice of syntactic structures.

   In the present case, I was able to obtain the cooperation of the parents of an exceptionally bright and verbal girl (Emily) who was 21 months at the onset of the study. Emily was in the habit of talking to herself, after her parents left the room, about significant events as well as about imaginative play with "friends" in the crib (i.e., stuffed animals) and reciting songs and fragments of stories from her books. On two or three occasions, during each week for the 4 months of the study reported here, her parents placed a cassette audio tape recorder under her crib and let it run until she fell asleep. The recordings were first monitored by her mother who made rough transcriptions and noted the meaning of references or memories, including approximate dates for experiences that were mentioned if they could be identified. Tapes have thus far been transcribed and analyzed from a period of 4 months that included Thanksgiving, Christmas, a change in her bedroom, the birth of a baby brother, and her own second birthday. Using the mother's notes for guidance, all passages were transcribed and analyzed that appeared to refer to real life (rather than to imaginary games with "friends," songs, etc.).

   Before describing the data, it is important to give a general characterization of the child, her language, and the character of her monologues. Emily was a precocious child, advanced in both cognition and language, as will become evident. From all evidence she is friendly, happy, outgoing, emotionally stable. She attends—and has attended—a group care setting in a nearby home almost since birth as her parents are both full-time professionals. Her maternal grandmother (called "Mormor") lives nearby and frequently baby-sits. Thus, she has experienced multiple caretakers and also has a number of friends her own age. Both parents participate equally in childcare and the father is a particular favorite who is usually the last to see her at night before bed.

   During the course of this study, her language outside the crib was not recorded except for those segments that were included as part of the bedgoing routine before the parents left the room. Therefore, it was not feasible to obtain a reliable measure of mean length of utterance (MLU) or any other standard index of language competence, nor could a standard assessment of her crib language be made, because its characteristics were quite unlike those of her interactive speech. Her crib talk came, not in isolated utterances or sentences, but in long paragraphs maintained over a series of breath-groups that did not break at normal phrases but rather regrouped and rephrased in a continuous stream. Informal assessment, however, showed her to be far advanced in both semantic and syntactic competence.

   From the outset, her crib talk was differentiated into two distinct registers. One, low pitched and indistinct, accompanied her pretend play with her friends,the stuffed animals in the crib, and were often concerned with the state of their imaginary diapers. The second was high pitched and projected, a clearly recitative register that marked the occasion for recounting, anticipating, singing, or telling a story fragment. At first, this register was also marked by the use of "so" to introduce and connect the narrative parts. (This marking dropped out fairly early.) Thus "here and now" activity was in these ways clearly marked from "there and then" knowledge at the beginning. Although the raised pitch and volume helped in the transcriptions, her articulation—at least in this situation— lagged far behind her vocabulary and syntax; thus, even at the end of the period covered by this study, many words and whole phrases were not transcribable. This problem was more evident that it would be in a study in which the observer is present, can clarify ambiguous passages through queries, or use nonverbal context as a clue to interpretation. Although something has inevitably been lost thereby, enough is clearly interpretable to give strong indications of important developments.

Selective Recall and Rehearsal

Let us consider first the kinds of things Emily talked about in her recitative mode. Note that every memory evidenced in this study represents uncued recall or recall cued internally, as there were no cues in the room to the kinds of things talked about. Some possible exceptions to this generalization are her monologues about her bed and bedtime. But, on the whole, this is a unique opportunity to observe early spontaneous recall of past experiences.

The Routine and the Novel. There were clear themes in Emily's recitations that tended to appear more than once. Although the kind of exciting or disruptive events that we might expect to have an impact on her memories for the most part went unremarked, there were certain occasions that seemed to be highly important from her point of view. These were minor departures, for the most part, from her regular routine. Thanksgiving, when many relatives came to visit, including her paternal grandmother, had no discernible impact at the time and did not show up in later memories. The same was true of Christmas, when the only reference was to a new stuffed animal that went to bed with her (Rocky Raccoon). The birth of her brother, anticipated for a month or more, was rarely mentioned after the fact, and her own birthday did not show up in subsequent transcripts. In both the latter cases, transcripts were obtained either on the day of the event or the next day or both.

Not surprisingly, many of the recurrent themes were ones that involved changes in Emily's own life, whether large or small. Examples included visits to the doctor when Emily was sick; the change in her sleeping place which was engineered so that the new baby would have her old room which was closer to the parents, a change that took place many weeks before the baby's arrival but that continued to appear in Emily's monologues throughout the study; and a trip to the library with her grandmother which took place several months prior to the first tapes. These became subjects for monologues that were repeated many times over and sometimes popped up in the middle of other themes. Strong affect may have dictated memory for these events. One prominent example was a bad dream about alligators that was referred to over a period of months.

Other themes were simple variations on the general routine, for example, episodes involving play with her real friends, trips to Child World (a toy and baby equipment store) with her parents, and daddy making cornbread, of which she was fond. It appeared that these tended not to be repeated as frequently as the apparently more significant changes or disruptions.

Still other themes involved secondhand experiences, especially verbal explanations given by her parents for certain happenings, for example, the new baby coming. Others included mommy–daddy—her dual term for her parents—going to a cocktail party, an event later incorporated into her imaginative play; an episode from some months prior to the study involving one of the family cars being broken so that it could not be used; and daddy doing the laundry in the basement. In these cases, Emily appeared to be returning to these themes to rehearse the explanations of usual or unusual behavior, even though in many cases it was clear that she did not understand the significance of what was said. It might be that they were rehearsed *because* she only partially understood the references. For example, without knowing what a cocktail party involves from firsthand experience, the explanation that mommy–daddy are going to a cocktail party can be memorized and rehearsed in verbal form but remains a conceptually mysterious event. Likewise, if the child has not watched daddy doing the laundry in the basement but only seen him disappear in that direction, the mystery of what doing the laundry involves remains unsolved and apparently intriguing.

Thus, throughout the tapes events of varying degrees of novelty, from very minor play routines to major disruptions such as the change of rooms, were recalled. Some were firsthand experiences, others were secondhand reports and explanations. It was not possible from the samples obtained to come to any conclusion about the relation of degree of novelty and amount of rehearsal. However, the themes that continued to appear months later were the more novel or disruptive: the broken car, the change in rooms. Minor variations tended to appear and then not appear again.

The Old and the New. How long is long-term memory at 2 years?

As already indicated, some events persisted in recall over many months—for example, going to the library on the bus with grandmother appeared at intervals over a 6-month period. Others, which at least as far as we know were not frequently rehearsed, appeared for the first time weeks after they had been experienced. For example, the incident of daddy making cornbread was brought up 2 weeks later. Happenings from the same day were frequently mentioned but so were events from yesterday or last week, and no distinction was made among them. Thus, no relationship was apparent between the length of the memory and its likelihood of appearance in monologue. However, there was no evidence for a specific memory from more than 6 months previously. It should be noted that, according to parental report, Emily was talking quite well at 15 months, 6 months prior to the first records obtained.

The General and the Specific. Thus far, all of the material discussed can be tied to specific incidents in Emily's life. There is no evidence, however, that these incidents retained specificity or had an episodic quality for Emily. Some of the material that enters into the monologues is not event-organized at all. This is true of her recitations of stories (e.g., Peter Rabbit, Babar), songs, nursery rhymes, counting, and naming friends. These do not seem to differ from her episodic recitations except in form and on the several occasions her own memories were interspersed with these materials. This characteristic of the monologues is of considerable interest and is related to an apparent differentiation that takes place over time. Let us consider first the evidence for fusion and confusion among the different types of material before considering evidence for a growing differentiation and establishment of specific memory as such.

Fusion and Confusion. We speak of *fusion* of memories when two or more incidents apparently become reconstructed into one. *Confusion* occurs when an experience is poorly understood and becomes transformed in retelling. Not surprisingly, there is evidence of both in these transcripts. Let us consider some early examples of fusion.[1]

(1)   21;12 Mormor came afternoon. Read my books. *So*
           mommy–daddy to cocktail party *after* the [nap?]

Interpretation. Before leaving, her parents told Emily that Mormor, her grandmother, would come that afternoon to baby-sit and read books. Thus, this was a verbal memory. "Mommy–daddy to cocktail party"

[1]The transcripts are arranged so that periods mark definite sentence boundaries whereas ellipses (. . .) mark pauses. A question mark [?] refers to missing or uncertain words. Although emphasis and intonation are salient throughout and difficult to capture, words that are particularly emphasized are italicized. The numbers preceding the transcripts indicate the month and day of age at which they were spoken.

refers to an event 5 days earlier when Mormor baby-sat for her. Although this sequence has the surface appearance of an inference from past experience, other evidence from the transcripts during this time suggests that it is simply a fusion of the verbal input from one experience with another. "So" is an apparently contentless marker that drops out of the transcripts after a time. "After" is not common at this point but may be an early appearance of a future marker.

(2)   21;13 Daddy brings down the washing down the basement.
            Emmy so . . .
            Daddy brings [?] down the washing from the basement in
                the . . .
            So Emmy change . . .
            Daddy bring them back up . . .
            So daddy bring . . .
            My daddy bring my grocery . . .
            My daddy come home . . .
            So my daddy Emmy daddy don't go work.
            Emmy daddy ca[m]e.
            I don't why my daddy ca[m]e.
            So Emmy move down to outside.
            I ca[m]e see cousin and see trucks.
            I ca[m]e see rocks, dirt.
            So my daddy do washing.
            I ca[n] do my daddy . . . I can do my sleep.
            Go down there.
            My daddy in cellar.
            Go *down* there.
            So next week my daddy wanna not come store . . .
            My daddy wanna not come store.
            So why my daddy bring . . .
            I can[t] see why my daddy bring down the washing.

Interpretation. This excerpt illustrates characteristics of Emily's language as well as her stream of consciousness at this period. Although the transcription makes the talk appear to include both present and past tense as well as temporal markers (e.g., next week) and causal questions ("why?"), the articulation of her verb forms is such that past and present are rarely distinguishable and it is doubtful that Emily distinguishes them at this point. "Came," "can" and "can't" are rendered similarly and may be interpreted differently in different contexts. The present interpretation is only one of many that could be made of these forms. "I don't why" and "next week" are clearly formulas modeled after parental speech forms as is much else here. The daddy theme includes both usual (washing, groceries) and unusual ("not go work"—referring to the present day, i.e., the day after Thanksgiving). Interspersed or fused with the daddy activity is an account of Emmy seeing cousin, trucks, rocks, and dirt. The point to be emphasized is that bits of many different episodes are strung together here but lack a coherent narrative structure and do not refer to a single or similar experience or even a common theme. Now consider a case of fusion 6 weeks later.

(3)   22;31 Make my bed. Probably when I wake up and prob-
           ably my sleeping liking this bed. And Emmy felt the bed
           so good. Emmy saying Emmy felt the good bed. Emmy
           didn't like it. [?] Emmy, when Emmy fell down the bed
           and bring [?] and sometimes and make new bed for Emmy.
           And that be now [?] up. That [?] bed me. And new bed
           for me. And new bed for new baby. Make new. And after
           make new bed for baby. I [?] and make new bed for the
           for the my little baby. Maybe. I like that book. Mommy
           that book. I don't know.

   Interpretation. This segment is taken from the evening on which the new baby was brought home. It fuses a story about a father making a new bed for a new baby that was read to her weeks earlier with her own new baby and new bedroom. (Those interested in metalinguistics may note her "Emmy saying Emmy felt the good bed." This is not an isolated incident. She frequently quotes herself as well as others.) This monologue also illustrates the imprecise grammatical structure of her recitals, which run on in long paragraphs with pauses at junctures that apparently signal changes of direction of thought rather than sentential structure. Note here also the use of "probably," the present progressive, the past tense (still not always clear), "after," and "sometimes." We will return to these later. Although this segment displays fusion of story elements and real life experience, the theme is maintained and the narrative is more coherent than in the earlier segments.
   Another example of story and real life fusion is the following:

(4)   23;6 And Babar eating bad mushrooms. And Emmy very
           sick. [??] Ate mushrooms and I played and played. And
           then Emmy went to sleep and slept and on the blanket.
           And one day Emmy didn't feel so good. And just Emmy's
           daddy hold me tightly and tightly. Then I play, play and
           won't cry. Now my sleepy. Emmy play and play. Emmy
           just love to say play . . . that day. Then Emmy got sick
           [?] at dinner. Emmy ate one time. And one time Emmy
           sick. Emmy won't eat dinner. Emmy won't. And Emmy
           ate the ice and took dinner. And that Emmy played and
           played.

Interpretation. In a Babar story one of the elephants eats poisonous mushrooms and gets very sick. Mother has explained that there are bad mushrooms outside as well as the good mushrooms that Emily likes. She has also made a distinction between the ice outside that we do not eat and the inside ice that Emily likes to eat. Here, Emily fuses the Babar story with her own experience with illness, mushrooms, and ice. Note the increasingly sure command of the past tense and again the metalinguistic comment that she loves to say play. Again, in spite of the fusion, this example maintains a theme and presents a reasonably coherent narrative.

It might be objected that these examples do not display fusion of memory but rather the association of one memory with another of common content. However, the productions give no hints of comparison or conjunction but rather a mixture of elements from different sources, in the last two examples from stories and from real life. These verbalizations are good candidates for the mechanism behind the transformation of hearsay memories from early life into a conviction of personal experience. This phenomenon has been not infrequently commented upon (among others, Piaget) and has often been cited as a reason for not believing in the veracity of any early memories (e.g., Neisser, 1982). Early memories may indeed be particularly vulnerable to this sort of transformation; however, this feature should be studied as carefully as any other and not simply dismissed or made the reason for not studying early memories.

Confusion differs from fusion in that only one memory is involved, but its parts are rearranged, omitted, or substituted. A simple example is the following:

(5)   24;4 Mormor brought this. But the tiger got something
           wrong. [?] Mormor bought the cheetah. Just for Emily.
           But I don't know who bought the tiger. Maybe Mormor
           or daddy or mommy. Mormor bought the cheetah. I don't
           know what came, where the tiger [yawn] . . . But Mormor
           bought the cheetah. That's what Mormor bought . . . the
           cheetah . . . the tiger.

Interpretation. Emily refers here to a visit by grandmother and a friend. The friend bought the cheetah as a present for Emily. Emily appears to be aware at some level of confusion in her repetitive assertion that Mormor bought the cheetah.

A more striking example of confusion followed a before-nap explanation by daddy that after nap they would go to Child World and buy an intercom so that they could hear the baby when he cried in other parts of the house. This explanation was repeated three times at Emily's insistence. After daddy leaves the room she rehearses:

> 23;15 Daddy said buy diapers for Stevie and Emmy and
> buy something for Steven plug in and say "ahah" [imi-
> tating his cry] and put that in . . . on Saturday go Child
> World buy diaper for Emmy and diaper for the baby and
> then buy something for the Emmy see for that baby plug
> in and that diaper for anybody. And buy moon that day
> at Child World and buy coats and maybe Child World
> cause that one at broken at Tantas. The one that's broken.
> The one that's broken here . . . the infant seat . . .

Interpretation. Emily tries to repeat what she has been told but gives up and talks about other more familiar things they can buy at Child World, including diapers, coats, and an infant seat to replace the one that is broken. Note here the use of "maybe" and the relative "that," but note also the continued jumble of syntax (e.g., "buy something for the Emmy see for that baby plug in . . .") in spite of these sophisticated forms. This jumble is not evident in her interactive before-bed speech.

Differentiation of Past, Present, and Future

Although fusions and confusions are evident throughout the tran-scripts, the character of the recounts gradually changes. They become more clearly thematic and episodic, focused on a particular happening or on the anticipation of a promised event, with fewer apparently irrelevant intrusions from other experiences (as were evident in the laundry se-quence [2], for example). That is, they seem to be more definitely recon-structions or plans rather than free-floating fragments. An interesting cor-related development is evident in Emily's language use over this period.

As already noted, at the outset Emily's verb forms were neither clearly past nor present. Terminal phonemes and whole syllables tended to be swallowed so that it was difficult to say with certainty that she did not have -ed or -s morphemes, but there was no clear evidence that she did. From the beginning, she used what appeared to be empty forms to mark and guide her narratives. The use of "so" in the early selections has been noted and also occasional temporal markers such as "next week" and "after" (see [1] above) were found. Although these forms are re-markable for the fact that they tend to be appropriately placed, they are uncommon in use; in particular "so" drops out after a few weeks and does not reappear. In contrast, the temporal markers do begin to be used with consistency between 22 and 25 months.

Table 1 shows the use of temporal markers in different discourse contexts over the 3-month period in question. Numbers in parentheses

Table 1. Use of Temporal and Conditional Markers in Transcripts

Session	Age (months;days)	Present	Future	Past	Possible/ conditional	General
1	21;12		after			
2	21;13		next week			
3	22;2	now (1)	after my nap (1)	yesterday (2)		
4	22;11	now (4)			maybe (4)	
5	22;17	(to)day (1) now (1)	then (2) after my nap (1) not right now (2) now (1)			
6	22;18	now-not (1) nighttime (1)	morning time (1) not time (1) after . . . not now (1)			
7	22;20		when . . . then . . . not right now (1) next year (2)			
8	22;23		tomorrow morning (1)			
9	23;1	now-now (1) now today (1) today (1) now time (1)			I don't know (1) how 'bout (1) probably (2) sometimes (1) maybe (1) maybe (3)	
10	23;2		just a minute (1) [to]day (1) not now (1) that day (1)			
11	23;4		pretty soon (1) afternoon (1) after . . . after (2)			
12	23;5	now (1)	soon (1)			

13	23;6	now (5)		when I woke (2) yesterday night (2)	maybe (4) I don't know (3)	in the morning (1) now . . . sometimes (1)
14	23;7		Saturday	one day (1) one time (2) yesterday (1) yesterday (4)		
15	23;8					
16	23;10					
17	23;11					
18	23;15		Saturday (1) that day (1)		maybe (9) I don't know (4) actually (1) actually (1)	
19	23;23	now (1)		one day (1) different time (1) one day (1)	maybe (5)	
20	24;1					
21	24;2		yesterday (?)	one day (1) today (1)	how 'bout (3) maybe (18) I don't know (2)	
22	24;3		tomorrow (1) today (1)			
23	24;4			one day (1)		in the nighttime (1) in the morning (1) afternoon (1) night (1)
24	24;6	now (3)		afternoon (2) yesterday (1)	maybe (3) I don't know (4) what if (1)	
25	24;7		pretty soon (1)		maybe (6) I don't know (2) probably (2)	
26	24;9					

indicate the frequency of use of that form in the transcript. Note that at
22;2 the present begins to be differentiated from the future by the use of
"now" and "after my nap." At the same time, the progressive verb form
(without auxiliary) comes in and is clearly differentiated from the simple
present. The progressive appears to be used primarily at first aspectually
as an alternative for the present (for example, in "Now Emmy going" or
"Now Emmy sleeping" or "Daddy coming"). However, the present is
also used in future contexts at least as frequently as the progressive. As
can be seen from Table 1, from 22;11 through 23;4 increasing numbers of
present and future markers are introduced and serve to differentiate between accounts of what is now and what will happen after nap. Both, of
course, are based on past experiences. (This analysis does not include
talk based on ongoing play activities in the crib.) For example:

(7)   22;20 When daddy comes then daddy get Emmy then
           daddy wake Emmy up then then Carl [close friend] come
           play. Only not right now. Emmy sleeping. Emmy sleep-
           ing. Next year. Next year. Carl come. And the baby come.
           Carl sleeping.

In addition to "now," Emily uses "today" and "nighttime" to mark the
present. She uses "not right now," "now now," "morning time," "not
time," "when . . . then," "next year," "tomorrow morning," "just a
minute," "that day," "soon," "pretty soon," "after," and "afternoon"
to designate future time. Table 1 shows the relative frequency of these
forms over the course of the period. The fact that there are more forms
for the future and that they are used more frequently probably reflects
both her parents' emphasis on what will happen later, as well as the need
to differentiate the future from the present.

During this 23rd month, forms referring to neither the past nor the
past tense are evident except for fleeting appearances. Moreover, even
when she talks about an event in the past, it is fused with the present and
general. An example, which includes one of the first uses of the past tense
and refers to an event that has occurred twice, once 2 weeks and once 6
weeks earlier, is as follows:

(8)   22;23 Daddy didn't make some corn bread for Emmy . . .
           Daddy didn't make that corn bread for to Emmy eat.
           Daddy. Not that bread for who for Emmy. That bread
           not for Emmy. Emmy like corn bread and too. I don't
           like many other things. I like toast and milk and food I
           like. And not too . . . I don't like anything cept cept for
           that that bread. Daddy has. I just like that bread. Some-
           thing. Daddy don't like. Emmy don't like. Daddy and
           mommy drink it. Nothing.

Contrast this with a more organized and coherent account from the same session about a plan for the future:

(9)   22;23 Tomorrow morning when I wakes up then daddy helps Emmy washes the dishes. Morrow morning when my wake up then daddy all clean then puts some juice on cups then Emmy have cock[tail] party, then Emmy drink the cocktail up.

This plan is based on a frequent imaginary game of Emily's of playing cocktail party. Note that this constitutes a true planning function. That is, although many of Emily's references to future activities are based on her parents' accounts prior to bed, here is evidence that she can independently anticipate a future activity based on her past experience.

Beginning at 23;6 (about 1 month after present and future were first consistently marked), temporal markers for the past begin to be consistently used along with past tense forms, both regular and irregular (see the Babar excerpt [4] above). At that point Emily again uses "now" frequently to mark the present, as though the introduction of a clear past needed the contrast of a clear present. Thereafter, past markers become very common (see Table 1) and include terms such as "one day," "one time," "in the morning," "different time," "when," "today," "afternoon," as well as "yesterday." Moreover, at this point her episodic recounts also become more coherent in structure and form with few intrusions or associative bypaths. For example, an account of a variation on her regular routine that took place earlier the same day went as follows:

(10)   23;8 When Mormor make pretty mommy had a help my slept and mommy came and mommy said "get up time go home." [Emily imitates mommy's call.] Then my slept and to wake Mormor coming. Then get up time go home. Time to go home. Yesterday did that. Now Emmy sleeping in regular bed. Yesterday my slept in in Tantas house and mommy woke me and Emmy go "time a go *home*." Then daddy bring P water[2] up. And yesterday daddy and mommy and Mormor and daddy bring me in my regular bed. Actually mommy got me. [True] Daddy and mommy threw my kitten in and mommy–daddy make my bed. Threw threw mommy kitten in. Bring my, bring, bring . . . I sleeping Tanta house. Mommy come and woke me up and call me "Time go home!" Woke [?] and mommy said time bring P water. Then mommy–daddy put me in the bed in my regular bed. Actually, actually mommy did it.

[2]Perrier water.

Or, consider her account of a trip to the library that took place 4 months previously:

(11)   24;9 Go library. I sat in Mormor's lap. I went to the
            library. Probably that's what we did. Probably we did in
            the *bus*! I sat on top of the bus and I wait for my bus.
            Cause the. . .I did sit in the regular bus I not in school
            bus. I wait for the school bus. I waited and waited and
            waited and waited and waited. The last buses are
            for. . .that's too much [?] outside. But mostly. . .But mostly
            one more time.

These correlated developments in language terms and forms and in the organization of her narratives around defined episodes and anticipated happenings contrasted with the present suggest a developmental progression. It appears at the outset that past, present, and future are not differentiated, that what Emily knows to be the case in terms of her own experience and what she has been told are entered into a general knowledge store where knowledge is loosely organized around events, novel and routine, and where similar happenings or events with common components are related to each other and in some cases become fused into a single, loosely organized structure. Strictly speaking, we cannot call these memories at this point because they seem to be neither remembered nor anticipated. Rather they form a general undifferentiated knowledge base that serves as a background for present experience. Out of this base, first present and future, and then past are differentiated. Before considering further implications of this postulated development, let us consider two further developments that appear to take place at the same time or shortly after the personal past appears. These are also displayed in Table 1.

The General and the Probable

Shortly after Emily's future is established in her monologues, she begins to generalize and consider alternative possibilities. As with the temporal differentiations, these segments are linguistically marked. In the case of generalization, they are marked by the use of the term "sometimes." The following two segments from the same night are the first to appear; the second one first explains the move to her new room two months previously and then generalizes.

(12)   23;11 Emmy you can't see Emmy here. . .when Emmy
            go. . .in bedroom that's what Emmy do *sometimes*.
            Sometimes Emmy go sleep and have dream.

(13)   Daddy didn't bring in the baby room cuz the baby bassinet
            in the room that's where the baby room was. Daddy–
            mommy move Emmy in this room cuz the baby sleeping
            in own room. Daddy brought this in the mo[ther] goose
            room Emmy sleeping in this mo[ther] goose room cause
            the bassinet and the baby in the. . .that Emmy's [last
            name] room. That's where that baby. This is Emmy's
            room. This where Emmy sleeps. Lot times Emmy go bed
            and naps. Sometimes Emmy take napping. Sometimes
            Emmy say bedtime. Time go bed. Sometimes Emmy say
            that. Now sometimes Emmy say. . .[?]. . .And Danny C.
            and Leif B. me say sometimes. That Emmy say. Some-
            times say my say *Yucky Danny*.

A week later she generalizes in a similar way about her friend Carl:

(14)   23;20 Carl sleeps like that. Carl likes his blanket and Carl
            friends in the bed. Then Carl can go [?] and mommy–
            daddy say in to the blankets and said them and Carl take
            the really nice little nap. And Emmy mommy and Emmy's
            daddy and Emmy came home. That in Carl blanket in Carl
            bed so Carl can hold that whole thing in Carl bed go cause
            it *yes*. Emmy and baby this is kind of bed that Emmy
            blanket go . . . [She continues with her own bed schema
            of various blankets and "friends" that sleep with her.]

A bit later still she verbalizes part of a script:

(15)   24;4 I can't go down the basement with jammies on. I
            sleep with jamas. Okay sleep with jamas. In the nighttime
            I only put big girl pants on. But in the morning we put
            jamas on. In the morning gets up. But afternoon I wake
            up and play.

Although the temporal markers are interchanged ("big girl pants" are
worn at nap and jamas are worn at night, not put on in the morning), she
is clearly articulating to herself the day's script requirements. (In the light
of such evidence it is hardly surprising that we find children of three years
able to narrate their "day scripts" so well.)

Even before the general or usual begins to appear as a form in its
own right, possible courses of action and plans show up. These differ
from the future noted previously in that they include alternatives. They
are marked by the terms "maybe," "probably," "I don't know." These
terms are used first with the past (see [11] above) and simple future but
gradually come to mark specifically uncertainty and possibility. The first

use for possibility in the transcripts is in the context of explaining an event the cause of which is unknown to her, as follows:

(16)   23;6 That the daddy. Coming up and running downstairs. And running and running and running downstairs. Daddy running and running down here get some dinner. I don't know. Maybe daddy getting food for muffins. *Maybe.* I don't know what daddy getting downstairs. Maybe daddy getting some books or getting blanket. I don't know what daddy doing. Maybe getting some books.

The following excerpt occurs at naptime when she has been told that she will visit the doctor for her checkup after nap. This is pure speculation because her parents said nothing about her clothes and she has not previously been to the doctor in her pajamas.

(17)   24;9 Maybe this doctor put my jamas . . . maybe . . . maybe we take my *jamas* off. But we leave diaper on. Take my jamas off. And leave them off at the doctors with my checkup so we take my jamas off. My jamas need to be off there. And we maybe take my jamas off. I don't know what we do with my . . . maybe the doctor take my jamas. My jamas off cause I maybe get checkup. Have to take my jamas.

Even more striking is the following excerpt from nighttime as she considers who will bring what book to the baby-sitter's the next day:

(18)   24;2 I don't want to like the Hansel & Gretel book. Maybe that . . . Maybe Carl turn or maybe Emmy's turn or maybe Stephen's turn or maybe Lief's turn or maybe Danny's turn. I know . . . I don't knew which boy bring book tomorrow. Maybe Lief. I don't know which boy brings book today. Maybe Danny, maybe Carl, maybe me, maybe Lief, maybe Julie. How bout Lief bring books? [?] Books. One for Julie and ones for me. Carl brings back Dr. Seuss books for me. Carl can bring one for Julie, one for Carl and Dr. Seuss for me. Maybe my get Dr. Seuss for Carl maybe bring book to me. And Carl maybe bring books. Maybe Carl. Maybe Julie the books maybe bring.

Thus by 24 months, Emily is not only able to recount a specific episode but also to use her knowledge of the past to generalize and to speculate about future possibilities.

Implications

What I have observed in following the monologues of this child is her emergence from an undifferentiated experiential knowing to the establishment of, first, a clear future and present, and, later, a personal past, followed by the establishment of general scripts and optional possibilities that utilize knowledge of the past and present to provide explanations and make plans. Each of these is marked linguistically as well as in its content and discourse form. Before considering the implications of these developments for our understanding of memory in infancy and early childhood, we need to consider two possible qualifications that would prevent drawing any conclusions on the basis of the present data. The first involves the question of whether the observed development involves only language and not memory, and the second is the question of how representative Emily is of other children her age.

The first question cannot be answered unequivocally. At 21 months, when taping began, Emily was very verbal and had been talking to herself in her crib from as early as she could babble. Her command of vocabulary was considerably greater than the average child her age, and although her syntax was still in a primitive state, having some of the "telegraphic" look so frequently described, she could formulate quite complex thoughts even then. The early tapes are full of incomprehensible passages as well as fragments of thoughts whose reference is unknown. They also contain much talk about play with her "friends" in the crib, interspersed with recitations from books, songs, and real life. Although it is difficult to argue conclusively that the later segments do not simply reflect a better command of narrative form, syntax, and vocabulary, the impression they convey is one of greater intentionality with respect to reminiscing, anticipating, explaining, and planning. The earlier linguistic markers, such as "so" and "yesterday", disappear from the narratives for a time and then reappear at a time when their usefulness to the distinction of past, future, and causation are realized. What once seemed to be empty forms take on meaning in appropriate discourse contexts. That is, the linguistic developments appear to interpenetrate the cognitive ones. The inevitable conclusion from these observations is that the cognitive and linguistic advances proceed together. It may even be that the newfound ability to talk distinctively about the past and the future enables the child to establish these as separable domains. Although the tapes in question are taken from bedtime monologues, it must be borne in mind that they reflect a great deal of general modeling and even direct imitation of parental talk about the past and future. It seems quite possible that talking with others about these domains is essential in order for the child to differentiate them.

The question of how representative Emily is can only be answered through future studies that replicate this one and converge on its findings. Emily is clearly an unusual child. Although the use of terms such as "before" and "after," "when," "so," "because," "if-then," "but," and "or" has previously been documented in 3- and 4-year-old speech (French & Nelson, 1982; see also Hood & Bloom, 1979), their use at that age has been infrequently observed, and understanding of these terms even by school-age children has often been called into question. Their appearance in transcripts from children below the age of 2 years is virtually unheard of. Even though some primitive usages remain apparent in Emily's talk at 25 months, such as the use of her name or "my" in place of the first person subject pronoun, in general her syntax is very advanced by ordinary standards. She uses both relative clauses and conjoined clauses and phrases. She has mastered tense and aspect, as well as negatives and interrogatives, although there is little evidence of the latter in the tapes because she does not use questions to herself. She can also count to 10 and identify colors. She listens to and remembers many stories and songs. All of these accomplishments are unusual at her age, being more typical of children at 2½ or even 3. The question then is, Are the developments observed here representative but advanced? That is, would we expect to see the same course of development in most children but at a somewhat later age, correlated with their mastery of the tense system? Or, are these developments typical of children between 18 months and 2 years but have only become visible here because Emily is able to articulate them? Or, is Emily unique in respect to these memory abilities?

Although these are at present unanswerable questions, my own guess is that though Emily is advanced, the progression observed here is representative of developments that all children go through in the transition from infancy to childhood.[3] We should also note that these developments have taken place over a very brief time period—3 months in fact. Is this typical? What does it imply with respect to the relation of language and thought?

The importance of these observations lies in their implications for understanding the nature of infant memory and its relationship to later memory process and organization. Research on infant memory in the laboratory and through observation of natural memory phenomena has shown that information obtained through experience is retained for long periods of time and is available for recognition and cued recall. In this

[3]That the progression from present to future to past is typical is affirmed by observations of Ames (1946) and Stern (1930) (reported in Friedman, 1978) although the age of emergence was considerably later (during the 3rd and 4th year). But Friedman (1978) appears to agree with Lewis (1937) that past and future were undifferentiated at first, a position that would also accord with the observations presented here.

study, we have observed spontaneous recall of information about novel episodes and routine events, verbal accounts from parents, both general and specific information, experiences from the same day, last week, or months earlier, all existing at first on what appears to be the same plane of undifferentiated recounting. We noted that Emily distinguished her present activities from her recitations by her vocal register—high sustained recitative tone versus low, more conversational tone. At first, the different types of recounting were not otherwise distinguished from one another and often were produced interspersed with one another, which led me to hypothesize an early undifferentiated knowledge system.

To the extent that this hypothesis is correct, it appears to be more accurate to talk about the infant's representational system than about a memory system *per se*. Clearly, the infant does represent past experiences as evidenced in both recognition and cued recall. But we have no evidence that these become part of a "memory" (episodic in Tulving's sense, and dated) rather than simply "knowledge." Rather, the infant system appears to make no distinction between general and specific, distant and recent, routine and novel. According to this view, fusion and confusion are probably the rule, because the system attempts to coordinate knowledge derived from different experiences, including verbal input of all kinds. This proposal is consistent with the claim that memory is cognition (Flavell, 1971). Under this hypothesis "real" memory (memory in the narrow sense according to Piaget, 1973) becomes differentiated from the undifferentiated representational system sometime after the infancy period. The present evidence indicates that memory for past follows after the prior differentiation of anticipated future from the present and is followed by the differentiated general from the specific episodic and the possible plan. Each of these then—past, present, future, schema or script, and plan—becomes a distinguishable domain within the general representational system. Under this account, we can speak of experientially based representation in infancy, but not of memory *per se* (see Chapters 3, 6, & 8). On the other hand, it would be wrong to argue that children below the age of 3 or so do not remember; they remember much from their experiences but it is not systematized. The differentiation and integration of a memory system, and of the use of representation for problem solving and planning, is no doubt greatly aided by the ability to talk about what did happen and what may happen. This is precisely what we have observed in the case of Emily.

The relation of the specific to the general under this account is not simply one of which comes first. Rather, the general form, like the specific, emerges out of the undifferentiated sytem. This form may then take over for all experiences of a routine nature, thus producing the blocking of specific episodes that we have observed in our script research.

Although this hypothesis appears to account for the presently available data, it obviously needs to be subjected to direct test and the observational data base needs to be greatly expanded. It should also be noted that the present account refers to one type of memory only—spontaneous recall of meaningful personal experience. Its relation to the commonly tested memory for object locations, word lists, and pictures is not clear nor does it have any clear bearing on deliberate memorization of material for later use. Certainly Emily's selection of what to rehearse reveals that what is important or salient to the child may not match what seems important to the adult. The implication for memory research with infants and young children is clear and needs emphasis: to understand memory in its full complexity we need to understand the child's selection of what is memorable. In other words, we need to get inside the head of the child, and we need to discover more ways of doing this. The present effort is a start in this direction.

More generally, what we call memory needs to be considered as one form of representation of experience that has different functions. Each function—anticipation, planning, guiding action, reminiscing—may dictate a different kind of organization of material. The last function—memory of the past for its own sake—may be a product of social, cultural, language-dependent exchanges. We would not expect to see it in infants, although we would expect to observe the infant's use of the past in present contexts. Thus, in order to understand memory development in general and particularly memory in infancy and early childhood, we need to understand the functions that representation of experience is serving.

ACKNOWLEDGMENTS

Special thanks are due Emily and her parents, whose contribution to this research has been invaluable. The paper has benefitted from discussions at the Erindale Conference and with the members of my research group at CUNY. Lucia French suggested editorial revisions that substantially improved it.

References

Ames, L. B. The development of the sense of time in the young child. *Journal of Genetic Psychology*, 1946, *68*, 97–126.
Anglin, J. *Word, object, and conceptual development.* New York: Norton, 1977.
Ashmead, D. H., & Perlmutter, M. Infant memory in everyday life. In M. Perlmutter (Ed.), *Children's memory: New directions for child development* (No. 10). San Francisco: Jossey-Bass, 1980.

Bell, S. M. The development of the concept of the object as related to infant-mother attachment. *Child Development*, 1970, *41*, 291–311.

Black, R. W. Crib talk and mother-child interaction: A comparison of form and function. *Papers and Reports on Child Language Development* (Stanford University), 1979, *17*, 90–97.

Campbell, B. A., & Jaynes, J. Reinstatement. *Psychological Review*, 1966, *73*, 478–480.

de Loache, J., & Brown, A. Looking for big bird: Studies of memory in very young children. *The Quarterly Newsletter of the Laboratory of Comparative Human Cognition*, 1979, *1*(4), 53–57.

Fivush, R. *Learning about school: The development of kindergartener's school scripts*. Unpublished doctoral dissertation, City University of New York, 1982.

Flavell, J. H. First discussant's comments: What is memory development the development of? *Human Development*, 1971, *14*, 272–278.

French, L., & Nelson, K. Taking away the supportive context: Pre-schoolers talk about the then and there. *The Quarterly Newsletter of the Laboratory of Comparative Human Cognition*, 1982, *4*, 1–6.

Friedman, W. J. Development of time concepts in children. In H. W. Reese & L. P. Lipsett (Eds.), *Advances in Child Development and Behavior* (Vol. 12). New York: Academic Press, 1978.

Hood, L., & Bloom, L. What when and how about why: A longitudinal study of early expressions of causality. *Society for Research in Child Development Monographs*, 1979, *44*(6).

Hudson, J., & Nelson, K. *Scripts and autobiographical memories*. Paper presented at the biennial meeting of the Society for Research in Child Development, Detroit, April 1983.

Istomina, Z. M. The development of voluntary memory in preschool-age children. *Soviet Psychology*, 1975, *13*(4), 5–64. (Originally published, 1948)

Keenan, E. Conversational competence in children. *Journal of Child Language*, 1974, *1*, 163–183.

Kintsch, W. *The representation of meaning in memory*. Hillsdale, N.J.: Erlbaum, 1974.

Lewis, M. M. The beginning of reference to past and future in a child's speech. *British Journal of Educational Psychology*, 1937, *7*, 39–56.

Neisser, U. *Memory observed: Remembering in natural contexts*. San Francisco: W. H. Freeman, 1982.

Nelson, K., & Brown, A. L. The semantic-episodic distinction in memory development. In P. Ornstein (Ed.), *Development of memory*. Hillsdale, N.J.: Erlbaum, 1979.

Nelson, K., & Gruendel, J. Generalized event representations: Basic building blocks of cognitive development. In A. Brown & M. Lamb (Eds.), *Advances in developmental psychology* (Vol. 1). Hillsdale, N.J.: Erlbaum, 1981.

Nelson, K., & Ross, G. The generalities and specifics of long-term memory in infants and young children. In M. Perlmutter (Ed.), *Children's memory: New directions for child development* (No. 10). San Francisco: Jossey-Bass, 1980.

Nelson, K., Fivush, R., Hudson, J., & Lucariello, J. Scripts and the development of memory. In M. T. H. Chi (Ed.), *Trends in memory development research*. Contributions to Human Development Monograph Series. Basel, Switzerland: S. Karger, A. G., 1983.

Perlmutter, M. (Ed.). *Children's memory: New directions for child development* (No. 10). San Francisco: Jossey-Bass, 1980.

Piaget, J. *Play, dreams and imitation in childhood* (C. Gattegno & F. M. Hodgson, Trans.). New York: Norton, 1962.

Piaget, J. *Memory and intelligence*. New York: Basic Books, 1973.

Rovee-Collier, C. K., & Fagen, J. W. The retrieval of memory in early infancy. In L. P. Lipsitt (Ed.), *Advances in infancy research* (Vol. 1). Norwood, N.J.: Ablex, 1981.

Spear, N. E. Experimental analysis of infantile amnesia. In J. F. Kihlstrom & F. J. Evans (Eds.), *Functional disorders of memory*. Hillsdale, N.J.: Erlbaum, 1979.

Stern, W. *Psychology of early childhood*. New York: Holt, 1930.

Tulving, E. Episodic and semantic memory. In E. Tulving and W. Donaldson (Eds.), *Organization of memory*. New York: Academic Press, 1972.

Weir, R. *Language in the crib*. The Hague: Mouton, 1962.

CHAPTER 6

What Do Infants Remember?

Robert S. Lockhart

Department of Psychology
University of Toronto
Toronto, Ontario, Canada

The title of this chapter is intended to reflect my concern with the content and function of infant memory rather than with process and mechanism. Being neither a student of infancy nor a developmental psychologist, I will comment from the viewpoint of someone interested in adult memory. I do so with some hesitation: my reading of work in infant memory suggests that the area has already been too greatly influenced by concepts drawn from the study of adults.

Theories of memory abound with dichotomies: long-term and short-term, primary and secondary, episodic and semantic, to mention just a few of the more common ones. Chapters and review papers on infant memory (which seem almost to outnumber papers with original data) have made liberal use of these distinctions in an effort to provide the area with a suitable taxonomy of memory types and systems. I would like to begin by discussing several dichotomies.

Memories and Consequences

In adult memory, the distinction between the memory of an event and the more general class of consequences of that event is so obvious that we take it for granted and the fundamental nature of the distinction remains unexamined. Fatigue is a consequence of exercise, and pain is a consequence of injury; but we would not say that feeling tired constitutes a memory of the exercise, nor that feeling pain, in itself, constitutes a memory of being injured. Fatigue and pain are consequences of particular events (one may even think of them as traces of those events). They may serve as reminders or cues, but they are not memories of those events. This distinction, so taken for granted in the case of adult memory, is one that studies of preverbal infant memory force us to examine more closely. Are novelty effects following habituation examples of memories or consequences, and in any case, what is the essential difference?

Several misleading answers to this question must be rejected. One answer invokes that frequently exploited conceptual wildcard of psychological theory, *similarity*. According to this view, memory is a particular kind of consequence, one that is similar to the event that caused it. Fatigue and pain are not memories because they are not sufficiently similar to the events that caused them. But this use of the concept of similarity, like most of its uses in psychology, is a logical sleight of hand. To describe a memory as being similar to the event remembered is quite misleading. The only way in which an event and its subsequent memory can be described as similar to each other is in the sense that there exists a structural correspondence between the two, as, for example, between an event and a verbal description or pictorial representation of that event. (Indeed, this is all similarity can ever mean.) But such a structural correspondence will exist between an event and almost *any* consequence. Different exercises fatigue different muscles at different rates so that rules of correspondence could be drawn up even in this case, and it would make as much (or, rather, as little) sense to describe exercise and fatigue as possessing a certain degree of similarity. Thus, similarity is not a concept that can serve to distinguish memories from the more general class of consequences. This is not a particularly surprising conclusion. As Goodman (1972) remarks, similarity "is insidious . . . a pretender, an imposter, a quack . . . found where it does not belong, professing powers it does not possess" (p. 437).

A second misleading answer is to resort to the distinction between the mental and the physical. Memories are mental consequences, whereas such things as fatigue are physical consequences. Apart from the standard problems posed by this mind/body dualism (e.g., do we classify pain as mental or physical?), even if we concede that memories, whatever they may be, are in some sense mental, not all mental consequences can be considered memories. If they were, we would have to say that all mental development that is attributable to experience is the accumulation of memories. The term memory would become so general as to lose any usefulness.

We could, of course, have the worst of both worlds and combine the concepts of similarity and mental, in which case we would have a version of standard trace theory, probably still the most commonly held view. Memories are stored mental representations of events, residing in hypothetical boxes within a flow diagram. I will be returning to this misleading viewpoint at various points throughout the chapter, but for the present I will pursue the problem of distinguishing memories from consequences.

A final misleading, or at least inadequate, answer is to define memory in terms of certain experimental operations. (Memory, for example, is a differential responding to a previously presented stimulus.) Once again, memory becomes indistinguishable from more general processes of adaptation and development.

All this analysis may seem like so much logical hairsplitting, but the issue is important in the study of how infant memory develops. If the term memory is to have any significance, there must be a clear distinction between memory and consequences. I will argue that the proper basis of this distinction is not to be made in terms of properties of traces but by noting that memories are essentially inferences about the past. They are memories *of* something, that is, something to which the property of "pastness" is attributed. It is this attribution, and only this attribution, that distinguishes memory from such other cognitive functions as perceiving, learning, reasoning, or imagining.

If this argument seems familiar, it is because it is old. William James (1892, pp. 287 ff.) makes it very forcefully. Memory, says James, "is the knowledge of an event, or fact . . . with the additional consciousness that we have thought or experienced it before" (p. 287). Further on he says,

> A general feeling of the past direction of time, . . . a particular date conceived as lying along that direction, and defined by its name or phenomenal contents, an event imagined as located therein, and owned as part of my experience,— such are the elements of every object of memory. (p. 288)

In summary, we remember not when we recover traces but when present mental activity supports an inference about the past. This kind of inference, and only this kind of inference, distinguishes memory from cognition in general and enables us to distinguish memory from consequences. Inference should not, of course, be taken to mean conscious inference, although in the verbal child conscious inference may aid remembering. The term is used in Helmholtz's metaphorical sense. If we ask, "What is infant memory the memory of?" then by way of a first step toward an answer we can say that, if infants have anything that can legitimately be called memories, they are (to use a redundant phrase) the remembrance of things past.

In the adult or the verbal child, language makes the potential confusion between memories and consequences an apparently trivial problem. With the preverbal infant the matter becomes considerably more difficult. The use of the term *memory* to explain novelty effects in habituation paradigms, for example, is particularly problematical. Exposure to certain visual patterns clearly yields predictable consequences that outlast the physical presence of the pattern. There is, however, no more reason to invoke a concept of memory to explain this phenomenon than to invoke memory to explain learning in general. Of course, like Humpty-Dumpty we are entitled to use a word to mean whatever we wish it to mean, but there are several disadvantages to the use of the term memory in the context of habituation studies. First, it blurs the valuable distinction between learning and memory, a distinction I will develop later in this chapter as essential to a proper understanding of the ontogeny of memory. Second, the term *memory* tends to bring with it a great deal of surplus meaning—gratuitous conceptual baggage—that invites a joint attack from Occam's razor and Lloyd Morgan's canon, and justifies many of the Gibsonian arguments (cf. Chapter 3). A third disadvantage is more significant. By failing to distinguish memory from general adaptaive learning or attunement, research has been deflected from those developmental processes that relate peculiarly to memory. How does the developing infant or child come to accept present experiences as representing past experiences? How are these attributions or inferences validated? Such questions constitute the fundamental issue facing anyone seeking to explain how memory emerges as part of general cognitive development, yet strangely they seem not to have received much attention (cf. Chapters 4 & 5).

Memory as Retrieval

It will be clear by now that I am engaged in a crusade to save the term *memory* from ubiquity and preserve it for quite a narrow domain. I think this is in line with current trends in general memory theory. Adult memory research has gradually, if reluctantly, conceded that the aspect of remembering that establishes memory as a distinct subarea of cognition is the process by which thoughts and images are produced and accepted as valid representations of past experience. To use more common (but less satisfactory) terms, the distinctiveness of the memory area lies in the process of retrieval, recovery, or reconstruction, not in "encoding" or the laying down of traces. This is not to deny that encoding is of great interest to students of memory. Such processes, however, are not special to the area of memory. They are the proper subject matter of virtually every area of cognitive psychology.

This point has been made previously (Craik & Lockhart, 1972) in a paper that argued that, if we are to retain the concept of a memory trace, such a trace should be regarded not as a special product or output of the memory system, or as the placement of a mental representation in a memory store, but rather as a by-product of normal cognitive activities, such as perceiving, imagining, discriminating, reasoning, and the like. As William James (1892) saw clearly, there is nothing in such mental activity that is peculiar to memory and the meaning of such terms is to be established with reference to a general theory of cognitive functioning not within the more narrow confines of a theory of memory. Craik and I argued, therefore, that the study of memory should proceed not by instructing subjects to "try to remember" but by having them engage in incidental tasks that modeled basic cognitive skills. The task of a theory of memory is to offer an account of how such experiences are subsequently reconstituted as memories.

This argument for the use of incidental tasks is relevant to the study of infant memory. Obviously one does not instruct a 6-month-old infant to "try to remember," but implicit in this basic argument is a demand that these incidental tasks should capture and retain the essential features of normal cognitive functioning. Our argument was prompted in part by a distaste for the artificiality that often characterizes laboratory memory tasks.

The study of memory in natural settings or accurate models of natural settings is a noble goal eloquently advocated in Neisser's recent book (Neisser, 1982). It is easily realized in adult studies, but is much more difficult to achieve with the preverbal infant. Perhaps, though, it is not as difficult as many studies, putatively of infant memory, would suggest. These are studies in which a near motionless infant views a silent, motionless, untouchable, two-dimensional world of photographs or line drawings.

The argument that the feature that distinguishes memory from other areas of cognition is retrieval or "ecphory" (to use the term of Tulving, 1982) leads directly to a consideration of a dichotomy of great relevance to the study of infant memory: the distinction between recognition and recall.

Recognition and Recall

The distinction between recognition and recall has been a major feature of theories of adult memory and also plays a dominant role in accounts of early childhood memory. Piaget (1968), for example, distinguishes sharply between recognition and evocation and argues that, whereas recognition can rely solely on perception and sensorimotor schemes, evocation entails the use of symbolic functions such as language and imagery. Piaget then goes on to argue that, whereas evocative memory does not emerge before the age of 1½ or 2 years, recognition memory can be observed during the first few months of life. The ontogenetic priority of recognition is paralleled in phylogeny; recognition, says Piaget, can be seen even in lower invertebrates. Why Piaget stops at the lower invertebrates is unclear. He might well have gone on to list plants (that can clearly "recognize" the sun; some can even recognize insects) or indeed, any mechanical device that can respond differentially to a stimulus as a function of prior exposure to that stimulus.

In its general outline, Piaget's account seems to be the position most generally accepted. Recognition can occur at a very early age and in organisms low on the phylogenetic scale. Recall or, more generally, evocation demands symbolic functions.

Piaget describes a third kind of memory that he regards as intermediate between recognition and evocation, both ontogenetically and phylogenetically. This he terms *reconstruction memory*. An example of a task calling on reconstruction memory would be to reproduce a previously presented figure by arranging its elements, the elements being provided by the experimenter and remaining available to the subject during performance of the task.

This taxonomy of memories based on the task set for the subject is totally unsatisfactory. There is nothing in the logic of the classification that compels one to stop at three types of memory. Indeed the logic forces one to posit an indefinitely large number of memories, one for every degree and type of cue information.

The proper theoretical basis for distinguishing various memory tasks, of which different forms of recognition tests, cued-recall, and free recall are but a few examples, has caused a great deal of difficulty and confusion. Recent statements by Tulving (Tulving 1982, 1983) have gone a long way toward clarifying the matter conceptually. Tulving describes a process he terms *ecphory*, or *ecphoric information*, as the joint or interactive product of trace information and cue information. For any act of ecphory, the relative contributions of trace and cue information may vary, so that ecphoric information can be thought of as being located in a two-dimensional space, the axes of which represent degree of trace and cue information. Ecphory, however, is not itself memory. Remembering entails a third factor: a consideration of the particular question asked. A given degree or kind of ecphoric information may support the answer to certain questions but not others. Consider the situation of eyewitness identification in a police lineup. Ecphory will depend jointly on the nature of the learning resulting from the orginal encounter with the target person and the nature of the perceptual experience of the lineup. Our ability to identify the villain (assuming that is the question to be answered) will also depend on who else is in the lineup.

Clearly, we cannot develop an adequate taxonomy of memory systems by classifying tasks and cue conditions. It might reasonably be argued, however, that the infant's memory capabilities show a gradual development over time, beginning with recognition tasks in which there is rich cue information together with small demands on trace information and moving through successive degrees of development until the child is capable of pure evocation in which the cue information is generated symbolically without the presence of external cues.

As a general framework for thinking about early memory development, I think this point of view has merit. In other words, the task of a theory of early memory development within a general theory of cognitive development is to explain how ecphory emerges from trace and cue information and then to explain how ecphory is used as the basis for solving problems, answering questions, and accomplishing other acts of remembering. However, I must return to the point that the essential component of construction of memory out of ecphory is that there be an attribution to the past, that is, a capacity to discriminate (at least to some degree) the contributions of trace and cue information to the ecphoric experience. Otherwise ecphory is nothing more than the modification of a response as a consequence of exposure to a prior stimulus. One way of conceptualizing the emergence of memory is as the developing capacity of the child to partition ecphory into its trace and cue components.

Episodic and Nonepisodic Memory

I am obviously restricting the term *memory* to what is commonly termed *episodic memory*, and it is to this topic we now turn. Although the distinction between personal, autobiographical memory, or memory in the strict sense as Piaget describes it, and other cognitive skills such as knowledge of facts has only recently played an important role in theories of memory, the distinction itself is quite old and rather obvious. Philosophers such as Bergson, Russell, and Ayer made extensive use of it (see Locke, 1971). Nonetheless, the distinction is not without its difficulties, as many psychologists (e.g. Norman, 1976) have pointed out. A major problem is the nebulous and largely contradictory nature of the category I have termed *nonepisodic memory*. The frequently used term *semantic memory* is even worse, because not only is nonepisodic memory not memory, it is not peculiarly semantic either.

When we use the term *memory* to refer to knowledge, skills, and other products of learning, we so so only in the peculiar sense of denoting the absence of forgetting; when, for example, the possibility of forgetting seems to be at issue, and, as with the pragmatics of most negative assertions, there is the denial of a plausible alternative. Thus, the statement "I remember that Paris is the capital of France" is not quite synonymous with the statement "I know that Paris is the capital of France." The former statement is really an assertion that I have not forgotten something I once knew and would be spoken in a context where such forgetting is plausible. But we should not confuse the term *memory* used to deny the forgetting of some known fact or skill with *episodic memory*.

A major reason why such a confusion has existed is because a great deal of memory theory of the past 20 years has its roots in the earlier traditions of verbal learning. Since elements of the same history threaten to work themselves out in studies of infant memory, the matter is worth further examination.

Consider a typical experiment in which a subject is presented with a list of discrete items (words, say) and is subsequently asked to recall them. This procedure is normally considered an experiment in episodic memory since the words themselves are well known and what needs to be remembered is the event represented by the subjects' perception of the word at this particular time and place. Suppose we now modify the experiment slightly and present the list two or more times before asking for recall. If an item is subsequently recalled, is the subject remembering an episode, several episodes, or has the subject learned a new fact, for example, that the word *house* was on the list, either by reference to the episodes constituted by the item's presentation and perception or by reference to a knowledge structure that entails no direct recollection of such episodes? With respect to the distinction between episodic and nonepisodic memory, the typical word list experiment has an ambiguous status, and I think it is the legacy that such paradigms have left that has led to much of the confusion surrounding the conceptual status of episodic memory.

Let me make one further point in this matter and then turn to a consideration of the implication of my argument for the study of infant memory. No act of remembering, however autobiographical and however strong the sense of the personal past, is purely episodic, isolated from other aspects of cognition. Bartlett (1932) established that point some time ago. In fact, it is in many ways misleading to speak of episodic memory as a distinct system. Such a view smacks too much of the notion that episodic memories exist as intact entities, waiting to be revived, Penfieldlike, at the appropriate signal. It is much more fruitful, especially, I believe, in the study of early development, to think of memory as learning with an episodic component. The *episodic component* is the component that affords the subjective sense of the past and thus creates the essential difference between a consequence and a memory.

Some Conclusions

Learning Is More Fundamental than Memory and Precedes Memory

Learning is the foundation on which memory is built. The study of infant learning is therefore highly relevant to our understanding of how memory emerges. Nothing that has been said thus far should be taken to suggest that studies of infant recognition, habituation and novelty effects, and the conjugate reinforcement paradigm of Rovee-Collier are of no value to the study of memory. To the contrary, such studies serve to document the conditions under which infants are capable of responding differentially to a stimulus as a function of past exposure to that stimulus. Such differential responding constitutes the evidence (for the infant) from which memory develops.

Such studies, however, do not take us far enough. There remains the missing link of explaining how pastness is attributed to a present idea and how some ideas warrant this attribution and others do not. How do we as *adults* distinguish memories from imaginings? This question has teased many a philosopher and will no doubt continue to do so. (See, for example, the account by Ross & Kerst, 1978, of Wittgenstein's comments on this question.) I believe that the most promising approach to this question is through a study of memory's early development, the use of genetic epistemology as a method of answering questions in the best Piagetian tradition. In many ways the issue can be thought of in terms of the emergence of metamemory in the sense that there can be no real memory until there is a self-awareness, a conscious concept of having and using memory.

Let me try to clarify this rather confused statement by exploiting some ideas from James Mark Baldwin. Baldwin (1906, 1920) was quite clear in presenting the view that learning, and in particular imitation, is the precursor of memory. Like William James, he emphasized that memory is necessarily a conscious experience that implies the identification of something past. But the concept from Baldwin that I would like to mention is *memory validation*. How is a present thought or image accepted as a valid account of a past experience? This is clearly an important question, analogous to the question of how perceptual experience is validated against the external world and accommodates to that reality. Baldwin describes three stages of memory validation: physical, social, and psychical (see Ross & Kerst, 1978, for a brief description). Physical validation entails the verification of memory through perception by the physical reinstatement of the original external occurrence. In the second stage, social validation, the child makes use of parents and others to establish the veracity of his or her memory. Memories are checked against the opinions of others and against generally accepted truths. Finally, memories can be validated internally, checked against other memories and known facts.

Physical validation is of most interest to the student of infant memory since for the scarcely verbal infant, most validation will be of this kind. The basis of physical validation is the contingency between past and present actions. A current mental state, if it is a memory (and not, say, a felt need, a wish, or an act of imagination), will support or afford certain kinds of behavioral anticipations, as when an object that the infant places out of view is subsequently located without trial and error. The successful locating of the object validates *as a memory*, the later experience of having placed it there, and in so doing serves the ongoing process by which memories are differentiated from other mental states.

The concept of validation should not be taken to imply that memories appear fully formed and are then checked. As with all cognitive development, validation is an integral part of the developmental process itself and assumes that concepts of accommodation, assimilation, and equilibration are as relevant to our understanding of the emergence of memory and its differentiation from other mental states as they are to other areas of development.

In arguing that learning is prior to memory I am clearly supporting the view that memory develops through a process of differentiation and that learning does not entail the integration of memories for specific experiences. The integration point of view seems to be a particular realization of the general theory of abstraction, the view that conceptual development proceeds through a process of abstracting, or drawing out, common or defining features.

It has been known to philosophers for some time, and to many psychologists as well (e.g., Piaget), that the theory of abstraction will not work. It cannot be correct because it presupposes what it purports to explain. I cannot acquire the concept of dog by noticing what dogs have in common since I have no way of knowing to which of the infinitely many features I should attend unless I already possess the concept. Similarly, learning does not develop through abstracting common elements from specific experiences. Rather, memory develops through the increased differentiation of experiences, a differentiation that eventually supports an awareness of the uniqueness of an event, the event thereby becoming distinct from knowledge, which exists as part of a general script or frame (cf. Chapter 5).

These theoretical issues are difficult to address empirically since it is usually impossible to distinguish between integration on the one hand and a failure to differentiate on the other. I was very interested, however, in some results reported recently by Nelson and Ross (1980) and by Nelson (Chapter 5). Admittedly the data are from preschoolers rather than infants, but the results clearly demonstrate that such children have more difficulty in reporting specific episodes than in answering questions about the general case. Even in answering specific questions about past events, they used the present tense from 10% to 50% of the time. "They often slipped from past to present in the specific condition but rarely did the reverse— slip from present to past in the general condition" (Nelson and Ross, 1980, p. 97).

What is also interesting about these data is that they provide hints about how specificity emerges. It would seem that to be reported as a specific memory, an event must be sufficiently novel to avoid the fate of being incorporated or assimilated into a familiar script or scheme. According to Ross and Kerst (1978), Baldwin held a similar view, arguing that memory progresses by the breaking up of large undifferentiated happenings into smaller separable units.

The Study of Infant Memory

My final comment is that the development of memory should be studied, not only as an isolated skill, but in the broader context of general cognitive development. I have argued elsewhere (Lockhart, 1978) that adult memory has suffered greatly by placing too much emphasis on controlled, and frequently contrived, laboratory paradigms. Too often the paradigms themselves become the object of study rather than a tool for answering more fundamental questions. At times, this fate seems to threaten the various habituation paradigms used so frequently in infant research. I do not mean that laboratory paradigms should be discarded or that there should be a rush to the nursery to observe memory in action, *au naturel*. There are, however, several naturally occurring phenomena that have been subject to intensive investigation and that are likely to be of particular interest to memory theorists because they are phenomena within which embryonic memory is likely to be observed in action. The most obvious example is object permanence. The various developmental stages of this phenomenon are perhaps the clearest example of Baldwin's concept of the physical stage of memory validation, and the paper by Sophian (1980) is a good example of what I have in mind. A second example is the development of the concept of self. Not only does the development of this concept seem to be essential to the development of memory, but conversely it is difficult to imagine the development of such a concept without an associated development of memory. A third example of potential interest is the possible role of memory in the development of self-control and in particular the role that memory might play in coping with an imposed delay of gratification. Freud (1900/1953, pp. 564–568), for example, suggested that in order to cope with delay (such as feeding) the infant will "re-establish the situation of the original satisfaction" with mnemonic images of the potential source of reward—mother's breast, for example. Although there is little direct evidence that such ideation occurs in the infant, Freud's idea constitutes an interesting suggestion for a developmental context within which to study the emergence of memory. What I find particularly promising about this topic is that learning to cope with an externally imposed delay of gratification clearly entails the development of understanding of temporal concepts: past and future, memory and expectation, each opposite sides of the same coin. These ideas have been explored with young children in some interesting papers by Karniol and Miller (e.g., Karniol & Miller, 1981). What they have shown is that reward-focused ideation increases tolerance of an externally imposed delay of gratification, a delay that is outside the control of the child. Because such externally imposed delay is more characteristic of the infant's experience than self-imposed delay would be, the phenomenon should be of general interest to students of cognitive development and to memory theorists in particular.

There are undoubtedly other, and perhaps better, examples that will occur to those more familiar with infant development than I am. I wish merely to point out that the study of early memory development should not be isolated from those developmental phenomena in which it is imbedded.

References

Baldwin, J. M. *Thought and things: A study of the development of meaning and thought or genetic logic.* New York: Macmillan, 1906.

Baldwin, J. M. *Mental development in the child and the race* (3rd ed.). New York: Macmillan, 1920.

Bartlett, F C. *Remembering.* Cambridge: Cambridge University Press, 1932.

Craik, F. I. M., & Lockhart, R. S. Levels of processing: A framework for memory research. *Journal of Verbal Learning and Verbal Behavior,* 1972, *11,* 671–684.

Freud, S. *The interpretation of dreams* (Vols. 4–5) (J. Strachey, Trans.). London: Hogarth Press, 1953. (Originally published, 1900.)

Goodman, N. *Problems and projects.* New York: Bobbs-Merrill, 1972.

James, W. *Psychology.* London: Macmillan, 1892.

Karniol, R., & Miller, D. T. The development of self-control in children. In S. S. Brehm, S. M. Kassin, & F. X. Gibbon (Eds.), *Developmental social psychology.* New York: Oxford University Press, 1981.

Locke, D. *Memory.* London: Macmillan, 1971.

Lockhart, R. S. Method and content in the study of human memory. In J. P. Sutcliffe, (Ed.), *Conceptual analysis and method in psychology.* Sydney: Sydney University Press, 1978.

Neisser, U. *Memory observed.* San Francisco: Freeman, 1982.

Nelson, K., & Ross, G. The generalities and specifics of long-term memory in infants and young children. In M. Perlmutter (Ed.), *Children's memory: New directions for child development* (No. 10). San Francisco: Jossey-Bass, 1980.

Norman, D. A. *Memory and attention* (2nd ed.). New York: Wiley, 1976.

Piaget, J. *On the development of memory and identity.* Barre, Mass.: Clark University Press, 1968.

Ross, B. M., & Kerst, S. M. Developmental memory theories: Baldwin and Piaget. In H. W. Reese & L. P. Lipsitt, (Eds.), *Advances in child development and behavior* (Vol. 12). New York: Academic Press, 1978.

Sophian, C. Habituation is not enough: Novelty, preferences, search, and memory in infancy. *Merrill-Palmer Quarterly,* 1980, *26,* 239–256.

Tulving, E. Synergistic ecphory in recall and recognition. *Canadian Journal of Psychology,* 1982, *36,* 130–147.

Tulving, E. *Elements of episodic memory.* Oxford: Oxford University Press, 1983.

CHAPTER 7

Infantile Amnesia
A Neurobiological Perspective

Lynn Nadel   and   Stuart Zola-Morgan

Cognitive Sciences Program   *Veterans Administration Medical Center*
School of Social Sciences   *and*
University of California   *Department of Psychiatry*
Irvine, California   *School of Medicine*
                    University of California at San Diego
                         La Jolla, California

Groucho: Chicolini, when were you born?
Chico: I don't remember, I was just a little baby at the time. (*Duck Soup*)

Introduction

Few facts about infancy are so obvious as the apparent inaccessibility of memories from the months and years just after birth. Explanations offered to account for this absence of early memories have ranged from psychoanalytic formulations to mechanisms grounded in neurobiology. In this chapter, we will suggest that the postnatal maturation of a specific neural system—the hippocampal formation—lies at the root of infantile amnesia. This argument is based on the points outlined below, each of which will be developed in the sections to follow.

The research described in this chapter was supported by NINCDS grant NS 17712 to Lynn Nadel.

145

1. Studies of the ontogeny of memory indicate that it is a nonunitary phenomenon; that is, there is more than one memory system. Some memory systems are functional at birth or shortly thereafter, whereas others become functional following a period of postnatal neurogenesis.
2. Studies of disordered memory function have demonstrated that the nervous system honors distinctions between different types of learning and memory; that is, localized brain damage typically leads to selective, rather than general, memory defects. The hippocampal formation seems necessary for only certain kinds of learning/memory, whereas other kinds remain intact even in the absence of normal hippocampal function.
3. The hippocampal formation in adults seems central to just those learning/memory functions whose absence characterizes infantile amnesia. Further, the existence and time course of this amnesic condition seem to match, in those species studied to date, the postnatal maturation of the hippocampal region.

Why Study Memory Ontogeny?

One studies the ontogeny of memory both for its own sake and as well for the light it might shed on more abstract issues: Are all memory systems alike? Do they go through similar developmental sequences? What can be said about the properties of these memory systems as they mature through time? One might be excused for asking: Why study the ontogeny of memory in animals? Isn't it hard enough to study it in children? What can we gain by looking at birds, rats, monkeys, and the like in their development of memory capacities, which might, in any case, differ from that which we seek to understand in human infants?

We take it as a matter of established fact that there is continuity in neural function through evolution. Although specialized memory systems may be found in humans alone, most of human memory would seem to function according to principles, and be mediated by physiological processes, indistinguishable from those studied in other animals. This being the case, one can avail oneself of the advantages offered by the study of animals other than humans. The special kinds of possibilities permitted by animal studies include (1) precise manipulation of experimental variables that cannot be so readily controlled in humans; (2) unusual rearing regimes; and (3) analyses of the biological bases of the memory through controlled lesion, stimulation, and recording studies. But, beyond these well-known and generally accepted advantages is the likelihood that certain meaningful generalizations about the ontogeny of memory will emerge only through comparative studies. Human memory and its development will, we assume, be best understood in a biological framework that considers capacities such as learning/memory in terms of their adaptive value to the organism. But this biological context presents a number of problems that must be discussed first.

Some Caveats

The study of infant memory and its neurobiological bases is plagued by special methodological problems. Many of these difficulties arise from the fact that one studies organisms at a time when the underlying mechanisms responsible for their behavior are in a dynamic, fluctuating state. This fact and its diverse implications are brought out most forcefully in the study of disordered memory resulting from brain damage in either laboratory or clinical settings.

Consider Teuber and Rudel's (1962) study of perceptual motor performance in brain-damaged children. On one task, the effects of infant lesions were not apparent before the age of 11 years but became increasingly obvious thereafter. On a second task, a deficit was seen at all ages. The third task revealed effects of early injury only up to 11 years; no abnormalities in performance were seen beyond that. There are lessons here relating both to the interpretation of these kinds of studies and to the course of memory ontogeny. One traditional framework for understanding the effects of brain damage in the young was supplied by Kennard (1938, 1940, 1942) in her classic series of studies on the effects of damage in motor systems of primates (humans and monkeys). She suggested that early brain damage has less of an effect than comparable lesions made in adults. The Teuber and Rudel study and many others show that this notion is "deceptively simple" (Teuber, 1971). One might as easily argue that damaging a neural system in the young, thereby depriving the developing organism of its contributions to ontogeny, could actually be more devastating than a comparable manipulation in adulthood, in which case the organism would have had the benefit of that system for most of its life. To the extent to which a neural system contributes to reorganization and plasticity in other neural systems (not directly disturbed by the brain lesion), one will expect some such result. Yet another possibility is that a brain lesion could have no effect at all, which might occur if the subject is tested at an age when the damaged region does not normally contribute to task performance and if the lesion was not made early enough to interfere (indirectly) with the development of other brain areas that are essential to performance. Thus, generalizations about the ontogeny of memory from the study of the effects of brain lesions must be qualified. Where is the lesion? At what age is the lesion made? What manner of system is disrupted? What is the nature of the task, and how does its solution relate to the disrupted system? At what age is testing carried out? How does adultlike performance on the task develop during ontogeny?

Two additional variables should be noted. First, the maturation of brain/behavior proceeds at different tempos in males and females, and this could have consequences for the study of infant memory. For example, male rhesus monkeys with orbital prefrontal neocortex lesions are impaired on certain behavioral tasks (object reversal learning and delayed response) at 75 days of age, whereas similar deficits are not detected in females with comparable lesions until 15–18 months of age (Goldman, Crawford, Stokes, Galkin, & Rosvold, 1974). Second, environmental stimulation during infancy is certain to be a potent factor governing an organism's capacity to perform on various tasks. Animals reared in complex, "enriched" environments have "better" brains—more synapses and more dendritic spines, for example—than others reared in ordinary laboratory environments (Greenough & Chang, in press).

Even if we were to account for all these factors, we still might not be as close as we thought to obtaining clarification of the way behavioral ontogeny maps onto neural ontogeny or vice versa. Some general examples will make this point clearer. The order in which neurons in various brain regions are laid down may bear little relation to the onset or nature of the functions of these regions. For instance, prefrontal granular neocortex and primary visual neocortex are formed at roughly the same time, but these areas ultimately mediate quite different functions, which develop over widely different intervals of time (Goldman, 1976; Rakic, 1974). As another example, the deposition of neural elements is completed in cerebral neocortex long before it is in the cerebellar cortex, but the emergence of mature cerebellar function most likely precedes that of neocortical function (Goldman, 1976). A more specific example is provided by Goldman and Alexander (1977), who demonstrated a pattern of increasing sensitivity to cooling of the dorsolateral prefrontal neocortex among groups of monkeys tested at different ages (see Figure 1). Monkeys 19–31 months of age during cooling were significantly worse on the delayed response task than were monkeys 9–16 months of age. In turn, monkeys 34–36 months of age made more errors during cooling than did the 19–31-month-old animals. The authors concluded that the dorsolateral neocortex does not participate significantly in the mediation of delayed response performance during the first 16 months of life and that subsequently the region

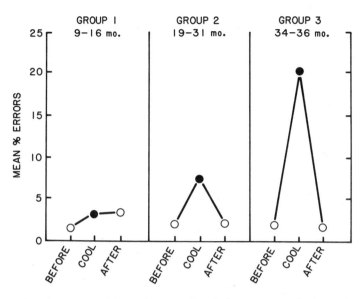

Fig. 1. Delayed response (DR) performance in relation to cryogenic depression of the dorsolateral prefrontal neocortex (DLC). Mean percent errors on DR trials presented before, during, and after DLC cooling for three different groups of monkeys in the age spans indicated. The ability to perform DR did not change across the ages sampled. However, the involvement of the DLC in DR did change in ontogeny, as indicated by the greater impairment induced by cooling in the older animals (adapted from Goldman & Alexander, 1977).

is progressively more involved until by 36 months the process of maturation seems essentially complete. But notice that during this transition from minimal to maximal dependence on the dorsolateral neocortex there was no evidence of change in the ability to perform the task. We must conclude that dorsolateral neocortex plays an integral role in mediating delayed response performance in fully mature organisms but that neonates can achieve adult levels of performance even though this brain region appears to be minimally functional at the time. Other brain systems must be mediating performance during the maturation of the dorsolateral neocortex, after which the latter could augment or replace the former. Perhaps detailed behavioral analyses would demonstrate that good delayed response performance is being mediated by fundamentally different underlying behavioral strategies at different ages (cf. Goldberger, 1974).

The foregoing discussion points out some of the difficulties one must face in trying to interpret data from ontogenetic studies. Even when the time course of development of good performance on specific tasks is well delineated, there is no guarantee that it can be directly related to the concomitant maturation of some neural system. The crucial missing step concerns the relation between neural systems and their specific functions, and the behavioral requirements of particular tasks. Notwithstanding these difficulties, many facts are available to help us understand infantile amnesia, and it is possible, indeed profitable, to begin putting them together. In the following section, we focus on a number of studies that have demonstrated the existence of multiple cognitive systems, each with its own maturational calendar.

Multiple Memory Systems

When we study the ontogeny of memory, are we looking at a single, monolithic function or at many different capacities united primarily by the shared properties of plasticity and storage? Following a period during which memory has often been considered a univocal function, many contemporary approaches embody distinctions between forms of memory differing either in terms of processes or contents[1] (cf. Chapter 8).

Dichotomies of this sort are useful insofar as the distinctions they draw between kinds of memory are interesting. What do we mean by this? By interesting we mean that the distinctions could (1) be confirmed by a particular pattern of memory development during ontogeny, (2) converge with data from developmental neuroanatomy and neurophysiology, (3) give rise to predictions concerning the characteristics of the behaviors resting on different systems, or (4) make informative predictions about the way memory will fragment in dysfunctional states. Uninteresting dichotomies fail to connect with biological reality, reflecting instead the arbitrary ways in which laboratory studies are done. As we see shortly, the data from ontogenetic studies indicate that there are different kinds

---

[1]For example, process dichotomies include primary/secondary, short term/long term, working/reference, and possibly selectional/instructional. Content dichotomies include verbal/nonverbal, episodic/semantic, taxon/locale, and possibly procedural/declarative. Each such characterization has its advantages and disadvantages. Process-oriented dichotomies concentrate on the movement of information through a computational system, often conceived in terms similar to those applied to general purpose computers. Content-oriented dichotomies stress the specific nature of the information being processed, often assuming that the brain is composed of a set of special-process modules. Data suggesting that there are multiple memory systems, each concerned with a distinct kind of information, are more consistent with content dichotomies (see Nadel & Wexler, in press). The distinctions expressed in process dichotomies could be realized as different states of activation within separate content-specific modules.

of memory, at least insofar as diverse time courses of development can be demonstrated for a variety of behavioral capacities. But, it is not so easy to know precisely how to define these different systems, and until recently little work has been done on animals using tasks that address the issue of memory directly. The data we discuss below relate to multiple cognitive systems, rather than multiple memory systems. Nonetheless, they address the same issue: How many systems are there?

Early work by Harlow and his colleagues (Harlow, 1949, 1959; Harlow, Harlow, Rueping, & Mason, 1960) provides a general framework within which we can view the abilities of developing monkeys. However, these investigations have not always clearly distinguished between two stages in the ontogeny of a given ability: the time when a particular problem can first be solved and the time when it can be solved in the adult manner with adult levels of proficiency. This seems to us a critical, but often neglected, distinction—we raise it here because it will help in understanding data from studies on the effects of early brain damage in monkeys.

Goldman has carried out an extensive series of investigations concerned with the effects of damage in the dorsolateral prefrontal neocortex (of monkeys) on performance in a delayed response (DR) task. When extensive lesions are made in this region within the first 2 months of life and the animals are tested before they become a year old, the characteristic DR deficit induced by similar damage in adults is not observed (Goldman, 1971). However, when these early lesioned monkeys are retested in their second year of life, they demonstrate impaired performance on the DR task. This difficulty is not due to any deterioration in the performance of the lesioned monkeys. Rather, it reflects the growing efficiency with which their age-matched controls can now perform the task. That is, the ability to perform DR tasks with adult proficiency is not present in the neonatal monkey and develops only gradually over an extended postnatal period. Visual pattern discrimination and object discrimination reversal apparently do not depend on the integrity of this region since its removal either in infancy or adulthood has no effect on the learning/performance of these tasks.

The same point is made in more complex fashion in work carried out by one of us (Zola-Morgan) in collaboration with Mahut at Northeastern University. Damage to the hippocampal system via bilateral fornix section had different behavioral effects at 20–30 days of age than it did later, at 2–3 years. Specifically, although adult operated monkeys were impaired on a position reversal task, they were better-than-normal on a visual reversal task using 3-dimensional junk objects (Mahut, 1972; Schram, 1970; Zola & Mahut, 1973). Monkeys in whom comparable damage was made early in life, when tested a few weeks after surgery, showed only the impaired performance on the position task. They were indistinguishable from their age-matched controls on the visual reversal task (Mahut & Zola, 1977). We next compared the performance of normal infant monkeys to that of normal adults on both kinds of reversal tasks. As seen in Figure 2, normal infant monkeys at 3 months can perform the position reversal task as efficiently as adult monkeys. But, compared to normal adults, 3-month-old infant monkeys are impaired on the object reversal task and do not approximate adult levels of performance, even with repeated testing, until 2 years of age.

These data suggest that there are two separate systems: one matures very early (by 3 months) and is necessary for the performance of position reversal tasks, the other matures much later (between 12–24 months), delaying the onset of adultlike performance on visual reversals until it is complete. The facilitation of object reversals induced by lesions in the hippocampal system depends, in some way we do not understand at present, on the pre-existing function of this late-developing system.

Thus, within a single species, maturational scenarios can be described that suggest different time courses for the development of different cognitive abilities (i.e., position reversal vs. delayed response vs. object reversal). These differences obtain even for functions that appear on the

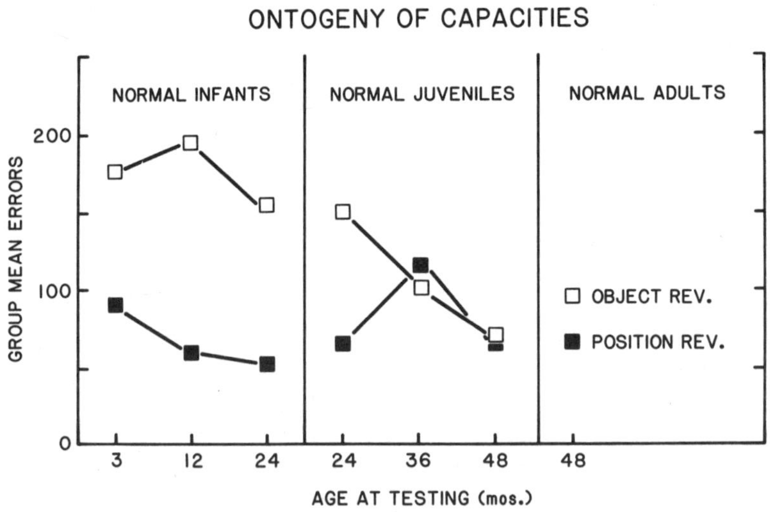

Fig. 2. The performance of normal infant, juvenile, and adult rhesus monkeys on two types of reversal task. Position reversal capacity appears fully developed by 3 months of age. Animals did not achieve adultlike performance on the object reversal task until 2 years of age (adapted from Mahut & Zola, 1977).

surface to share significant characteristics. Table 1 lists the behavioral tasks used in investigations with monkeys for which we know the age of onset of adultlike performance. The data are consistent with the view that there is a temporal dimension to the emergence of complex cognitive abilities, such as those underlying reversal learning and delayed response. We will argue that this maturation of function is intimately related to the maturation of areas in the central nervous system (the dorsolateral prefrontal neocortex and the hippocampal system in the two cases just discussed). Timetables of the ontogeny of mature forms of behavior may be indispensable in uncovering the status of the central nervous system at a particular point in development.

The studies just reviewed do not directly address the issue of different memory systems (see Squire & Zola-Morgan, 1983, for a discussion of reversal learning and delayed response tasks as they relate to issues of memory). A recent preliminary report (Bachevalier & Mishkin, 1982) extends this view of separable systems to the study of memory and its ontogeny. Three-month-old normal infant monkeys learned and retained an object discrimination task exactly like adult monkeys. But, on a one-trial recognition task, requiring a judgment of novelty, adult levels of proficiency were not achieved even after a year. (At this time we do not know when in development young monkeys can perform this task the

Table 1. Ontogeny of Capacities in the Monkey

Task	Adult performance
Left–right spatial discrimination (Harlow, 1959; Mahut & Zola, 1977)	15–45 days
Spatial discrimination reversal (Mahut & Zola, 1977)	< 90 days
Object discrimination (Harlow, Harlow, Rueping & Mason, 1960; Mahut & Zola, 1977)	4–5 months
Delayed response (5 min) (Harlow, Harlow, Rueping, & Mason, 1960)	8–9 months
Object discrimination reversal (Goldman, 1974; Mahut & Zola, 1977)	2 years
Object learning set (Harlow, Harlow, Rueping, & Mason, 1960)	2–3 years

way adults do.) The authors conclude that their results "provide some support for the view that infantile amnesia may be due to the absence of a functional memory system in early childhood."

The same conclusion of separately developing learning/memory systems has been reached by many others. Sussman and Ferguson (1980), for example, have shown that infantile amnesia can appear present when one measure is used but be apparently absent with another. Rats trained in avoidance at 23–25 days of age showed rapid forgetting when instrumental responding was assessed but normal forgetting when the fear-induced decrease in activity was measured. Misanin and co-workers (Misanin, Nagy, Keiser, & Bowen, 1971; Misanin, Brownback, Shaughnessy, & Hinderliter, 1980) came to the same view from their study of the ontogeny of escape behavior. Experiments such as these have led Spear (1979) to state in his recent review that "although the data are not yet conclusive, they do suggest that young organisms store fewer and different memory attributes than adults store" (p. 147). But which "attributes" of any situation get stored and which fail to get stored? Or, to use Bachevalier and Mishkin's language again, which "functional memory systems" are absent in infancy? Next, we discuss studies of exploratory behavior in rats. It will be our contention that primary among those attributes that are not stored by infants are those pertinent to environmental contexts.

Habituation, Exploration, and Novelty Reactions

When an animal is exposed to an unfamiliar situation it will, after some initial caution, explore its new environs. This exploration is not a haphazard wandering about. Rather, animals explore in a structured fashion, going first to one place then to another, rarely returning to locations and objects already visited before the others have been sampled. This pattern suggests the existence of internal representations that capture the spatial structure of the environment. Tolman's (1948) notion of a "cognitive map" seems closest to this idea, and one of us has proposed an updated version of cognitive map theory that discusses issues related to exploration at some length (Morris, 1982; O'Keefe & Nadel, 1978, especially Chapter 6).

Habituation of exploration lasts for a considerable time (Cheal, Klestzick, & Domesick, 1982) indicating that the knowledge underlying such behavior is maintained in memory to be referred to in the future should the organism return to that place. We can contrast the long-lasting habituation of exploration (and the neural systems underlying it) with the response decrements following repetition in systems such as those involving the startle reflex. These latter decrements are influenced by different pharmacological interventions and are probably dependent on different neural systems (Williams, Hamilton, & Carlton, 1974).

The dissociation between repetition-induced decrements in startle reactions and behavioral exploration is of interest here because the two capacities show different ontogenetic patterns. Decrements within reflex systems, such as startle or forelimb-withdrawal, can be largely intact in neonates at a very early age (cf. Campbell & Stehouwer, 1979, who report decrements in 3-day-old rat pups). Normal exploration and its decrement over time are not seen until postnatal day 18 or later (Campbell & Stehouwer, 1979; Feigley, Parsons, Hamilton, & Spear, 1972; File, 1978; Williams, Hamilton, & Carlton, 1975). These results are consistent with data from the study of spontaneous alternation. When an animal is allowed to choose between two alternatives and its choice is not determined by such factors as hunger, thirst, or the need for a mate or safety, the likelihood is quite high that it will alternate its choices. Such behavior is easily demonstrated on the T-maze, where rats choose to go to opposite ends of the maze on successive choices. We have interpreted this kind of behavior in terms of exploration, a view which is supported by findings that the same neural systems implicated in alternation are involved in exploration. Studies of the development of spontaneous alternation indicate that this capacity develops relatively late in ontogeny (Douglas, Peterson, & Douglas, 1973; Egger, 1973a, b; Egger, Livesey, & Dawson, 1973; Frederickson & Frederickson, 1979a, b; Kirkby, 1967; Somerville, 1979[2]). In rats, significant levels of alternation are not achieved until the fourth week of life, whereas in cats reliable alternation appears during the second month. As we see later, these behavioral signs of exploration emerge just as the hippocampal system approaches maturity. Most interesting, perhaps, is the fact that the guinea pig, a precocial animal whose central nervous system (including hippocampal formation) is essentially mature within a week of birth, shows reliable alternation at this early age as well (Douglas et al., 1973).

Pilot work by one of us (Nadel) confirms the view that spatial exploration develops late in ontogeny. In our task, rats explore an open arena containing an array of several objects; their behavior is monitored and subsequently scored for both its spatial and temporal patterning. The rats are lowered into the center of the arena inside a box that then serves as a home base. The typical rat, if we can be excused for speaking of such an abstraction, does the following in the arena situation: initial cau-

[2]In her comprehensive Ph.D. thesis (1979), E. Somerville investigated various concomitants of postnatal hippocampal maturation. We refer in several places to her extensive findings, which are in strong agreement with the position adopted in this chapter. Interested readers are referred to this work for further details.

tion is followed by a burst of activity during which time the entire arena is explored, typically (but not always) beginning with the regions nearest the home base. Special attention is paid to objects. When the entire arena has been explored, inactivity returns. This pattern is reflected in the proportion of time spent by the animal in the delivery box, or home base. Initially quite high (caution), this value decreases dramatically (exploration), only to rise again later (habituation). In terms of specific patterns of exploration, most rats begin their exploring near the home base, moving outward as familiarity increases. They usually do not return to the same areas repetitively, preferring to distribute their exploration throughout the area. In short, they act as though they are "mapping" the arena. Most rats show relatively complete decrement in exploration within 3–4 sessions—this change being both long lasting and specific. On the day following what appears to be the cessation of exploration, the rat is reintroduced into the arena, but with some change in the location or nature of one or more of the objects. Its ability to detect and respond to these changes provides a behavioral assay of the qualitative nature of the representations formed during exploration. Adult rats react to a variety of such changes, including addition of a new object, deletion of an old one, and the spatial rearrangement of several of the old ones. This latter finding is crucial; it shows that the rats are storing information not only about the occurrence of objects but also about their locations within a specific environment. Our pilot studies on neonates indicate that patterned exploration, decrements in exploration over time, and reactions to novel changes in now-familiar environments do not show up until at least postnatal day 19, if not somewhat later. Much the same picture emerges from the study of the ontogeny of exploration in primates (Menzel & Menzel, 1979).

What conclusions can we draw from these various studies on the ontogeny of exploration? First, it must be emphasized that habituation, like memory, is not a univocal function; response decrements within different systems develop at different times in ontogeny. Indeed, it may not be correct to apply the same term—*habituation*—to the decrements seen in startle reflexes and in exploration. They are different in all relevant respects. Second, what appears to be developing late is a system responsible for the exploration of environments and the formation of internal representations of these experienced environments. To return to the questions posed at the close of the previous section, it appears as though among the functional memory systems absent in infancy is one that is concerned with environmental attributes (i.e., where things are located and, as we shall see, in which environment events transpire).

Thus far, we have suggested that work with rats and monkeys points to the existence of multiple memory systems and that these separable systems appear to mature at different rates. In addition, we have suggested that infantile amnesia might be associated with the late development of a memory system concerned with information about places and the events that occur within them. One way of testing this notion might be to identify situations in which this late-developing system has been disrupted after maturation and see if the behavioral effects resemble those characteristic of infantile amnesia. Recent studies of this sort from the areas of clinical and comparative neuropsychology are consistent with the notion that memory is not a monolithic entity, showing that only certain kinds of memory are affected in organic or experimentally induced amnesia.

It has been known for some time that amnesic patients with damage either in the medial temporal region or in midline diencephalic structures can, under certain circumstances, exhibit good learning and retention across long intervals. The best-known examples of this observation come from the learning of perceptual-motor skills. In the past few years, tests that are less clearly perceptual motor have been identified that can also elicit signs of retention in patients who by other indications are profoundly amnesic (see Cohen, 1981; Parkin, 1982; Squire, Cohen, & Nadel, in press). The capacity for preserved learning in amnesia appears to extend to perceptual skills like mirror reading (Cohen & Squire, 1980), purely cognitive skills such as learning a numerical rule (Wood, Ebert, & Kinsbourne, 1982), and the solution to certain puzzles (Cohen, 1981; Cohen & Corkin, 1981). By contrast, the development and consolidation of knowledge comprising the facts of conventional memory studies, and daily life, appear to be severely compromised in amnesia.

The facts from cases of human amnesia suggest that only a particular kind of memory system is affected. In the intact adult, this system affords the basis for knowledge about specific events, the time and place of their occurrence, and facts about the world obtained in the course of (or subsequently derived from) such experiences. We believe that in the absence of the medial temporal region (most prominently the hippocampal formation but possibly also including the amygdala[3]) organisms maintain the capacity to acquire skills but cannot establish memory of the specific events that led to the perfection of these skills. That is, representations

[3]Mishkin (1978) suggested that conjoint damage to the hippocampal formation and amygdala is necessary for the full expression of amnesia. More recent work (Murray & Mishkin, 1982; Parkinson & Mishkin, 1982; Squire & Zola-Morgan, 1982) suggests that these two structures contribute differentially to memory functions. Hippocampal damage alone can cause significant memory impairment. In this chapter, we refer specifically to the hippocampal formation, though we remain aware that its neighbor in the medial temporal region, the amygdala, could play some role in the formation and stabilization of memories as well.

can develop that change how organisms respond to the external world without affording access to information about where and when the instances that led to this change occurred.

Recent work has demonstrated parallel findings in adult monkeys with brain damage in areas implicated in human amnesia. Monkeys with damage to either the diencephalic or medial temporal (including hippocampal) regions of the brain were impaired on tests constructed to be parallel to those sensitive to amnesia in humans (Zola-Morgan & Squire, in press, b). They were unimpaired on other tasks, analogous to the skill-learning tasks unaffected in human amnesia (Zola-Morgan, in press; Zola-Morgan & Squire, in press, a). Mishkin and his co-workers recently demonstrated a dissociation after damage in the hippocampal region in adult monkeys; some tasks were affected (Parkinson & Mishkin, 1982), others were not (Murray & Mishkin, 1982). These data are particularly interesting because they show that hippocampal damage results in a loss of memory for the places in which objects are to be found, a result consistent with the data reviewed above indicating that it is environmental information that is most severely affected by such damage. Similarly, research by one of us in adult rats has demonstrated the selective impairment of place learning, but not cue learning, after hippocampal damage (Nadel & MacDonald, 1980; O'Keefe, Nadel, Keightley, & Kill, 1975).

Thus, data from both humans and nonhumans suggest that there are at least two kinds of memory systems. One is left intact in amnesia, the other is not. The selective disruption seen in amnesia resembles the pattern of partial memory capacity characteristic of infantile amnesia. We elaborate on the features of the memory system implicated in these phenomena in a later section. First, we present evidence that the hippocampal formation is indeed a late-developing system, whose tardy maturation could plausibly underlie infantile amnesia.

Developmental Neuroanatomy

The hippocampal formation is portrayed in Figure 3. At what age is this neural system functional in the various species under consideration? We can start out with a simplistic comment: If the machinery is not there, the system will not function. The difficult part is that even if the machinery is there, we cannot be sure that it is functioning. At this point in the development of our technical sophistication we may be able to describe the birth and growth of the neural machinery, but we still do not know how to relate these events to behavior. To put the issue most concretely:

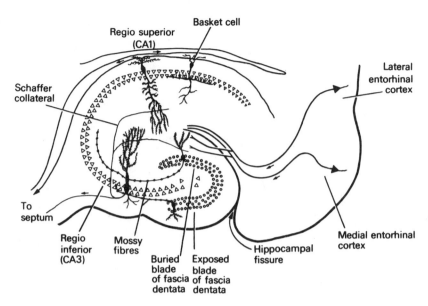

Fig. 3. Schematic diagram of a horizontal section through the right hippocampus of a rat (from O'Keefe & Nadel, 1978).

What does synaptogenesis or the formation of complex dendritic spines mean for the performance of delayed response?[4]

Our intent here is to describe briefly the state of knowledge about some of the indices of hippocampal ontogeny. We imagine that there is a dynamic interplay between the various components of the hippocampal formation maturing at different rates as well as interplay between these components and other areas of the brain. Neural systems may become partially functional and begin to assert influence (or give it up) long before they are completely mature. There would appear to be a kind of "developmental overlaying" both within and between brain areas that are at varying stages of maturity at any given moment (cf. Lanier & Isaacson,

[4]Neural systems and the behaviors they support rarely come "on-line" all of a sudden. In her thesis, Somerville (1979) contrasts the time at which a capacity first appears in any member of a population of developing rat pups with the time when it is prevalent in the population as a whole. There is a spread across a few days in some cases, and across a week or longer in others. It is likely that capacities primarily depending on the internal wiring of a system would precede those that depend on precise interconnection between separate systems. Thus, learning/memory for environmental information, as measured in place learning tasks, seems to mature fastest, whereas the improved retentive capacities that rest on precise interaction between such an environmental coding system and other, separate circuits continue to develop for some weeks longer.

1977). It is presently impossible to relate these subtle aspects of development to the time course of appearance of particular forms of behavior.

Relative simplicity has made the dentate gyrus (fascia dentata) of the hippocampal formation (see Figure 3) the focus of considerable attention in the developmental neurosciences. The majority of its cells are of a uniform type and their perikarya are arranged in a single layer, the stratum granulosum. There is also a broad plexiform zone, the stratum moleculare, in which the dendrites of the granule cells ramify and in which most of the afferent fibers to the dentate gyrus terminate. The cytoarchitecture of this region is not its only appealing feature. The fact that each of the extrinsic afferents and some of the association pathways to the dentate terminate on different portions of the granule cell somata or their dendrites makes the study of the development of such connections manageable. For instance, we now know that two of the critical factors determining the final pattern of connectivity in the dentate gyrus are the time of arrival of its various afferent pathways and the time at which the appropriate postsynaptic structures on the granule cells and their dendrites are generated (Gottleib & Cowan, 1972a, b).

The dentate gyrus of the rat contains about 600,000 granule cells, generated from the 14th day of gestation (E14)[5] through the second postnatal week (P14+) (Schlessinger, Cowan, & Gottleib, 1975). Three distinct morphogenetic gradients have been described in the gyrus: (1) cells in the dorsal blade form earlier than those in the ventral blade; (2) cells in the more caudal (temporal) portion of the gyrus are generated earlier than those in the more rostral (septal) regions; and (3) in all regions the more superficial neurons in stratum granulosum are formed earlier than the deeper granule cells. These varying time courses have an impact on the development and organization of the dentate gyrus that we cannot discuss here.

There is information about other parts of the hippocampal formation and other species, as well. In monkeys, whereas cells in the hippocampus proper are generally born by E78, the time course of origin in the stratum granulosum extends to approximately P60. Neurogenesis in humans appears to proceed at least through 2 years. Synaptogenesis is another well-studied index of dentate gyrus development. Most synaptogenesis in the rat occurs postnatally, and by P25 the animal has reached essentially the adult level (Crain, Cotman, Taylor, & Lynch, 1973). For the monkey, however, the story is an intriguing one. Synaptogenesis develops considerably before birth, with a rapid increase occurring from E78 to birth (E165) (Eckenhoff & Rakic, 1981). In fact, at birth the density of synapses is not different from that seen in adults. Postnatally it begins to exceed

[5]We will follow tradition, using E to refer to gestational day and P to refer to postnatal day.

adult levels until it stops at about P64. From that time to P300 it decreases but even then exceeds adult levels (Nowakoski & Rakic, 1981). Other processes of development have been studied that similarly suggest a dynamic overlaying and shifting time course of maturing neural systems. The arrival of particular afferent systems to the dentate (Fricke & Cowan, 1977) and the laminar staining of the hippocampus, reflecting the termination of various fiber systems in these laminae (Zimmer & Haug, 1978), are two examples.

This brief review of the development of the hippocampal system establishes that its postnatal neurogenesis continues through the period during which infantile amnesia is most prominent in several species. Data from studies of the development of synaptic function, as measured physiologically, are largely in agreement with this picture (e.g., Baudry, Arst, Oliver, & Lynch, 1982; Creery & Bland, 1980; LeBlanc & Bland, 1979; Purpura, Prevelic, & Santini, 1968).

Ontogeny of Learning

We have argued that there are multiple memory systems and hence would expect a heterogeneous picture to emerge from the study of memory ontogeny. Learning unassociated with the hippocampal system, which we have elsewhere called *taxon* or *skill-like* learning, should be possible prior to maturation of the hippocampus. Learning about places and exploration of environments, on the other hand, depend on hippocampal function and should not appear until its maturation is sufficiently advanced. Further, we have postulated an interaction between these two kinds of learning systems that gives to the hippocampal system a special role in the "consolidation" of information in nonhippocampal memory circuits. In the absence of the hippocampal system, an organism might acquire some information about an event but not the knowledge of when and where it happened. This absence might cause it to forget what it has learned rather quickly (see Squire *et al.*, in press, for discussion of why this happens). In sum, we expect to see good learning of some tasks but poor learning of others in the altricial neonate. The rapid forgetting of some aspects of what seemed normally learned should appear whenever the hippocampal system is involved in the long-term consolidation of those particular features of memory.

Until quite recently, demonstrations of associative learning in neonates were rare; the development of sensitive behavioral techniques has been central to the spate of research indicating that learning is possible in the first days of life. Rather than attempting to condition infants in situations designed for the study of adult learning, these techniques have demonstrated learning and memory in neonates by taking advantage of their known behavioral capacities. Thus, considerable work has now attested to several kinds of learning, some occurring as early as P1, in the suckling situation (e.g., Johanson & Hall, 1982; Johanson & Teicher, 1980; Pedersen, Williams and Blass, 1982). This early functioning of the taste/odor modalities is mirrored, as well, in the presence of flavor aversion conditioning in the early days (P2–P4), though the possibility of long delays between conditional and unconditional stimuli that characterize this form of learning does not appear until a week or so later (Gemberling & Domjan, 1982; Gregg, Kittrell, Domjan, & Amsel, 1978; Martin & Alberts, 1982; Rudy & Cheatle, 1977). Neonates have been taught instrumental discriminations as early as P7 (again taking advantage of the suckling situation) and have the capacity to retain such learning (Kenny & Blass, 1977). Simple position habits can be learned and retained, though there is an unexpected (and unexplained) U-shaped developmental curve for this kind of learning (Nagy, 1979) that resembles some of the anomalous findings described earlier for the monkey. Amsel and Stanton (1980) review a series of experiments concerned with the ontogenetic development of various paradoxical reward effects.[6] Patterned alternation and the partial reinforcement extinction effect appear by day P15, whereas negative contrast and the overtraining extinction effect appear only after P21. The authors speculate that, at an early age, "learning, extinction and other reactions to reinforcement change occur without benefit of goal anticipation (cognitive mediation)" (p. 266). This corresponds to the form of learning we have attributed to nonhippocampal systems.

The absence of ordered spatial exploration until P19 or later is an example of difficulties with tasks in which place learning is central. A similar finding comes from the study of reactions to a painful stimulus (shock) in neonatal rats. One such reaction, freezing, has been taken as an index of place learning (Blanchard & Blanchard, 1969). The first signs of such freezing appear at P15 (Collier & Bolles, 1980), and fully adult patterns do not appear until P30 (Bronstein & Hirsch, 1976; Campbell & Stehouwer, 1979). Another example comes from the study of latent in-

---

[6]These studies were designed to test the notion that delayed maturation of some "inhibitory" function of the hippocampus lies at the root of infantile amnesia (e.g., Altman, Brunner, & Bayer, 1973; Campbell & Spear, 1972). This view has been criticized elsewhere (Nadel, O'Keefe, & Black, 1975). We agree with this early emphasis on postnatal maturation in attempting to understand infantile amnesia but not with the way in which hippocampal function was then conceived. The studies by Amsel's group (e.g., Amsel, Burdette, & Letz, 1976; Amsel, Letz, & Burdette, 1977; Chen & Amsel, 1975, 1980a, b) clearly show that many "inhibitory" functions are intact well before the hippocampal system is operational.

hibition in a Pavlovian conditioning situation. When an animal is preexposed to a conditional stimulus, subsequent conditioning of that stimulus to an unconditional stimulus will be impaired relative to controls that did not undergo preexposure (Lubow, 1973). This effect is environment specific (Channell & Hall, 1983; Lubow, Rifkin, & Alek, 1976; Nadel & Willner, 1980; Nadel, Willner, & Kurz, in press; Wagner, 1978) suggesting that it depends on the place learning system. Corroborating this view is the fact that hippocampal dysfunction interrupts the development of latent inhibition in several paradigms and species (Salafia & Allan, 1980; Solomon & Moore, 1975). Several studies investigating the impact of conditional stimulus preexposure on neonates have been reported. Two studies (Brennan & Barone, 1976; Wilson, Phinney, & Brennan, 1974) used a directional avoidance behavior and reported the absence of latent inhibition in their neonatal subjects. These data "suggest that environmental stimuli differ in their effect upon young and adult rats. Specifically, the data indicate that young subjects do not mediate environmental cues to the same extent as adults" (Brennan & Barone, 1976, p. 243). On the other hand, equivocal results were seen in a study of latent inhibition in the conditioned emotional response in 23-day-olds (Wilson & Riccio, 1973), although apparently normal latent inhibition was seen in flavor aversion conditioning in 20-day-old weanlings (Franchina, Domato, Patsiokas, & Griesemer, 1980). Most convincing are data from the study of place learning in a water maze (Sutherland, 1982), a task known to be sensitive to hippocampal dysfunction in terms of both postoperative acquisition and the retention of preoperatively acquired learning (Morris, Garrud, Rawlins, & O'Keefe, 1982). Appropriate place learning in the water maze shows up quite abruptly on P19. As already noted, spontaneous alternation, which typically rests on the use of place information, becomes noticeable after 3 weeks. Data on the ontogeny of place learning in the T-maze (pilot data from Nadel's lab; Smith & Bogomolny, 1983; Somerville, 1979) indicate that neonates use response strategies until approximately P20, after which they use predominantly place strategies. All the above confirm that tasks demanding place learning are beyond the capacities of infants, becoming manageable only after hippocampal maturation.

Finally, we predicted that, just as after hippocampal damage in adults (Thompson, 1981) and in amnesics (Squire *et al.*, in press), in neonates some tasks should yield normal learning conjoined with rapid forgetting. Such a pattern has been reported many times (e.g., Campbell & Campbell, 1962; Feigley & Spear, 1970; Kirby, 1963; Steinert, Infurna, & Spear, 1980). In our view such forgetting reflects the absence of a system that functions during memory consolidation and that is critical to the full development and stabilization of knowledge. We have characterized this system as one that represents environments and their contents, the "time-

and-place'' of things. The data from ontogenetic studies of learning just reviewed indicate that there are separate learning systems, some maturing early, others late. Memories formed by neonates do not include information about places. One consequence of this is that early learning transfers easily from one environment to another; such transfer diminishes as the hippocampus matures (cf. Miller & Berk, 1979) and as learning becomes tied to the specific environment in which it occurs. Although events certainly influence the organism and leave behind some residue, they will not be remembered "in place" until after the hippocampal system matures.

This ontogenetic sequence carries with it several seeming disadvantages. First, the learning that occurs prior to maturation of the hippocampal system will not be retrievable in an environmentally specific way. This learning will be embedded in the networks that develop out of the merging of information acquired in varied environments. Such mixing of aspects of acquired knowledge from different situations occurs in adults as well but is balanced by the availability of the hippocampal system, which in our view provides the basis for event-specific memories. Second, some of that that is acquired will be lost rapidly. Such forgetting is characteristic of infantile amnesia and hippocampal damage alike. We have argued that neural elements representing co-occurring aspects of an environment must be connected by some extrinsic coordinating framework for some time after learning. In the absence of this framework, specific patterns of interconnection fail to "consolidate" and forgetting results.[7] Given these disadvantages of delayed maturation, one wonders about the advantages. Daly (1973) has speculated that exploration of novel environments could be harmful to young animals. This difficulty might be avoided by delaying hippocampal maturation.

Developmental Perspectives

What, then, can we say about the sequence of developments in memorial capacities that we have uncovered here? Is there any rhyme or reason to it? One possibility is that the ontogenetic sequence "recapitulates" some phylogenetic sequence. This would seem true at some abstract level,

---

[7]At least some early experiences that appear forgotten can be "reinstated" by the appropriate manipulation later in life (Campbell & Jaynes, 1966). A number of psychopathological problems, such as the development of phobias, seem related to these early "memories" and their subsequent reemergence under certain, typically stressful conditions. Such phenomena are considered in the context of the present approach to infantile amnesia in Jacobs and Nadel (submitted).

because environment-specific memory, a late development in phylogeny, also appears to be a late-developing capacity in ontogeny. But this equation is too simple. If one compares species such as rat and monkey, one sees a heterogeneous pattern of onset of various kinds of learning. Even within a group of related species these patterns will be different. What is needed is a clear understanding of the particular needs of infant organisms at various stages of development for in those needs will be found the "reasons" for the timing of appearance of particular memory systems in ontogeny.

Research on development often assumes that infants are essentially "immature" adults and that infant capacities are poor versions of adult capacities. According to this view, infant memory is like adult memory, differing only in strength. We do not concur with this position. Rather, we believe that infants are prepared for their specific needs, much as adults are for theirs. This perspective, akin to Anokhin's (1964) "systemogenesis," has attracted others as well (cf. Galef, 1981; Turkewitz & Kenny, 1982). Consider the newborn rat. During the initial week of its life it must acquire information about certain things: the smell of its mother's pheromones and the taste of her milk, for example. It is therefore not surprising that the ability to remember smells matures very rapidly, providing the necessary base for this essential learning. Some time later, other kinds of cues take over in the control of the pup's interactions with its mother, and the capacity to remember such information can be seen to develop at the appropriate time to subserve these needs. For infant monkeys, the data might indicate a different sequence of availability of various cue–memory systems related to the kinds of information monkeys use to perform certain essential functions at particular ages. This latter point is crucial, as we have already seen: at different ages quite different processing/memorial capacities could underlie performance on a given task. In order to understand why infants have certain memory systems but lack others, one must consider what their situation requires.

The broad picture of memory ontogeny that emerges from this discussion is the following: memory is not one but many things. Different memory systems mature at different times in the life of the developing organism in ways which, given present scanty data, seem to relate to the needs of the organism at that time of its life. In more general terms, the capacity to store information about environments to be used either as the substrate for spatial exploration and place learning or to contribute time-and-place information to memory seems to develop relatively late in ontogeny. When this development is complete, it permits the encoding of events in terms of where they occur, increasing the memory capacity of that organism by providing the basis for separate representations of similar events occurring in different environments. The absence of this memory system in the neonate interferes with long-term consolidation and leads in many cases to rapid forgetting.

Memory systems, the substrate of behavioral plasticity, themselves show developmental plasticity. Is it too much to speculate that memory capacities come and go as the organism needs them? Nottebohm (1981) has shown that portions of the midbrain involved in the learning of bird song increase and decrease in size with the change of seasons, attaining maximal function each year when bird song is critical. Such an on-again/off-again pattern of memory capacity is probably unusual. But, it makes the point quite clearly that memory and its ontogeny must be considered within the context of the organism's natural history and ecological niche.

ACKNOWLEDGMENTS

This chapter reflects ideas generated in two distinct research programs and the compromises necessary to bring these into concert. It has benefitted from the comments of our colleagues and co-workers as well as from the prior work and writings of many who came before. Like the events of early life, the advances made by those who come first are often merged into "general knowledge," the specific contributions of many individuals being lost in the process. Past and present discussions with N. Cohen, H. Mahut, J. O'Keefe, and L. Squire have been invaluable in the development of these ideas.

References

Altman, J., Brunner, R. L., & Bayer, S. A. The hippocampus and behavioral maturation. *Behavioral Biology*, 1973, *8*, 557–596.

Amsel, A., & Stanton, M. Ontogeny and phylogeny of paradoxical reward effects. In J. S. Rosenblatt, R. A. Hinde, C. Beer, & M.-C. Busnel (Eds.), *Advances in the study of behavior* (Vol. 11). New York: Academic Press, 1980.

Amsel, A., Burdette, D. R., & Letz, R. Appetitive learning, patterned alternation and extinction in 10-day-old rats with non-lactating suckling as reward. *Nature*, 1976, *262*, 816–818.

Amsel, A., Letz, R., & Burdette, D. R. Appetitive learning and extinction in 11-day-old rat pups. Effects of various reinforcement conditions. *Journal of Comparative and Physiological Psychology*, 1977, *91*, 1156–1167.

Anokhin, P. K. Systemogenesis as a general regulator of brain development. In W. A. Himwich & H. E. Himwich (Eds.), *Progress in brain research: Vol. 9. The developing brain*. Amsterdam: Elsevier, 1964.

Bachevalier, J., & Mishkin, M. *The development of memories vs. habits in infant monkeys*. Paper presented to International Organization of Psychophysiology, 1982.

Baudry, M., Arst, D., Oliver, M., & Lynch, G. Development of glutamate binding sites and their regulation by calcium in rat hippocampus. *Developmental Brain Research*, 1981, *1*, 37–48.

Blanchard, R. J., & Blanchard, D. C. Crouching as an index of fear. *Journal of Comparative and Physiological Psychology*, 1969, *67*, 370–375.

Brennan, J. F. & Barone, R. J. Effects of differential cue availability in an active avoidance CS for young and adult rats. *Developmental Psychobiology*, 1976, *9*, 237–244.

Bronstein, P. M., & Hirsch, S. M. Ontogeny of defensive reactions in Norway rats. *Journal of Comparative and Physiological Psychology*, 1976, *90*, 620–629.

Campbell, B. A., & Campbell, E. H. Retention of learned fear in infant and adult rats. *Journal of Comparative and Physiological Psychology*, 1962, *55*, 1–8.

Campbell, B. A., & Jaynes, J. Reinstatement. *Psychological Review*, 1966, *73*, 478–480.

Campbell, B. A., & Spear, N. E. Ontogeny of memory. *Psychological Review*, 1972, *79*, 215–236.

Campbell, B. A., & Stehouwer, D. J. Ontogeny of habituation and sensitization in the rat. In N. E. Spear & B. A. Campbell (Eds.), *Ontogeny of learning and memory*. Hillsdale, N.J.: Erlbaum, 1979.

Channell, S., & Hall, G. Contextual effects in latent inhibition with an appetitive conditioning procedure. *Animal Learning and Behavior*, 1983, *11*, 67–74.

Cheal, M. L., Klestzick, J., & Domesick, V. B. Attention and habituation: Odor preferences, long-term memory, and multiple sensory cues of novel stimuli. *Journal of Comparative and Physiological Psychology*, 1982, *96*, 47–60.

Chen, J.-S., & Amsel, A. Durability and retention of persistence acquired by young and infant rats. *Journal of Comparative and Physiological Psychology*, 1975, *89*, 238–245.

Chen, J.-S., & Amsel, A. Retention under changed-reward conditions of persistence learned by infant rats. *Developmental Psychobiology*, 1980, *13*, 469–480. (a)

Chen, J.-S., & Amsel, A. Learned persistence at 11–12 but not at 10–11 days in infant rats. *Developmental Psychobiology*, 1980, *13*, 481–491. (b)

Cohen, N. J. *Neuropsychological evidence for a distinction between procedural and declarative knowledge in human memory and amnesia*. Unpublished Ph.D. thesis, University of California, San Diego, 1981.

Cohen, N., & Corkin, S. The amnesic patient H.M.: Learning and retention of a cognitive skill. *Society for Neuroscience Abstracts*, 1981, *7*, 235.

Cohen, N., & Squire, L. R. Preserved learning and retention of pattern analyzing skill in amnesia: Dissociation of knowing how and knowing that. *Science*, 1980, *210*, 207–209.

Collier, A. C. & Bolles, R. C. The ontogenesis of defensive reactions to shock in preweanling rats. *Developmental Psychobiology*, 1980, *13*, 141–150.

Crain, B., Cotman, C. W., Taylor, D., & Lynch, G. A quantitative electron microscopic study of synaptogenesis in the dentate gyrus of the rat. *Brain Research*, 1973, *63*, 195–204.

Creery, B. L., & Bland, B. H. Ontogeny of fascia dentata electrical activity and motor behavior in the Dutch belted rabbit (*Oryctolagus cuniculus*). *Experimental Neurology*, 1980, *67*, 554–572.

Daly, M. Early stimulation of rodents: A critical review of present interpretations. *British Journal of Psychology*, 1973, *64*, 435–460.

Douglas, R. J., Peterson, J. J., & Douglas, D. P. The ontogeny of a hippocampus-dependent response in two rodent species. *Behavioral Biology*, 1973, *8*, 27–37.

Eckenhoff, M. F., & Rakic, P. Synaptogenesis in the dentate gyrus of primates: Quantitative EM study in rhesus monkey. *Society for Neuroscience Abstracts*, 1981, *7*, 6.

Egger, G. J. Novelty induced changes in spontaneous alternation in infant and adult rats. *Developmental Psychobiology*, 1973, *6*, 431–435. (a)

Egger, G. J. The relevance of memory, arousal, and cue factors to developmental changes in spontaneous alternation by rats. *Developmental Psychobiology*, 1973, *6*, 459–468. (b)

Egger, G. J., Livesey, P. J., & Dawson, R. J. Ontogenetic aspects of central cholinergic involvement in spontaneous alternation behavior. *Developmental Psychobiology*, 1973, *6*, 288–299.

Feigley, D. A., & Spear, N. E. Effect of age and punishment condition on long-term retention by the rat of active- and passive-avoidance learning. *Journal of Comparative and Physiological Psychology*, 1970, *73*, 515–526.

Feigley, D. A., Parsons, P. J., Hamilton, L. W., & Spear, N. E. Development of habituation to novel environments in the rat. *Journal of Comparative and Physiological Psychology*, 1972, *79*, 443–452.

File, S. E. The ontogeny of exploration in the rat: Habituation and effects of handling. *Developmental Psychobiology*, 1978, *11*, 321–328.

Franchina, J. J., Domato, G. C., Patsiokas, A. T., & Griesemer, H. A. Effects of number of pre-exposures on sucrose taste aversion in weanling rats. *Developmental Psychobiology*, 1980, *13*, 25–31.

Frederickson, C. J., & Frederickson, M. H. Emergence of spontaneous alternation in the kitten. *Developmental Psychobiology*, 1979, *12*, 615–621. (a)

Frederickson, C. J., & Frederickson, M. H. Developmental changes in open-field behavior in the kitten. *Developmental Psychobiology*, 1979, *12*, 623–628. (b)

Fricke, R., & Cowan, W. M. An autoradiographic study of the development of the entorhinal and commissural afferents to the dentate gyrus of the rat. *Journal of Comparative Neurology*, 1977, *173*, 231–250.

Galef, B. G., Jr. The ecology of weaning: Parasitism and the achievement of independence by altricial mammals. In D. J. Gubernick & P. H. Klopfer (Eds.), *Parental care in mammals*. New York: Plenum Press, 1981.

Gemberling, G., & Domjan, M. Selective associations in one-day-old rats: Taste-toxicosis and texture-shock aversion learning. *Journal of Comparative and Physiological Psychology*, 1982, *96*, 105–113.

Goldberger, M. E. Recovery of movement after CNS lesions in monkeys. In D. G. Stein, J. J. Rosen, & N. Butters (Eds.), *Plasticity and recovery of function in the central nervous system*. New York: Academic Press, 1974.

Goldman, P. Functional development of the prefrontal cortex in early life and the problem of neuronal plasticity. *Experimental Neurology*, 1971, *32*, 366–387.

Goldman, P. Maturation of the mammalian nervous system and the ontogeny of behavior. In J. S. Rosenblatt, R. A. Hinde, E. Shaw, & C. Beer (Eds.), *Advances in the study of behavior* (Vol. 7). New York: Academic Press, 1976.

Goldman, P. S., & Alexander, G. E. Maturation of prefrontal cortex in the monkey revealed by local reversible cryogenic depression. *Nature*, 1977, *267*, 613–615.

Goldman, P. S., Crawford, H. T., Stokes, L. P., Galkin, T. W., & Rosvold, H. E. Sex-dependent behavioral effects of cerebral lesions in the developing rhesus monkey. *Science*, 1974, *186*, 540–542.

Gottlieb, D. I., & Cowan, W. M. Evidence for a temporal factor in the occupation of available synaptic sites during the development of the dentate gyrus. *Brain Research*, 1972, *41*, 452–456. (a)

Gottlieb, D. I., & Cowan, W. M. On the distribution of axonal terminals containing spheroidal and flattened synaptic vesicles in the hippocampus and dentate gyrus of the rat and cat. *Zeitschrift für Zellforschung*, 1972, *129*, 413–429. (b)

Greenough, W. T., & Chang, F. F. Anatomically-detectable correlates of information storage in the nervous system of mammals. In C. W. Cotman (Ed.), *Neuronal plasticity* (2nd ed.). New York: Raven Press, in press.

Gregg, B., Kittrell, E. M., Domjan, M., & Amsel, A. Ingestional aversion learning in preweanling rats. *Journal of Comparative and Physiological Psychology*, 1978, *92*, 785–795.

Harlow, H. F. The formation of learning sets. *Psychological Review*, 1949, *56*, 51–65.

Harlow, H. F. Learning set and error factor theory. In S. Koch (Ed.), *Psychology: A study of science* (Vol. 2). New York: McGraw-Hill, 1959.

Harlow, H. F., Harlow, M. K., Rueping, R. R., & Mason, W. A. Performance of infant rhesus monkeys on discrimination learning, delayed response and discrimination learning set. *Journal of Comparative and Physiological Psychology*, 1960, *53*, 113–121.

Jacobs, W. J., & Nadel, L. Stress induced recovery of fears and phobias. *Psychological Review* (submitted).

Johanson, I. B., & Hall, W. G. Appetitive conditioning in neonatal rats: Conditioned orientation to a novel odor. *Developmental Psychobiology*, 1982, *15*, 379–397.

Johanson, I. B., & Teicher, M. H. Classical conditioning of an odor preference in 3-day-old rats. *Behavioral and Neural Biology*, 1980, *29*, 132–136.

Kennard, M. A. Reorganization of motor function in the cerebral cortex of monkeys deprived of motor and premotor areas in infancy. *Journal of Neurophysiology*, 1938, *1*, 477–496.

Kennard, M. A. Relation of age to motor impairment in man and subhuman primates. *Archives of Neurology and Psychiatry*, 1940, *44*, 377–397.

Kennard, M. A. Cortical reorganization of motor function: Studies on series of monkeys of various ages from infancy to maturity. *Archives of Neurology and Psychiatry*, 1942, *47*, 227–240.

Kenny, J. T., & Blass, E. M. Suckling as an incentive to instrumental learning in preweanling rats. *Science*, 1977, *196*, 898–899.

Kirby, R. H. Acquisition, extinction and retention of an avoidance response in rats as a function of age. *Journal of Comparative and Physiological Psychology*, 1963, *56*, 158–162.

Kirkby, R. J. A maturation factor in spontaneous alternation. *Nature*, 1967, *215*, 784.

Lanier, L. P., & Isaacson, R. L. Early developmental changes in the locomotor response to amphetamine and their relation to hippocampal function. *Brain Research*, 1977, *126*, 567–575.

LeBlanc, M. O., & Bland, B. H. Developmental aspects of hippocampal electrical activity and motor behavior in the rat. *Experimental Neurology*, 1979, *66*, 220–237.

Lubow, R. E. Latent inhibition. *Psychological Bulletin*, 1973, *79*, 398–407.

Lubow, R. E., Rifkin, B., & Alek, M. The context effect: The relationship between stimulus preexposure and environmental preexposure determines subsequent learning. *Journal of Experimental Psychology: Animal Behavior Processes*, 1976, *2*, 38–47.

Mahut, H. A selective spatial deficit in monkeys after transection of the fornix. *Neuropsychologia*, 1972, *10*, 65–74.

Mahut, H., & Zola, S. M. Ontogenetic timetable for the development of three functions in infant macaques and the effects of early hippocampal damage upon them. *Society for Neuroscience Abstracts*, 1977, *3*, 428.

Martin, L. T., & Alberts, J. R. Associative learning in neonatal rats revealed by cardiac response patterns. *Journal of Comparative and Physiological Psychology*, 1982, *96*, 668–675.

Menzel, E. W., Jr., & Menzel, C. R. Cognitive, developmental and social aspects of responsiveness to novel objects in a family group of marmosets (*Saguinus fuscicollis*). *Behaviour*, 1979, *70*, 251–279.

Miller, R. R., & Berk, A. M. Sources of infantile amnesia. In N. E. Spear & B. A. Campbell (Eds.), *Ontogeny of learning and memory*. Hillsdale, N.J.: Erlbaum, 1979.

Misanin, J. R., Nagy, Z. M., Keiser, E. F., & Bowen, W. Emergence of long-term memory in the neonatal rat. *Journal of Comparative and Physiological Psychology*, 1971, *77*, 188–199.

Misanin, J. R., Brownback, T., Shaughnessy, L. D., & Hinderliter, C. F. Acquisition and retention of multidirectional escape behavior in preweanling rats. *Developmental Psychobiology*, 1980, *13*, 85–93.

Mishkin, M. Memory in monkeys severely impaired by combined but not by separate removal of amygdala and hippocampus. *Nature*, 1978, *273*, 297–298.

Morris, R. G. M. Neural subsystems of exploration in rats. In J. Archer & L. Birke (Eds.), *Exploration in animals and humans*. London: Van Nostrand, 1982.

Morris, R. G. M., Garrud, P., Rawlins, J. N. P., & O'Keefe, J. Place navigation impaired in rats with hippocampal lesions. *Nature*, 1982, *297*, 681–683.

Murray, E. A., & Mishkin, M. Amygdalectomy but not hippocampectomy impairs crossmodal delayed nonmatching-to-sample in monkeys. *Society for Neuroscience Abstracts*, 1982, *8*, 23.

Nadel, L., & MacDonald, L. Hippocampus: Cognitive map or working memory? *Behavioral and Neural Biology*, 1980, *29*, 405–409.

Nadel, L., & Wexler, K. Neurobiology, representations and memory. In G. Lynch, J. L. McGaugh, & N. Weinberger (Eds.), *The neurobiology of learning and memory*. New York: Guilford Press, in press.

Nadel, L., & Willner, J. Context and conditioning: A place for space. *Physiological Psychology*, 1980, *8*, 218–228.

Nadel, L., O'Keefe, J., & Black, A. H. Slam on the brakes: A critique of Altman, Brunner and Bayer's response–inhibition model of hippocampal function. *Behavioral Biology*, 1975, *14*, 151–162.

Nadel, L., Willner, J., & Kurz, E. M. Cognitive maps and environmental context. In P. Balsam & A. Tomie (Eds.), *Context and learning*. Hillsdale, N.J.: Erlbaum, in press.

Nagy, Z. M. Development of learning and memory processes in infant mice. In N. E. Spear & B. A. Campbell (Eds.), *Ontogeny of learning and memory*. Hillsdale, N.J.: Erlbaum, 1979.

Nottebohm, F. A brain for all seasons: Cyclical anatomical changes in song control nuclei of the canary bird. *Science*, 1981, *214*, 1368–1370.

Nowakoski, R. S., & Rakic, P. The site of origin and route and rate of migration of neurons to the hippocampal region of the rhesus monkey. *Journal of Comparative Neurology*, 1981, *196*, 129–154.

O'Keefe, J., & Nadel, L. *The hippocampus as a cognitive map*. Oxford: The Clarendon Press, 1978.

O'Keefe, J., Nadel, L., Keightley, D., & Kill, D. Fornix lesions selectively abolish place learning in the rat. *Experimental Neurology*, 1975, *48*, 152–166.

Parkin, A. J. Residual learning capacity in organic amnesia. *Cortex*, 1982, 18, 417–440.

Parkinson, J. K., & Mishkin, M. A selective role for the hippocampus in monkeys: Memory for the location of objects. *Society for Neuroscience Abstracts*, 1982, *8*, 23.

Pedersen, P. E., Williams, C. L., & Blass, E. M. Activation and odor conditioning of suckling behavior in 3-day-old albino rats. *Journal of Experimental Psychology: Animal Behavior Processes*, 1982, *8*, 329–341.

Purpura, D. P., Prevelic, S., & Santini, M. Postsynaptic potentials and spike variations in the feline hippocampus during postnatal neurogenesis. *Experimental Neurology*, 1968, *22*, 408–422.

Rakic, P. Neurons in the rhesus monkey visual cortex: Systematic relation between time of origin and eventual disposition. *Science*, 1974, *183*, 425–427.

Rudy, J. W., & Cheatle, M. D. Odor-aversion learning in neonatal rats. *Science*, 1977, *198*, 845–846.

Salafia, W. R., & Allan, A. M. Conditioning and latent inhibition with electrical stimulation of hippocampus. *Physiological Psychology*, 1980, *8*, 247–253.

Schlessinger, A. R., Cowan, W. M., & Gottleib, D. I. An autoradiographic study of the time of origin and the pattern of granule cell migration in the dentate gyrus of the rat. *Journal of Comparative Neurology*, 1975, *159*, 149–176.

Schram, D. D. *The effect of hippocampal and fornix lesions on the acquisition, transfer and reversal of a visual discrimination.* Unpublished Ph.D. thesis, University of Washington, 1970.

Smith, G. J., & Bogomolny, A. Appetitive instrumental training in preweanling rats: I. Motivational determinants. *Developmental Psychobiology*, 1983, *16*, 119–128.

Solomon, P. R., & Moore, J. W. Latent inhibition and stimulus generalization of the classically conditioned nictitating membrane response in rabbits (*Oryctolagus cuniculus*) following dorsal hippocampal ablation. *Journal of Comparative and Physiological Psychology*, 1975, *89*, 1192–1203.

Somerville, E. *Postnatal development of the hippocampus in the rat (Rattus norvegicus), Correlations between hippocampal anatomy, electroencephalogram and behavior.* Unpublished Ph.D. thesis, University College London, 1979.

Spear, N. E. Memory storage factors in infantile amnesia. In G. Bower (Ed.), *The psychology of learning and motivation* (Vol. 13). New York: Academic Press, 1979.

Squire, L. R., & Zola-Morgan, S. The neurology of memory: The case for correspondence between the findings for humans and the non-human primate. In J. A. Deutsch (Ed.), *The physiological basis of memory* (2nd ed.). New York: Academic Press, 1983.

Squire, L. R., Cohen, N., & Nadel L. The medial temporal region and memory consolidation: A new hypothesis. In H. Weingartner & E. Parker (Eds.), *Memory consolidation.* Hillsdale, N.J.: Erlbaum, in press.

Steinert, P. A., Infurna, R. N., & Spear, N. E. Long-term retention of a conditioned taste aversion in preweanling and adult rats. *Animal Learning and Behavior*, 1980, *8*, 375–381.

Sussman, P. S., & Ferguson, H. B. Retained elements of early avoidance training and relearning of forgotten operants. *Developmental Psychobiology*, 1980, *13*, 545–562.

Sutherland, R. Personal communication, Calgary, Alberta, July 1982.

Teuber, H.-L. Mental retardation after early trauma to the brain: Some issues in search of facts. In C. R. Angle & E. A. Bering, Jr. (Eds.), *Physical trauma as an etiological agent in mental retardation.* Bethesda, Md.: National Institute of Health, 1971.

Teuber, H.-L., & Rudel, R. G. Behavior after cerebral lesions in children and adults. *Developmental Medicine and Child Neurology*, 1962, *4*, 3–20.

Thompson, R. Rapid forgetting of a spatial habit in rats with hippocampal lesions. *Science*, 1981, *212*, 959–960.

Tolman, E. C. Cognitive maps in rats and men. *Psychological Review*, 1948, *55*, 189–208.

Turkewitz, G., & Kenny, P. A. Limitations on input as a basis for neural organization and perceptual development: A preliminary theoretical statement. *Developmental Psychobiology*, 1982, *15*, 357–368.

Wagner, A. R. Priming in STM: An information processing mechanism for self-generated or retrieval-generated depression in performance. In T. J. Tighe & R. N. Leaton (Eds.), *Habituation: Perspectives from child development, animal behavior and neurophysiology.* Hillsdale, N.J.: Erlbaum, 1978.

Williams, J. M., Hamilton, L. W., & Carlton, P.L. Pharmacological and anatomical dissociation of two types of habituation. *Journal of Comparative and Physiological Psychology*, 1974, *87*, 724–732.

Williams, J. M., Hamilton, L. W., & Carlton, P. L. Ontogenetic dissociation of two classes of habituation. *Journal of Comparative and Physiological Psychology*, 1975, *89*, 733–737.

Wilson, L. M., & Riccio, D. C. CS familiarization and conditioned suppression in weanling and adult albino rats. *Bulletin of the Psychonomic Society*, 1973, *1*, 184–186.

Wilson, L. M., Phinney, R. L., & Brennan, J. F. Age-related differences in avoidance behavior in rats following CS preexposure. *Developmental Psychobiology*, 1974, *7*, 421–427.

Wood, F., Ebert, V., & Kinsbourne, M. The episodic-semantic distinction in memory and amnesia: Clinical and experimental observations. In L. Cermak (Ed.), *Human memory and amnesia*. Hillsdale, N.J.: Erlbaum, 1982.

Zimmer, J., & Haug, F. M. S. Laminar differentiation of the hippocampus, fascia dentata and subiculum in developing rats, observed with the Timm sulphide silver method. *Journal of Comparative Neurology*, 1978, *179*, 581–618.

Zola, S., & Mahut, H. Paradoxical facilitation of object-reversal learning after transection of the fornix in monkeys. *Neuropsychologia*, 1973, *11*, 271–284.

Zola-Morgan, S. Toward an animal model of human amnesia: Some critical issues. In N. Butters & L. Squire (Eds.), *The neuropsychology of memory*. New York: Guilford Press, in press.

Zola-Morgan, S., & Squire, L. R. Intact perceptuo-motor skill learning in monkeys with medial temporal lobe lesions. *Society for Neuroscience Abstracts*, 1983, *9*, 27.

Zola-Morgan, S., & Squire, L. R. Medial temporal lesions in monkeys impair memory on a variety of tasks sensitive to amnesia. *Behavioral Neuroscience*, in press. (a)

Zola-Morgan, S., & Squire, L. R. Preserved learning in monkeys with medial temporal lesions: Sparing of motor and cognitive skills. *Journal of Neuroscience*, in press. (b)

CHAPTER 8

Infants, Amnesics, and Dissociable Memory Systems

Daniel L. Schacter and Morris Moscovitch

Department of Psychology
University of Toronto
Toronto, Ontario, Canada

Department of Psychology
Erindale College
University of Toronto
Mississauga, Ontario, Canada

The title of this book—infant memory—appears straightforward. On re-flection, however, it becomes apparent that the term *memory* applies to many different facets of an organism's ability to conserve and utilize the effects of its experiences. The multiple senses in which memory can be, and has been, used range from what Piaget and Inhelder (1973) labeled "memory in the wide sense," including acquisition of skills, vocabulary, and adaptive responses, to what they labeled "memory in the strict sense"— the ability to consciously reflect on a specific incident in one's personal past. Few would deny that it is possible to use the term *memory* in the foregoing manners. What are the consequences for the study of infant memory?

In this chapter we suggest that many students of infant memory have not distinguished among different senses of the term *memory* in their research, and argue that such distinctions may be important for under-standing what underlies patterns of infant performance on a variety of tasks. As students of adult memory and amnesia who became familiar with the infant literature in preparing for the conference that provided the basis for this book, we were surprised to find that infants' performance on what seemed to be fundamentally different tasks such as habitua-

This chapter was supported by a Special Research Program Grant from the Connaught Fund, University of Toronto, and by a Medical Research Council of Canada and an Ontario Mental Health grant to Morris Moscovitch.

tion–novelty preference, object search, and conditioning were all accounted for by invoking a unitary concept of memory. The exceptions that we uncovered, in which it was argued that performance on such different tasks might reflect the operation of different types of memory, were few (e.g., Fox, Kagan, & Weiskopf, 1979; Sophian, 1980; Watson, 1980). We hope to show that it is useful theoretically and heuristically to conceptualize infants' performance on various tasks that require utilization of past experiences in terms of the differential availability of different forms of memory or different memory systems.

We develop the argument by first considering data that demonstrate dissociations between forms of memory that are preserved and forms that are impaired in adult amnesic patients. Similar dissociations, we suggest, may be present in infants. We also consider data from normal adults that imply the existence of at least two distinct and dissociable forms of memory, and suggest that many manifestations of memory in the infant, like the amnesic, may be attributable to just one of these forms. We then turn to the infant literature and consider data from habituation–novelty preference, conditioning, and object search paradigms in light of the proposed distinctions. The general theme of our argument is in some ways similar to the one developed by Piaget and Inhelder (1973): A form of memory analogous to "memory in the wide sense" developmentally precedes a form of memory analogous to "memory in the strict sense." By examining infants' mnemonic capabilities in the context of adult memory and amnesia, however, we hope to provide a novel perspective on the development of different memory systems in infancy and to stimulate research that will provide more detailed understanding of the forms of memory that are available to the infant at different points in development.

Before examining the pertinent literature, one important terminological issue should be mentioned. The phrases *forms of memory, kinds of memory,* and *memory systems* will appear throughout this chapter. What do we mean when we use these phrases? A memory system, in our view, is an organized relationship among brain structures and processes that makes possible the acquisition, retention, and utilization of knowledge. We use the phrase *memory system* interchangeably with the phrases *form of memory* and *kind of memory.* The psychological and neurobiological reality of multiple memory systems is suggested by evidence from a variety of sources: psychological experiments that demonstrate functional dissociations between tasks that tap different kinds of memory, neuropsychological studies that provide evidence of differential effects of experimental lesions and brain damage on different classes of memory tasks and, perhaps, developmental studies that find evidence of retention on one class of tasks before there is evidence of retention on a different class of tasks. Not all researchers find it useful to interpret differential effects of experimental variables or neurologically based dissociations as evidence for different memory systems; some prefer to talk about differences in methods of testing or different processes operating within a unitary system (e.g., Jacoby, 1983). It is not easy at the current time to tease apart such interpretations from a "multiple systems" interpretation because the problem of delineating similarities and differences among memory systems is relatively new, and there are few extant criteria or rules for relating patterns of performance on experimental tasks to properties of postulated underlying systems (Schacter & Tulving, 1982b; Tulving, 1983). However, we believe that it is useful to entertain the hypothesis of multiple memory systems for at least two reasons. First, the idea is consistent with a wide range of data from cognitive psychology, neuropsychology, physiological psychology, and, we will argue, developmental psychology (see Chapter 7 for a similar perspective). Second, it provides a conceptual framework for posing questions about mnemonic dissociations observed in a variety of situations in which the specific tasks, subjects, and methods of testing differ widely, and hence encourages the development of theories and models that address fundamental questions about memory that are common to different research areas (Schacter, 1984).

Forms of Memory in Human Amnesia

The amnesic syndrome occurs in a variety of conditions including Korsakoff's syndrome, encephalitis, lesions of the medial temporal lobes, and closed-head injury. Amnesic patients often appear perfectly normal during informal conversation or when functions other than memory are probed. The intelligence of amnesic patients is in the normal range; cognitive abilities such as language and perception are usually intact or minimally impaired; social skills are well preserved; and even performance on digit span tasks is relatively good. However, the facade of normality crumbles when patients are briefly distracted and asked to describe recent events or occurrences: amnesics typically recall little or nothing of their experiences from minutes, hours, days, or weeks ago, sometimes fail to recognize people they met just minutes earlier, and perform extremely poorly on standard laboratory tasks of memory that involve conscious recall and recognition of many different types of recently studied materials. A sampling of studies of the amnesic syndrome, as well as an introduction to the numerous theories that have been put forward to explain it, can be found in the volumes edited by Cermak (1982) and Whitty and Zangwill (1977).

One of the most intriguing aspects of recent research concerning the amnesic syndrome is the finding that amnesics can perform normally or near normally on a variety of memory and learning tasks—even though they frequently fail to remember the learning episode that constituted the basis of their successful performance. The basic form of the dissociation is well illustrated in the often-cited clinical example of Claparède's (1911/1951) Korsakoff patient who, after having been pricked with a pin hidden in Claparède's hand, refused to shake it again in spite of her inability to say why she suspected that something was amiss; the patient could only conjecture that "sometimes pins are hidden in hands." Although the experience of the pinprick was retained, in the sense that it affected the patient's subsequent behavior, it was apparently not available for conscious recall.

Numerous other clinical anecdotes could be marshaled to make the same point, but controlled experiments are more convincing. Weiskrantz and Warrington (1979) have provided evidence of classical conditioning in two severely amnesic patients: the patients did not recognize the conditioning apparatus at the same time that the conditioned responses were elicited, although they had extensive experience with it during training. Some of the earliest evidence that amnesics possess some mnemonic abilities was provided by studies showing that the well-known patient H.M., rendered densely amnesic by bilateral excision of the temporal lobes, could learn a variety of motor skills in near-normal fashion (Corkin, 1965, 1968; Milner, Corkin, & Teuber, 1968). The striking feature of H.M.'s motor-skill learning was that on most new learning trials he failed to recall the events of the previous trial or even the fact that there *was* a previous trial, although just seconds or minutes had elapsed. Similar observations of preserved motor-skill learning in the absence of conscious memory for having previously performed a task have been reported in studies of other amnesic patients (Brooks & Baddeley, 1976; Cermak, Lewis, Butters, & Goodglass, 1973; Starr & Phillips, 1970).

Recent investigations have indicated that the domain of spared learning in amnesics is not confined to motor skills and includes what can be called perceptual and cognitive skills. Brooks and Baddeley (1976), for instance, found that amnesics reassembled a jigsaw puzzle faster on a second trial than they did on the first trial; the patients improved just as much as control subjects did. Wood, Ebert, and Kinsbourne (1982) report that amnesics were able to acquire and apply a complex mathematical rule (the Fibonacci rule) over an extended series of trials. Although amnesics showed considerable savings when relearning the rule after 17 weeks, all patients "claimed unequivocally that they had never seen or done this task before" (pp. 173–174). Cohen (1984) has found that some amnesic patients, including H.M., are able to learn to solve the Tower of Hanoi problem in much the same manner as normals, even though they seem to have little awareness of how they solved the problem, and frequently do not remember having performed the task from session to session. Cohen and Squire (1980) found that amnesics learned to read mirror-transformed script in an entirely normal manner. They acquired the reading skill as quickly as controls and retained it equally well over a 3-month interval. However, amnesics' recognition memory for the occurrence of specific words was extremely poor. Moscovitch (1982b) has reported similar results using the transformed-script task in a different population of amnesic subjects and in addition has provided evidence that facilitation of reading can be item-specific: Amnesics read repeated sentences significantly faster than nonrepeated ones, even though their recognition performance did not distinguish between the two types.

Evidence that amnesics retain some effects of a learning episode can be gleaned from their performance on other tasks that do not require conscious recall and recognition of the episode *per se*. In a well-known series of studies, Warrington and Weiskrantz (1970, 1974) found that amnesics' yes/no recognition of words presented on a list was severely impaired with respect to controls. In contrast, the amnesics benefitted as much as normals from prior presentation of these same words when they were simply required to complete fragmented versions of them at the time of test. Graf, Squire, and Mandler (1984) and Diamond and Rozin (in press) have also provided evidence that amnesics' fragment-completion performance is normal and have delineated some of the variables that affect completion performance. Jacoby and Witherspoon (1982) asked Korsakoff amnesics and university students questions that included a low-frequency homophone (e.g., What is an example of a reed instrument?). When later engaged in a spelling task, amnesics provided the low-frequency spelling of the presented homophones (reed vs. read) even more often than controls did. However, amnesics' recognition memory for the prior occurrence of the homophones was virtually nonexistent in comparison to the high level of performance of the controls. In addition, responding with the low-frequency homophone was independent of recognition or nonrecognition of the word in both amnesics and normals. Moscovitch (1982b) observed that amnesics' performance on a lexical decision task was facilitated just as much as the performance of controls by prior presentation of a word: patients were faster to decide whether a letter string was a word or a nonword when the letter string was repeated than when it was new. This normal priming effect, however, occurred in the absence of recognition memory on the part of amnesics. In a case study, Schacter, Tulving, and Wang (1981) told a closed-head injury amnesic unusual stories about a series of presented pictures. Later, the patient consistently chose titles for the pictures that reflected the themes of the stories but could not recall that he had been told any stories.

The data presented in the foregoing examples are subject to multiple interpretations that involve a variety of issues concerning the specific tasks and patient populations involved (see Cohen, 1984; Moscovitch, 1982a, 1982b, 1984; Schacter & Tulving, 1982b; Squire, 1982, for discussions). Theorizing about the observed dissociations in amnesics' performance has typically taken the form of advancing a binary distinction between two types of memory or knowledge and then arguing that amnesics possess one type of memory or knowledge but not the other. Among the ideas that have been proposed to accommodate some or all of the data that we have considered are notions that amnesics are victims of disconnection between cognitive and semantic memory (Warrington & Weiskrantz, 1982), can acquire procedural but not declarative knowledge (Cohen & Squire, 1980), show effects of prior experience on performance but not on awareness (Jacoby, 1982), have semantic but not episodic memory (Kinsbourne & Wood, 1975, 1982; Schacter & Tulving, 1982a), can establish horizontal but not vertical associations (Wickelgren, 1979), and possess skilled memory but not conscious recollection (Moscovitch, 1982b).

We do not intend to discuss, let alone settle, the numerous issues that arise when attempting to apply each of these formulations to existing data. Rather, we retreat from the task of differentiating analytically among the various theoretical accounts and instead point to a common theme found in all of them. The memory, or memory system, that is severely impaired in amnesics is one that entails conscious access to recently established representations of events and information. This is the kind of memory that has been studied in most of the extensive adult literature that makes use of tasks such as free recall, cued recall, and yes/no, or forced-choice, recognition and is usually referred to as "episodic" or "conscious" memory. But there is a second type of memory that seems to be relatively intact in amnesics. It is not consciously accessible, and its operation is inferred from observed facilitations in performance on tasks that do not require the organism to relate its performance on the task deliberately to any past experience and seems to be relatively intact in amnesia. This is the kind of memory that has been referred to as "procedural," "unconscious," or "semantic." Although we are aware that it may turn out to be incorrect to characterize this "other" form of memory in an undifferentiated manner that glosses over potentially important distinctions (for example, one would not want to argue that "semantic memory" and "procedural memory" are identical [cf. Schacter & Tulving, 1982b]), we take the somewhat more molar view in the present chapter for two reasons. First, there are few data that permit us to say whether and to what extent the type of memory indexed by tasks such as mirror reading and repetition priming are similar. Second, because the comparisons that we shall make between amnesics and infants are necessarily of a rather general nature, attempts to pin down the specific type of memory that may be common to both would probably be premature.

In order to avoid such premature specificity and in order to link our discussion of amnesics and normal adults to our later discussion of infants, we shall refer to the two systems that we have described as the *early system* and the *late system*. The *early system* corresponds to the "unconscious" or "procedural" memory that is preserved in amnesics and, we will argue, is available to the infant almost immediately after birth. The *late system* corresponds to the "conscious" or "episodic" memory that is impaired in amnesics. This memory system, we shall suggest, is not available to infants until the latter part of the first year.

Dissociations between Forms of Memory in Normal Adults

Some of the data discussed in the preceding section have prompted several researchers to ask whether dissociations found in amnesics can also be observed in normal subjects. The answer provided by recent research is that they can. Let us consider evidence provided by several relevant studies.

Partly relying on the observation that amnesics' performance reflects the effects of learning episodes that are not explicitly recalled and recognized, Jacoby and Dallas (1981; see also Jacoby, 1982) compared the effects of different experimental variables on recognition memory and perceptual identification tasks. On the recognition-memory task, subjects were required to say whether or not a particular word had previously appeared on the study list. On the perceptual identification task, there was no reference to the study context; subjects simply attempted to identify the word from a brief (35 msec) exposure. Jacoby and Dallas found that variables such as the number and spacing of repetitions affected recognition memory and perceptual identification in a parallel fashion: performance on both tasks was facilitated by increasing the number and distribution of repetitions. In contrast, manipulations that affected the level of processing of study materials substantially affected recognition memory (more elaborate processing led to better recognition) but had no effect on perceptual identification. Moreover, Jacoby and Dallas found that the effects of a single-study exposure to a word facilitated perceptual identification performance by about as much after a 24-hour delay as it did after an immediate test; in contrast, recognition-memory accuracy declined significantly over the retention interval. They also observed that priming of perceptual identification did not transfer across sensory modalities, a finding that also has been reported by Morton (1979). Recognition memory, in contrast, was less dramatically influenced by study–test sensory modality changes. Indeed, other research indicates that recognition memory can be unaffected by cross-modal changes between study and test (Hintzman, Block, & Inskeep, 1972).

Jacoby and Dallas noted that the kind of memory tapped by a perceptual identification task resembles the kind of memory that is available to amnesics: it does not depend on explicit retrieval of information about the study episode. Similar observations have been made by Tulving, Schacter, and Stark (1982). Their study was designed to provide information about the kind of memory that underlies performance on yes/no recognition and word-fragment-completion tasks. Subjects studied long lists of low-frequency words and were tested by yes/no recognition and fragment completion either 1 hour, or 1 week, later. The study words were selected so that after deletion of 3–4 letters, only one correct English completion was possible (e.g., the fragment for ASSASSIN was A _ _ A _ _ I N, and for LACROSSE was _ A C _ O S _ _). In half of the test conditions, the yes/no recognition task preceded the fragment-completion task; in the other half, the fragment-completion task preceded the recognition task. The experiment yielded several results of interest. First, exposure to a word on the study list facilitated subjects' ability to complete a fragment of it. Probability of fragment completion was about .31 for new words and about .46 for words that appeared once on the study list. Second, the magnitude of this priming effect did not change over time. Although recognition accuracy declined substantially from the 1-hour to the 1-week test, probability of fragment completion was virtually identical over the course of the retention interval. This result indicates that the pattern of performance that Warrington and Weiskrantz (1970, 1974) observed in amnesics—normal priming effects on fragment completion in spite of poor recognition memory—can be observed in normal subjects at a long delay (see Woods & Piercy, 1974, for similar results). Third, in the experimental conditions in which the fragment-completion test followed the recognition test, probability of fragment completion was stochastically independent of recognition performance. Subjects were about as likely to complete a fragment whether or not they recognized that the word represented by the fragment had appeared earlier on the study list.

The data from the Jacoby and Dallas (1981) and Tulving, Schacter, and Stark (1982) studies suggest a fundamental difference between the forms of memory that underlie performance on yes/no recognition tasks on the one hand, and perceptual identification and fragment-completion tasks on the other. Evidence from several other studies indicates that similar dissociations can be observed when other tasks are used. As noted earlier, Jacoby and Witherspoon (1982) found independence between recognition memory and priming of low-frequency homophones on a spelling task in both normals and amnesics. Eich (in press) has reported similar results in a divided attention study in which target homophones were presented on an unattended channel. Scarborough and his colleagues (Scarborough, Cortese, & Scarborough, 1977; Scarborough, Gerard, & Cortese, 1979) have found that the priming effect of a word's appearance on latency to make a lexical decision about the word does not decrease with increasing lag between successive appearances of the word. In contrast, recognition latencies increase significantly with lag. Kolers (1976) demonstrated that college students showed a savings when they read transformed script a year after they had acquired the reading skill. However, he also found that savings on the reading task was uncorrelated with the ability to recognize whether or not a sentence of text was old or new. Using a somewhat novel procedure, Kunst-Wilson and Zajonc (1980) exposed subjects to geometric shapes for extremely brief durations. Although subsequent forced-choice recognition of new and old shapes was at chance, subjects demonstrated a reliable preference for the old shapes on a two-choice test in which they stated which of two shapes—one old, one new—they liked better.

Data that are similar to those reported in the foregoing experiments are provided by studies in which normal subjects were rendered temporarily amnesic. In a hypnosis study, Williamsen, Johnson, and Eriksen (1965) found that free recall and recognition of a short list of words was impaired in hypnotized subjects relative to controls. However, hypnotized subjects' performance on a word-fragment-completion task was facilitated as much as control subjects' performance by the occurrence of a word on the study list. Kihlstrom (1980), using word-association and category-instance production tasks, also provided evidence for normal priming effects in hypnotized subjects, in contrast to impaired free-recall performance. Bennett, Davis, and Giannini (1981) presented tape-recorded suggestions to anesthetized surgical patients to the effect that they should touch their ears when interviewed postoperatively by one of the doctors. In the postoperative interview, patients who received this suggestion touched their ears far more frequently than control patients, but none of the patients was able to recall receiving the suggestion.

The studies of normal subjects that we have considered converge on a theme that is similar to the one that emerged from studies of organic amnesics: there is a form of memory that is manifested in improved or primed performance on a variety of tasks that does not require explicit memory for a study episode and can be dissociated experimentally from the more conscious forms of recall and recognition. Although numerous accounts of the observed dissociations are possible (see Jacoby, 1984; Jacoby & Witherspoon, 1982; Mandler, 1980), we think it is reasonable to postulate that the data provide evidence for a distinction between what we have referred to as the early and the late memory systems. The data suggest that the two systems are affected similarly by some experimental variables (number and spacing of repetitions) and differently by others (levels of processing and retention interval). Perhaps the most compelling experimental evidence favoring the multiple-system interpretation of the observed dissociations is the independence of priming effects and recognition memory observed by Jacoby and Witherspoon (1982), Scarborough *et al.* (1979), and Tulving *et al.* (1982). If priming-recognition dissociations are attributable to differing methods of test or to different retrieval processes operating on a common memory trace, one would expect to find some degree of positive association between tasks. The observed independence by no means rules out such explanations, and research that involves a greater variety of tasks is clearly necessary before firm conclusions can be drawn. The data that we have considered so far, however, are consistent with a multiple-systems interpretation.

Studies of Infant Memory

Studies of infant memory are now considered in light of the distinctions put forward in the foregoing sections. Rather than attempt to review exhaustively the sizable literature associated with various approaches to infant memory, as has been done ably by others (e.g., Fagan, Chapter 1; Cohen & Gelber, 1975; Olsen, 1976; Rovee-Collier & Fagen, 1981; Werner & Perlmutter, 1979), our discussion is selectively guided by two major themes. First, it is argued that the kind of memory tapped by habituation-novelty preference tasks as well as by one class of conditioning paradigms is mediated by the early memory system, whereas the kind of memory tapped by object search tasks and by another class of conditioning paradigms is mediated by the late memory system. Second, it is argued that converging evidence derived from several sources suggests that the late memory system begins to emerge in infants at an age of about 8–9 months. Other researchers who have noted that substantial changes in mnemonic abilities occur at this time have tended to interpret such changes in terms of a transition from recognition to recall (e.g., Schaffer, 1972; Fox *et al.*, 1979). We attempt to show that they can be better understood in the context of the early/late memory system distinction.

Habituation–Novelty-Preference Tasks

The majority of studies of infant memory have employed habituation and novelty-preference paradigms. The logic underlying the application of these somewhat different yet related procedures to the study of mnemonic processes has been spelled out in other chapters of this volume (Chapters 1, 2, 3) as well as in numerous articles in the literature (e.g., Cohen & Gelber, 1975; Olsen, 1976; Sophian, 1980). The key idea seems straightforward: infants' preference for looking at and manipulating novel patterns and objects can be used to gauge the degree to which information about a stimulus has been encoded and stored in memory. If, for example, attention to a repeatedly exposed face declines over trials, but recovers on presentation of a novel face, then this pattern of habituation and recovery is taken as evidence of memory for the original face. Similarly, greater attention to a novel than to a previously exposed face in paired comparison paradigms would be regarded as an index of memory for the familiar face: infants "remember" the prior occurrence of the familiar face and hence attend more to the novel one.

The use of quotations around the term *remember* points toward a central question that needs to be raised about habituation and novelty preference paradigms: What kind of memory is tapped by these procedures? With the exception of several papers that will be discussed shortly, the articles in the literature concerning habituation and novelty-preference paradigms that we encountered fell into two general classes. One class of papers was empirically oriented and did not address systematically the problem of the nature of the memory process or system that underlies infants' performance on habituation and novelty-preference tasks; the term *recognition* was invoked in these papers without explicit consideration of exactly how it was achieved. This class of papers constituted a substantial majority in our examination of the literature and probably reflects the largely atheoretical nature of research on infant memory that has been noted by Fagan (Chapter 1). The second class of papers portrayed infants' recognition abilities in terms that are strikingly similar to the theoretical constructs applied to adult recognition memory. For example, Cohen and Gelber (1975) conceptualized infants' habituation to repeatedly exposed stimuli as a buildup of an internal representation or memory trace of the stimulus that is matched to stimuli that subsequently appear. When a match between the stimulus and the representation occurs, the infant is less likely to look at the recognized stimulus; when a match does not occur, the infant explores the novel stimulus. Similarly, Olsen (1976) proposed a model of infant recognition memory that shares much in common with adult information-processing models. He viewed the phenomenon of habituation as a consequence of memory search and matching processes as well as decision rules that are stored in long-term memory.

In recent years, some researchers have cast a critical eye on the assumptions underlying habituation and novelty-preference paradigms. Sophian (1980) argued that novelty preferences and memory are partly confounded in both paradigms and also noted that these tasks permit examination of a restricted range of memory phenomena (see Carter & Strauss, 1982 for reply). Rovee-Collier and Fagen (1981) also pointed to the narrow scope of mnemonic abilities that can be explored with habit- uation and novelty preference procedures. Jeffrey (1976) questioned the usefulness of invoking the construct of "memory" to account for patterns of infants' habituation, and similar conceptual concerns have been ex- pressed by Lockhart and Ruff (Chapters 3 and 6).

We share some of these concerns. In particular, we want to focus on the question of what kinds of mnemonic capacities are needed to show evidence of "recognition memory" on habituation and novelty-preference paradigms. Is it necessary to invoke the kinds of storage, search, and matching notions that are used to describe adult recognition memory in order to provide an account of infants' differential fixation of novel and familiar stimuli? We do not think so. Consider the types of queries that can be put to an adult participant in a memory experiment when he or she is shown, at the time of test, an experimental item (e.g., a word) that occurred earlier in a study list. One question that can be posed concerns the status of the item in the subject's personal past: Does the person recognize the item as one that he or she encountered on the study list? A positive answer to this question, or an ability to choose the old item when it is paired with a new item, is usually taken as evidence that the subject recognizes that the item appeared earlier in the experimental con- text. However, as noted in previous sections of the chapter, there are other queries that can be put to the subject that do not require recognition of an item's occurrence in a studied list. For example, a subject can be asked whether or not a string of letters constitutes a word. The fact that subjects make such decisions faster for old than for new words need not imply recognition of an item's prior occurrence—in fact, as pointed out earlier, facilitated processing of the old item can be independent of rec- ognition memory.

It seems reasonable to suggest that infants' performance on habit- uation–novelty-preference tasks can be conceptualized in terms of facil- itated processing of old (familiar) stimuli, rather than in terms of gaining access to information about the prior occurrence of the familiar stimulus in the experimental context and performing some sort of matching op- eration on it. Ruff (Chapter 3) has offered a similar analysis. She contends that, during periods of stimulus familiarization, infants explore objects and pick up information about their invariant features. When a previously exposed object is again presented, infants detect the invariants more quickly and hence spend less time exploring the object; more time is spent exploring a novel object, whose invariants are not so quickly detected. Ruff argues that this facilitation could be referred to as memory, but there would be no need to talk about comparison of present input with past input, even though the effect of prior experience is evident.

Similarly, Lockhart (Chapter 6) has proposed that a distinction between memories and consequences of experiences may be useful for understanding infants' performance on habituation–novelty-preference tasks. Lockhart acknowledges that "exposure to certain visual patterns yields predictable consequences that outlast the physical presence of the pattern" (p. 134). However, these consequences of a study exposure (differential fixation of novel and familiar stimuli) must be distinguished from memory of the study experience, which entails an attribution of "pastness."

The spirit of the ideas put forward by both Ruff and Lockhart closely resembles our hypothesis that differential attention to novel and familiar stimuli is a consequence of modifications of perceptual-cognitive processes or procedures. This notion also has much in common with the view of amnesics' spared learning capacities that was discussed earlier. The studies that were reviewed demonstrate clearly that amnesics' ability to make lexical decisions or to read transformed script is enhanced by prior exposure to the relevant material in the experimental context. However, amnesics are unable to recognize whether or not a particular item previously appeared in the experiment in spite of their facilitated processing of it. On the basis of similar dissociations observed in normals, it was suggested that the early memory system underlies certain priming effects and procedural facilitations, whereas the late memory system underlies the ability to recall and recognize specific incidents from the past. There is a striking resemblance between the requirements of tasks on which normals and amnesics demonstrate facilitated processing as a function of prior experience and the habituation–novelty-preference tasks on which infants differentially attend to old and new stimuli: successful performance on these tasks need not entail explicit knowledge that an item occurred in the study context; indeed, subjects can perform well without making any reference to the study context. This striking similarity leads us to suggest that infants' "recognition memory" may be mediated by the early memory system.

There are two issues that immediately arise in connection with the foregoing contention. The first concerns what might be called the "missing link" in our argument so far. It is possible to speak confidently about dissociations between two types of memory in adult subjects because normal performance on tasks that tap one form of memory co-occurs with impaired performance on tasks that tap the other (as observed in amnesics), and because there is independence of performance on the two types of task in normal subjects. The situation is different with habituation and novelty preference tasks. Although these tasks yield evidence of retention that we have argued can be mediated by the early memory system, there is an apparent lack of corresponding data indicating that infants—like amnesics—perform poorly on tasks that are mediated by the late memory system. Without such data, the force of our argument would be weakened considerably. However, we suggest in the next two sections of the chapter that supportive evidence is provided by paradigms other than those that rely on habituation and novelty preferences.

The second issue that requires discussion concerns the relation between the ideas that have been suggested here and existing data concerning infants' performance on habituation and novelty-preference tasks. Is there anything in the data that either supports or discredits our hypotheses concerning the early and late memory systems? One way to approach this question is to compare the effects of variables on tasks that tap the early and late systems in adults with their effects on habituation and novelty preference tasks. Such an approach, of course, may be problematic; the vast procedural differences between the tasks used in infant and adult research preclude fine-grain comparisons among the effects of the independent variables that are common to the two areas. We are well aware of these problems and hence constrain ourselves to a rather broad level of analysis in the comparisons that we make.

Consider the interpretation of cases in which experimental variables have parallel effects on adults' and infants' performance. A point that was made earlier in the chapter is relevant in this context: some experimental variables influence "early system tasks" and "late system tasks" in parallel fashion. This is an important point because parallel effects of an independent variable on the performance of adults and infants can lead to the conclusion that infants' performance may be attributed to the same processes that underlie the kind of adult memory that is mediated by the late memory system (cf. Chapter 1). This need not be so. To take just two examples, it has been observed that infants' preference for novel stimuli is heightened by increasing both the *number* and *spacing* of repetitions of items during familiarization trials (Cornell, 1980). Because of the ubiquity of repetition and spacing effects in the adult literature on "late system tasks," such as free recall and yes/no recognition, these results have been viewed as support for the idea that infant recognition memory is similar to adult recognition memory (e.g., Cornell, 1980; Chapter 1). However, increasing the number and spacing of repetitions facilitates perceptual identification performance as well as recognition performance in adults, even though performance on the two tasks can be independent of one another. Thus, results of studies of infants in which parallel effects are obtained may not be useful for teasing apart the influences of the early and late memory systems, because tasks that tap the two systems in adults may also show parallel effects with respect to a particular independent variable.

More interesting for our purposes would be cases in which an independent variable influences infants' novelty preferences in a manner that *selectively* mimics its effects on adults' performance of tasks that tap the early memory system. Although the existing data are neither abundant nor clear-cut, a number of studies do furnish some highly suggestive evidence. Consider the effects of length of retention interval. One of the most consistent findings in all of adult memory research is that performance on the classical late system tasks, such as free recall, cued recall, and yes/no recognition, declines with increasing delays between study and test. In contrast, studies that were discussed earlier have demonstrated little or no forgetting over time on "early system tasks," such as perceptual identification, word-fragment completion, and lexical decision, although yes/no recognition accuracy declined significantly as a function of delay in these studies. Indeed, even amnesics' performance on word-fragment completion (Warrington & Weiskrantz, 1968), mirror-reading tasks (Cohen & Squire, 1980), and complex puzzles such as the Tower of Hanoi (Cohen, 1984) is characterized by robust retention over time, in contrast to their highly fragile recognition memory.

How does retention interval affect infants' performance on habituation and novelty-preference tasks? Although an answer to this question depends on the exact conditions of the experimental situation, there is now a solid body of evidence indicating that the effects of a study exposure on subsequent processing of novel and familiar stimuli can be surprisingly immune to the length of the study–test interval. An early experiment by Fagan (1971) found that 5-month-old infants exhibited no forgetting over a brief retention interval (30 sec) in a paired-comparison paradigm. Length of retention interval was extended to 24 hr and 48 hr in two subsequent experiments (Fagan, 1973, Exp. 1 & 2), but no evidence of forgetting was observed across a variety of stimulus conditions; infants fixated a novel object, pattern, or face about as frequently after 24- and 48-hr delays as they did on immediate test. Although Fagan (1973, Exp. 3, 4, & 5) was able to obtain some evidence for disruption of delayed recognition through interference manipulations, the persistence of novelty preferences over time constitutes the most striking feature of his data. Similar results were reported in a later study by Fagan (1977), who concluded that "the biggest lesson to learn from the present report is that loss of recognition seems to be the exception rather than the rule in infant memory, occurring as it does only under rather circumscribed conditions" (p. 77). Resistance of habituation and novelty preferences to manipulations of delay and interference also has been observed by Cohen, DeLoache, and Pearl (1977) and McCall, Kennedy, and Dodds (1977). Cohen *et al.* concluded that "by eighteen weeks of age infants' visual memory is remarkably durable" (p. 96).

This apparent durability fits well with observations of long-lasting facilitations observed on such "early system tasks" as mirror reading, lexical decision, and fragment completion. It is also interesting to note that long-term habituation effects—on the order of weeks and months—have been observed in a variety of lower organisms, including *Aplysia* (Castelucci & Kandell, 1976), earthworm (Gardner, 1968), and rat (Leaton, 1974). One would probably not want to resort to search and matching processes to account for long-lived habituation effects in *Aplysia* or earthworms; it seems more plausible to refer to a modification in the processes or procedures used to analyze sensory input or to effect motor output. The long-term retention of habituation by lower organisms encourages the view that the persistence of habituation and novelty-preference effects observed in infants might be mediated by a somewhat primitive, procedurally based early memory system.

Not all studies, of course, have found robust retention over time, and the exceptions in the literature are instructive. It has been observed that retention may be somewhat fragile in habituation and novelty-preference paradigms if stimulus familiarization periods are relatively brief. Novelty preferences observed on an immediate test disappear after just a 1- or 2-min delay (Cornell, 1979; Lasky, 1980; Rose, 1980, 1981). Whereas experiments that found evidence of long-term retention used familiarization times on the order of 120 sec, these studies employed familiarization times ranging from 5–20 sec.

The powerful effect of duration of stimulus familiarization raises an important issue. Given the argument that experimentally induced novelty preferences are mediated by the early memory system, and given the observation that familiarization time influences retention of novelty preferences, one might expect that a variable analogous to familiarization time would exert parallel effects on "early system tasks" in adults. The scant evidence available seems to suggest otherwise. Although it is well known that length of presentation time affects such tasks as free recall, cued recall, and yes/no recognition, the one study (Jacoby & Dallas, 1981) that has examined the effect of presentation time on an "early system task" (perceptual identification) reported little or no effect of this variable; perceptual identification accuracy was enhanced about as much by a short study exposure as by a long one.

The discrepancy, however, may be more apparent than real; close inspection of the literature reveals that familiarization time in infant studies is not in fact analogous to presentation time in adult studies. When presentation time is manipulated in studies of adult memory, subjects continuously fixate an item for different amounts of time. In contrast, it is clear that in infant experiments familiarization time is comprised of a series of *discrete* fixations, the sum total of which constitutes length of familiarization. Existing evidence indicates that infants spend much of the familiarization period fixating stimuli other than the experimental target. For example, in one of Fagan's early studies, infants spent a total of 50–55 sec fixating the target during a 120-sec familiarization period (Fagan, 1971); in another experiment, they fixated the target for only 40–45 sec out of the 120 sec allowed for familiarization. In light of the fact that infants sporadically focus on the target during the familiarization period, recent studies have operationally defined familiarization time in terms of the combined length of the individual fixations of each infant relative to predetermined criterion (e.g., Cornell, 1980; Lasky, 1980; Rose, 1981). Thus, it seems most appropriate to view the length of familiarization time in studies of infant memory as a manipulation of number of stimulus exposures or repetitions. As noted earlier, number of repetitions affects adults' performance on "early system tasks" as well as "late system tasks." This leads us to suggest that the observed effects of familiarization time on infants' performance are not inconsistent with our hypothesis.

Some persuasive evidence that differential fixation of novel and familiar stimuli can be mediated by the early memory system is furnished by studies of infants' cross-modality recognition. It was noted earlier that in studies of adult memory, "early system tasks," such as perceptual identification, are more sensitive to modality shifts than are "late system tasks," such as yes/no recognition (Jacoby & Dallas, 1981; Morton, 1979). What do the data suggest about infants' cross-modal mnemonic abilities?

A number of studies have examined infants' novelty preferences under conditions of *cross-modal* shift, in which modality of presentation is switched from study to test (e.g., tactual familiarization and visual preference test), and under conditions of *intermodal* change, in which familiarization occurs in two modalities (e.g., visual and tactual) and novelty preferences are tested in one (e.g., visual) or the reverse procedure is used (e.g., visual familiarization, visual-tactual test). These studies have demonstrated that novelty preferences of 6–9-month-old infants are eliminated by cross-modal and intermodal changes between study and test, whereas novelty preferences of 12-month-old infants are largely unaffected by them (Gottfried, Rose, & Bridger, 1977, 1978; Mackay-Soroka, Trehub, Bull, & Corter, 1982; Rolfe & Day, 1981; Rose, Gottfried, & Bridger, 1978, 1979). However, in *intramodal* conditions—when stimuli are studied and tested within one and the same modality—younger and older infants in the foregoing studies exhibit reliable novelty preferences of the same magnitude. Indeed, infants as young as 4–5 months exhibit significant novelty preferences in the face of various intramodal transformations of stimuli between familiarization and test, including changes in orientation (Cornell, 1975; Fagan, 1979), representational format (Dirks & Gibson, 1977), and motion (Chapter 3).

The differential vulnerability of younger and older infants to study–test changes of modality, in conjunction with the aforementioned finding that priming effects in "early system tasks" in adults can be eliminated by study–test modality shifts, is consistent with the hypothesis that younger infants' performance on novelty preference tasks is mediated by the early system whereas older infants' performance is influenced by the emerging late system. A further finding reported by Rose *et al.* (1978, 1979) provides additional evidence that is congenial to this interpretation. They observed that 12-month-old *preterm* infants, who are characterized by slow development of various neurological and psychological functions (Parmelee, 1975; Sigman & Parmelee, 1974), perform much like 6–9-month-old full-term infants: novelty preferences of preterm infants are robust in intramodal conditions but are eliminated by cross-modal and intermodal changes between study and test. In the absence of such data, it could have been argued that cross-modal transfer is observed in 12-month-old but not 6-month-old full-term infants because the older infants have had more experience gaining knowledge about cross-modal properties of objects. The modality-bound performance of 12-month-old preterms makes it difficult to maintain such an argument and instead suggests that the achievement of cross-modal transfer depends on the occurrence of maturational events in the nervous system that develop slowly in preterm infants.

It should be noted that several studies have claimed that cross-modal transfer in novelty-preference paradigms can occur as early as 6 months (Bryant, Jones, Claxton, & Perkins, 1972; Rose, Gottfried, & Bridger, 1981; Ruff & Kohler, 1978) and 1 month (Meltzoff & Borton, 1979). There are, however, several reasons for viewing these data with caution. First, the cross-modal transfer data reported by Bryant *et al.* (1972), Rose *et al.* (1981), and Ruff and Kohler (1978) indicate that the phenomenon is not nearly as robust in younger infants as has been observed in older infants. For example, in the Bryant *et al.* (1972) and Ruff and Kohler (1978) experiments, the evidence for cross-modal transfer was obtained only with one of the experimental objects and was manifest in a slight preference for the *familiar* stimulus, a finding that is not easy to interpret. Moreover, in the Rose *et al.* (1981) and Ruff and Kohler (1978) studies, only 6-month-old infants were studied, so we do not know if older infants would have shown *more* cross-modal transfer than the younger ones, or for that matter, whether the younger infants showed any cross-modal transfer at all. The single study that furnishes evidence suggesting that cross-modal transfer occurs in 1-month-old infants (Meltzoff & Borton, 1979) has not been replicated (Baker, Brown, & Gottfried, 1982). In light of this nonreplication and the other evidence that has been reviewed, we agree with Bushnell's (1981) suggestion that the Meltzoff and Borton data must be viewed with caution. However, it is entirely conceivable that future studies will establish the occurrence of cross-modal transfer in very young infants. Infants aged 3–4 months are capable of cross-modal perception (e.g., Lawson, 1980; Lyons-Ruth, 1977; Spelke, 1976), and conditions may be uncovered in which they show cross-modal memory. Such a finding would not be inconsistent with our hypothesis, so long as older infants showed *more* mnemonic transfer across sensory modalities under similar experimental conditions.

Taken together, the results of habituation–novelty-preference studies provide suggestive, though not conclusive, evidence that infants' differential fixation of novel and familiar stimuli may be based on the early memory system, at least until the closing months of the first year. Future studies that explore the similarities and differences between the performance of younger (e.g., 6–7-month-old) and older (e.g., 11–12-month-old) infants may help to delineate more precisely the nature of the mnemonic changes that occur during what seems to be a critical transitional period.

Conditioning and Learning

The studies that we have reviewed so far assessed infant memory by examining how spontaneous behavior (such as looking) is modified by previous experience (such as exposure to a particular visual event). Another way of assessing memory is to examine the organism's learning ability in traditional conditioning paradigms. Here the organism demonstrates its memory by learning to associate responses with a particular stimulus or event. In classical or Pavlovian conditioning, a conditioned stimulus (CS) through successive pairings with an unconditioned stimulus (UCS), comes to elicit a conditioned response (CR) that resembles the unconditioned response (UCR). In operant or instrumental conditioning, an outcome that is contingent on a prior response increases the probability of emitting the response if the outcome is positive, and lowers it if it is negative. Although there have been many studies of conditioning in infants (for reviews see Fitzgerald & Porges, 1971; Hulsebus, 1973; Sameroff, 1971), there have been only a handful of these in amnesics (Oscar-Berman, 1980; Prisko, 1966; Sidman, Stoddard, & Mohr, 1968; Weiskrantz & Warrington, 1979). Extensive comparison of the types of variables that affect conditioning in the two groups is, therefore, impossible. However, we can gain some understanding of the possible roles of the early and late memory systems in conditioning by reviewing studies of nonhuman species, primarily rats. To do so we must depart from our reliance on purely functional dissociations between memory systems and consider briefly the neurological substrates that may underlie them.

Amnesia in adult humans arises from a variety of etiologies associated with damage to various neural structures (for review, see Barbizet, 1970). The structures most often implicated are the anterior-mesial temporal lobes and hippocampus, and the diencephalic structures, such as the mammillary bodies and dorsomedial nucleus of the thalamus, which are closely related anatomically to the hippocampus. Because there is some doubt as to which of the latter two structures is critical and because amnesia following bilateral hippocampal damage is so profound, most investigators searching for an animal model of human amnesia have concentrated on the hippocampus. Consequently, we will assume in the subsequent discussion that the functions of the late memory system in mammals depend on the integrity of the hippocampus and related structures and that conditioning in animals with a damaged or undeveloped hippocampus is of necessity mediated by the early memory system (see Chapter 7). If there is a phylogenetic continuity in the functions of the hippocampus, we would expect that conditioning in human infants without a fully developed late memory system would resemble that of other mammals with a damaged or undeveloped hippocampus. We are aware that the problems of comparing infants with adults in a given species are compounded when comparisons are made across species (Schacter, 1982, Chapter 7; 1984). The danger with this type of analysis is that many structures have not reached adult levels of functioning in infancy. It is possible that the deficits that we attribute to an incompletely developed hippocampus might well result from the absence of fully developed parietal or frontal lobes. However, our comparisons are not meant to be conclusive, but merely suggestive; they are meant to stimulate further research. With this proviso in mind, let us briefly examine the literature. We will rely primarily on O'Keefe and Nadel's (1978) excellent and thorough review of the literature on learning and conditioning in adult hippocampal animals as a base for our comparisons between these animals and human infants.

Simple operant conditioning on a schedule of continuous or conjugate reinforcement has been demonstrated in newborn infants (Sameroff, 1971). Thus, shortly after birth, infants can modify their sucking responses to receive milk as reinforcement (Sameroff, 1971). This type of instrumental conditioning has also been observed in neonatal rats and cats (Blass, Kenny, Stoloff, Bruno, Teicher, & Hall, 1979; Rosenblatt, 1979; Chapter 7) as well as in amnesic patients (Oscar-Berman, 1980) and in adult rats with hippocampal lesions (for review, see O'Keefe & Nadel, 1978). Surprisingly, it is difficult to find good evidence of simple classical conditioning until the human infant is about a month old, but this too occurs well before we hypothesize that the late memory system develops. Amnesic humans (Claparède, 1911; Weiskrantz & Warrington, 1979) as well as neonatal mammals with underdeveloped hippocampi (see Spear, 1979, for review) or adult mammals with damaged hippocampi can acquire simple classically conditioned responses with no difficulty (O'Keefe & Nadel, 1978, p. 316). What happens when certain variations in the simple operant or classical conditioning paradigm are introduced? The answer to this question is complex. As O'Keefe and Nadel (1978) remarked, departures from normal performance can be evident or absent depending on the demands that ostensibly similar tasks make on what we have called the organism's early or late memory system. For example, in maze tasks in which spatio-temporal contextual cues and long intertrial intervals bias the rat toward adoption of what we might call a late memory system strategy, extinction is impaired in rats with hippocampal lesions. These same rats, however, will extinguish normally in continuous-reinforcement operant tasks carried out in a Skinner box in which the diminished importance of spatio-temporal contextual cues may enable them to rely on the early memory system. In the latter case, the rat simply associates responses with rewards without regard to other contextual information.

In reviewing the human infant literature, we have found few conditioning tasks in which infants are required to attend to the temporal and spatial context of the conditioning situation. Typically, the environment is extremely impoverished except for the stimuli that are being conditioned. There is little opportunity for the infant to use temporal and spatial context, which we would consider to be in the domain of the late memory system, while responses are being conditioned or extinguished. Thus, on continuous fixed reinforcement schedules, it is possible to demonstrate quite complex conditioning phenomena in infants (Hulsebus, 1973). The interesting series of conditioning studies by Rovee-Collier, Fagen, and their colleagues, concerned primarily with 3- to 5-month-old infants, provide a striking example of this type of research (for reviews see Rovee-Collier & Fagen, 1981; Fagen & Rovee-Collier, 1982). Their basic paradigm, which they call mobile conjugate reinforcement, consists of making the movement of a mobile contingent on the infant's kicks by tying a ribbon to the mobile and the infant's ankle. Reinforcement is immediate, continuous, and varies in strength with the infant's kicks. Conditioning, as assessed by increases in kicking rate over baseline, is rapid and can be maintained for days. Changing the mobile after delays of up to a few days after initial learning leads to changes in the kicking response, indicating that the infant retains information about the initial mobile. By 4 days after acquisition, however, kicking responses to the new mobile are indistinguishable from those to the old, suggesting that responding is maintained by prototypical or general cues rather than by ones associated with a specific item. The infants are also sensitive to shifts in reward magnitude (they find some mobiles more attractive than others) and show definite positive and negative contrast effects (Rovee-Collier & Capatides, 1979). Because comparable experiments were not conducted with infants about a year old, it is difficult to know whether the performance of the 3- to 5-month-old infants in Rovee-Collier and Fagen's studies differs from that of older infants, who according to our hypothesis would have a functional late memory system. What is certain, given the extensive literature on conditioning and learning in rats with hippocampal lesions (see O'Keefe and Nadel, 1978, Chapters 7, 9, 10), is that acquisition and maintenance of these behaviors can be mediated by the early memory system.

The following intriguing result in one of Rovee-Collier and Fagen's experiments reinforces the impression that 3- to 5-month-old infants learn only associations between stimuli and responses but do not remember, in the ordinary language use of the term, the spatial-temporal context—the particular episode—in which learning occurred. Rovee-Collier and Fagen trained their subjects to discriminate between two mobiles, one that shook when the infant kicked (S+) and one that remained immobile (S−). The S+ clearly elicited more CRs than the S−, but even the conditioned response to the positive stimulus decayed to baseline levels after a 2-week delay between training and test. Simple presentation without reinforcement of the S+ on Day 13, but not of the S−, reinstated the conditioned response to its former high level. Apart from demonstrating that appropriate cues can reinstate a conditioned response, this study shows that the response only reflects the association the infant formed to a particular stimulus, and not its memory for a particular event. If the response was an index of the infant's memory of the spatial and temporal context of the conditioning situation, then the S− should have reinstated the memory for the response as well since it, too, was part of the episode in which learning occurred. What is reinstated, clearly, is not a memory of an episode but a conditioned response that exists, so to speak, outside of any temporal-spatial context. Rovee-Collier and Fagen's (1981) claim that their paradigm tests "retrieval and recall" in infants must therefore be viewed with some skepticism if they wish the terms to conform to their usage in the human literature on episodic memory. In the latter case, recall is assumed to be initiated by the subject, and cues act as guides, rather than purely as elicitors of appropriate responses. Moreover, in attempting to recall a particular stimulus or occurrence, subjects also try to remember the episode of which the event was a part, and are consciously aware of having experienced the episode in the past. Recall and retrieval as used by Rovee-Collier and Fagen bear a somewhat remote resemblance to this process. The infants in their experiments do not so much recall as perform under the demands of the situation; and they do not retrieve information, but rather responses are elicited from them by specific stimuli. In short, this kind of "retrieval and recall" is characteristic of the early memory system, whereas "retrieval and recall" of episodic memories is characteristic of the late system.

An even more dramatic demonstration of responses getting locked into specific stimuli comes from Papousek's (1967) study of conditioned head turning in 5-month-old infants. Using a mixture of operant and classical conditioning techniques, he trained infants to turn their head to the right to receive a squirt of milk when they heard a tone. After they had acquired the response, he continued the procedure until they received enough reinforcement to be satiated. Even then, the infants kept turning to the right on hearing the tone, though they refused to drink any milk. In another study, Papousek substituted quinine for milk after training had reached asymptotic levels. Despite ordinarily hating quinine, these infants would nonetheless turn and accept the quinine on hearing the positive conditioned stimulus.

These behaviors bear a striking resemblance to those of rats with hippocampal lesions. Kimble (1969) trained rats to run for water reward in the bright or dark arm of a Y maze until they were satiated. Both normal and hippocampal animals stopped drinking at the same time, but whereas normal animals stopped running a few trials later, hippocampal animals continued to run for the next 100 trials! Persistence of this sort is not uncommon in rats with hippocampal lesions and suggests that these conditioned responses, as well as those of the infants, are locked into the cues associated with reward without regard to the overall context in which this behavior occurs. These phenomena may be characteristic of behavior mediated by the early system and seem to appear in dramatic fashion only when the late memory system is not functional.

On what we would call late memory system tasks, such as delayed matching-to-sample, in which reference to a particular episode is necessary for successful performance, infants younger than age one perform very poorly, as do amnesics, monkeys, and rats with hippocampal lesions (O'Keefe & Nadel, 1978; Chapter 7). Brody (1981) trained 6- and 12-month-old infants to choose which one of two panels matched a previously presented panel. Whereas the 12-month-olds performed above chance at delays between 250 msec and 12 sec, which was the longest delay used in the experiment, the 6-month-olds were correct only at the 250 msec delay. On delayed matching-to-sample of materials that were difficult to code verbally, similar results were obtained with the well-known patient H.M., who became amnesic following surgical excision of the hippocampus bilaterally (Prisko, 1966; Sidman *et al.,* 1968). In Prisko's study, in fact, H.M.'s performance resembled that of the 6-month-old infant in that he was perfect only at the 0-sec delay condition, whereas in Sidman *et al.*'s study his performance deteriorated to chance levels by 25 sec, which was still well below that of controls. These findings, in conjunction with Brody's data, are consistent with our hypothesis that the late memory system is not operative before 9–12 months in infants.

These results also underscore the necessity of the late memory system for long-term retention of particular events or episodes. The absence of a functioning late memory system may create difficulty even in simple conditioning tasks when reinforcement is delayed or when the intertrial interval is lengthened. Ramey and Ourth (1971) found that vocalization rate could be increased in infants 3–9 months of age only if the reinforcer was immediate, but not if it was delayed by as little as 3 sec. Similarly, Millar (1972) found that 6- to 8-month-old infants failed to discriminate between contingent and noncontingent reinforcement of a hand-pulling response if the reinforcement was delayed by more than 2 sec, whereas older infants were not affected by these small delays. Again, the period from about 9 months to a year seems to be a watershed for overcoming these deficits.

In a subsequent study, Millar and Schaffer (1972) found that simply displacing reinforcing feedback spatially by 60° from the operant manipulandum disrupted conditioning in 6- and 9-month-old infants but not in 12-month-olds. All groups were conditioned normally when feedback was spatially contiguous with response. Spatial displacement forces the infant to attend to and integrate information from sources that are spatially separate, creating both a memory and cognitive load that may be beyond the capacities of the early memory system. Simply increasing the intertrial interval in conditioning tasks may have similar effects (Watson, 1967), because the infant must now retain information about reinforcement contingencies of particular episodes for a time span that exceeds the retention capacities of the early system. Significantly, intertrial interval (Nadel, Black, & O'Keefe, 1975; O'Keefe & Nadel, 1978, pp. 282, 344), spatial contiguity of rewards and responses (O'Keefe & Nadel, 1978, p. 320), and delays of reinforcement (O'Keefe & Nadel, 1978, pp. 323–325; Oscar-Berman, 1980) can all have disruptive effects on the behavior of amnesics and rats with hippocampal lesions.

One type of test that causes considerable problems both for Korsakoff amnesics and for monkeys with hippocampal lesions is object and spatial reversal learning (Chapter 7; Oscar-Berman, 1980). In object reversal learning, the subject is trained to choose one object and ignore the other until a criterion is met; the positive and negative stimuli are then reversed.

In spatial reversal learning, choosing the location, rather than the object, is reinforced.

In the next section, we discuss object search studies that show that young infants fail on similar tasks, whereas older infants easily master them.

Searching for Hidden and Visible Objects: The Role of Forgetting

The AB̄ Error and Infant Memory

We suggested earlier that remembering the locations of different stimuli is an activity that requires more of the organism than is provided by the early memory system; the results of several operant conditioning experiments provided some support for this view. How do infants perform when objects are hidden in different locations? Piaget (1954) observed that 8- to 10-month-old infants can find an object hidden at an initial location (A). However, after several successful searches at A, many infants continue to search there when an object is hidden at a different location (B), even though the displacement is visible and the infant attends to it. This phenomenon is known as the AB̄ or Stage IV error (Gratch, 1976).

There has been a great deal of research concerning the AB̄ error since Piaget's (1954) initial description of it. Among the factors contributing to the error that have been explored are the influence of the infant's own actions (Evans, cited in Gratch, 1976; Landers, 1971), the effect of hiding the same or a different object at the search locations (Evans & Gratch, 1972; Schuberth, Werner, & Lipsitt, 1978), the role of the number of search locations (Cummings & Bjork, 1983; Schubert & Gratch, 1981), and the effects of various spatial transformations (Bremner, 1978a, 1978b; Bremner & Bryant, 1977; Butterworth, 1975, 1976; Butterworth & Jarrett, 1982).

The findings of these studies have not always agreed with one another, and many empirical controversies about the AB̄ error are as yet unsolved. Theories about the error are also diverse. Piaget (1954) argued that the AB̄ error could be interpreted as evidence for an incompletely developed object concept in Stage IV infants: infants search perseveratively at A when the object is hidden at B because their "concept" of the object is embedded in their own prior actions related to it. A number

of investigators have supported Piaget's contention that the $A\overline{B}$ error reflects an incomplete object concept (Frye, 1981; Gratch & Landers, 1971; Schuberth *et al.,* 1978), whereas others have argued that it can be best understood as a consequence of incomplete development of spatial frames of reference (Butterworth, 1975, 1976), in terms of contingencies established between location of the object and subsequent rewards (Cornell, 1978), or as a function of violations of object identity rules (Moore & Meltzoff, 1978).

Although the somewhat disorderly state of the literature indicates that the $A\overline{B}$ error is not yet completely understood, we believe that it makes both empirical and theoretical sense to point toward rapid forgetting as a major source of the $A\overline{B}$ error. The evidence that favors a forgetting interpretation derives from studies that demonstrate that the frequency of the $A\overline{B}$ error varies as a function of the delay between the hiding of the object at B and the infant's search for it. In an early and briefly described study, Luria (1959) found more evidence of the $A\overline{B}$ error in a 10-sec delay condition than in a no-delay condition. Gratch, Appel, Evans, Lecompte, and Wright (1974) observed more $A\overline{B}$ errors after delays of 1, 3, or 7 sec between hiding and search at B than in a no-delay condition. Although the frequency of $A\overline{B}$ errors did not increase systematically as a function of length of delay, as might be predicted by a forgetting explanation, 26 of 36 infants in the three delay conditions committed the $A\overline{B}$ error, in comparison to just 1 of 12 infants in the no-delay condition. Failure to observe the $A\overline{B}$ error under conditions of no delay has also been reported by Miller, Cohen, and Hill (1970). Similarly, Harris (1973) found that perseverative search at A occurred more frequently when B trials included a 5-sec hiding–search delay than when no delay was used.

Recent research by Fox *et al.* (1979) provides compelling evidence that the length of delay can influence frequency of the $A\overline{B}$ error. In a longitudinal study of 8 infants, they found no evidence at 9 months of the $A\overline{B}$ error with a hiding–search delay of 3 sec; the infants searched successfully for the object at B when it was hidden there after three consecutive A trials. However, when a 7-sec delay was used, all of these 9-month-old infants committed the $A\overline{B}$ error. At 10 months there was no evidence of the $A\overline{B}$ error with either 3- or 7-sec delays. Fox *et al.* then replicated their procedure with a cross-sectional sample of 8- and 10-month-old infants. They found that 7 out of 8 of the 8-month-old infants and 0 out of 10 of the 10-month-old infants made the $A\overline{B}$ error with a 7-sec delay.

A study reported recently by Cummings and Bjork (1983) further implicates a role for forgetting in the genesis of the $A\overline{B}$ error. These investigators argued that the perseverative nature of the $A\overline{B}$ error may

be attributable to the fact that in the standard two-choice hiding paradigm, errors are by definition perseverative (see Schubert & Gratch, 1981, for a rejoinder). Cummings and Bjork presented 8–10-month-old infants with an array of five possible hiding places, and hid objects in three different locations on A, B, and C trials. There were five successive searches at each location. Cummings and Bjork found that infants searched less accurately on the first B trial than the last A trial and less accurately on the first C trial than the last B trial. However, they found little evidence for perseverative error: inaccurate searches on B and C trials tended to be at spatially proximate locations and not at the prior hiding locations. They also noted a tendency for more accurate search with increasing age and suggested that the observed patterns of performance could be attributed to easily disrupted memory processes that become more resistant to distraction and interference with age.

In a study of somewhat older infants that employed three hiding locations, Webb, Massar, and Nadolny (1972) report evidence of perseverative search. Using delays of 5, 10, and 15 sec, they found that 14- and 16-month-old infants searched accurately on the A trial at each delay roughly 80% of the time and that performance dropped to chance or below (indicating perseverative search) when the hiding location was changed on subsequent trials. Webb et al. also found that after a search error, second choices of the 16-month-old infants achieved above-chance accuracy; in contrast, 14-month-old infants' second choices were at the chance level. Although some have argued that such a finding does not favor a memory deficit interpretation of the A$\overline{\text{B}}$ error (Harris, 1975), it seems reasonable to interpret the chance level of 14-month infants' second choices on B and C trials as evidence of memory failure in this age group. The improved second-choice performance of the older infants can be attributed to a corresponding development of mnemonic processes. What does seem surprising about the Webb et al. data is that the A$\overline{\text{B}}$ error was observed in relatively old infants; task and situational demands may account for the apparent discrepancy from other studies.

Data that are also consistent with the forgetting interpretation of the A$\overline{\text{B}}$ error are furnished by studies that have examined infants' search for a mother who has recently left the room. Corter, Zucker, and Galligan (1980) found that when the mother departed through Door A on Trial 1, 9-month-old infants directed more visual and motoric search to Door A than to Door B. When the mother departed through Door A on Trial 2, search remained accurate; but when she left through Door B on Trial 2, most infants engaged in perseverative search at Door A. Zucker (1982) has recently extended these observations using a similar paradigm. In addition to replicating Corter et al.'s finding with 9-month-old infants, Zucker examined 7-month-old infants' search for a departed mother. When

she left through Door A on Trial 1, the infants tended to gaze *initially* at
the correct door—indicating that they registered the place of disappearance—but subsequent visual search behavior was randomly divided between Door A and Door B. In addition, 7-month-old infants were much
less distressed by the mother's departure than 9- to 10-month-old infants.
We interpret these data as providing evidence for the view that 7-month-
old infants do not possess the mnemonic abilities afforded by the late
memory system that are required to remember the place of their mothers'
disappearance. By 9–10 months, the late system is developed sufficiently
for infants to remember the place of disappearance on Trial A. But the
emerging system is still rather fragile and sensitive to interference, as
reflected in perseverative search on B trials. More generally, we suggest
that this description of the A$\overline{B}$ error as a consequence of the developing
late memory system that is still easily disrupted by delay or interference
accords reasonably well with the effects of delay on the developmental
trends observed in the foregoing studies. There are, however, several
studies in which the investigators claim to have provided evidence that
refutes a memory-deficit interpretation of the A$\overline{B}$ error. Let us examine
each of them.

Frye (1980) evaluated the hypothesis suggested by Harris (1975) that
forgetting attributable to proactive interference from A trials accounts for
perseverative search. Frye contended that distracting the infant during a
90-sec interval between A and B trials should reduce proactive interference and hence also reduce frequency of the A$\overline{B}$ error. Although Frye
argued that his data lend support to this contention, there are grounds
for questioning his conclusion. First, Frye's data are equivocal. The frequency of the A$\overline{B}$ error did not differ between controls and distraction
groups on the *first* B trial, but distraction subjects searched at A less
frequently than control subjects on four subsequent B trials. Second, it
is not clear that one would expect much difference between the groups
because there was no attempt to focus the attention of control infants on
the A location during the A–B interval; these infants may well have been
distracted during the A–B interval. In fact, Frye noted that infants who
became restless during the interval played with the experimenter—presumably a form of distraction itself. These data do not seem to provide
strong evidence against a forgetting interpretation of the A$\overline{B}$ error.

Harris (1974) reasoned that if infants search perseveratively at A with
the object *visible* at B, then it would be difficult to invoke a forgetting
explanation of perseverative search at A. Based on the results of an
experiment in which the object was visible at B, Harris concluded that a
memory deficit explanation of the A$\overline{B}$ error was no longer tenable.

The evidence that constituted the basis for this conclusion, however,
is not entirely convincing. Harris observed that only 3 out of 24 infants

initially approached the prior location A when the object was visible at B. Thus, there was in fact little evidence for the classical pattern of perseverative search. Harris also observed that many infants went back to the empty A location after initial search at B and argued against the memory hypothesis on the basis of this finding. But it seems clear that numerous interpretations of this behavior are possible. One attractive possibility emerges from consideration of the contingency between search and reward that had been established on A trials: "Good things" had previously happened when the infant searched at A (cf. Cornell, 1978). Thus, a return to A after encountering the object at B need not be inconsistent with the "memory deficit" interpretation. In a similar study, Butterworth (1977) examined the frequency of the A$\overline{\text{B}}$ error in three different experimental conditions: hidden object, object visible through a transparent cover, and object uncovered and visible. The 3-sec hiding–search delay was used in each condition. Butterworth reports that the A$\overline{\text{B}}$ error occurred most frequently in the hidden object condition (25 out of 48 infants), less frequently when the object was placed under a transparent cover (20 out of 48), and still less frequently when the object was entirely visible (11 out of 48). Although the ordering of the experimental conditions does not provide evidence counter to a forgetting hypothesis—fewer infants committed the A$\overline{\text{B}}$ error when the object was visible than when it was not—the fact that nearly one-third of the infants in the two object-visible conditions searched perseveratively at A cannot be ignored. If the A$\overline{\text{B}}$ error is attributable to forgetting, why do so many infants search at A when the object is visible at B?

One clue that points toward a potential answer to this question emerges from a comparison of the Harris (1974) and Butterworth (1977) studies. Harris, who observed the A$\overline{\text{B}}$ error in only 13% of his infants, did not include a delay between object placement and search; Butterworth, who observed nearly three times as much perseverative search in visible object conditions, did. These data can be accommodated by a forgetting hypothesis that postulates that during the delay in the Butterworth study some infants were distracted from the visible object at B, and that this interference was sufficient to lead to forgetting of the *entire episode* in which the object was placed at B.

Mnemonic Precedence: An Analogue of the A$\overline{\text{B}}$ Error?

Although it may seem that the foregoing hypothesis requires the infant to forget much in a short period of time, precisely this kind of rapid and extensive forgetting would be expected if infants do indeed perform like amnesics on tasks that require the late memory system. In an attempt to provide more substance to this conjecture, we have examined the performance of amnesic patients on two hiding tasks that are similar to those that have been administered to Stage IV infants.[1]

The first task consisted of two phases. In Phase 1, the patient sat across a testing table from the experimenter, who indicated that he would put some objects in different parts of the room, and that the patient should try to remember their location. The experimenter then got up and placed an object in back of some books that were on a desk located about 10 feet directly behind the patient (Location A). After the experimenter returned to the testing table, the patient was queried about the present location of the object and then asked to walk to where he or she thought the object was hidden and to show it to the experimenter. This constituted an immediate test. The experimenter and patient then conversed for 2½ min. The retention interval was terminated by the following request from the experimenter: "A little while ago, I put an object somewhere. Do you remember where I put it?" This cycle of hiding, immediate test, 2½-min retention interval, and delayed test was repeated until the patient searched correctly for the object at Location A three successive times. A different object was hidden at A on each occasion, randomly chosen from a set of common objects including a fork, pencil, cassette tape, cup, and stapler. The same series of events occurred in the trial that followed, except that now the object was hidden at Location B—behind a book or a plant that was on top of a filing cabinet located about 6 feet to the left of and slightly behind the patient.

Immediately after the B trial, Phase 2 was initiated. The experimenter moved to a chair next to the desk that served as Location A; the patient's chair was turned around so that he or she would face the experimenter. Location A was now in direct view of the patient. The experimenter then hid objects at Location A exactly as he had in Phase 1. After two successful searches at A (behind the books on the desk), an object was placed at Location C—in *front of* the books on the desk, plainly visible to the patient. Location C was chosen so that it was difficult, if not impossible, to look at A without seeing the object at C. On half the trials, a large Styrofoam cup was "hidden" at C, and on the other half a ball point pen was "hidden" there.

Six severely amnesic patients and six patients with mild cognitive deficits but no significant memory loss participated in the study. The severely amnesic group consisted of four patients in the early stages of Alzheimer's disease, one who had undergone an operation for a ruptured

[1]This research was conducted in collaboration with Endel Tulving and Morris Freedman. Donald MacLachlan provided access to the early Alzheimer patients, and Marlene Oscar-Berman provided access to frontal-lobe patients.

aneurysm of the anterior communicating artery, and one patient without a firm neurological diagnosis. These patients are characterized by gross deficits of recall and recognition that are disproportionate to other cognitive deficits. The group of patients with mild cognitive deficits consisted of two patients who had suffered a left-sided stroke, one anterior communicating artery aneurysm patient, one early Alzheimer, and two patients without a neurological diagnosis. The amnesic patients' performance on the Wechsler Memory Scale was significantly impaired with respect to control patients, but the two groups did not differ on age, education, or IQ.

All of the amnesic patients remembered the location of the object at A on the first three delay trials; they were also successful on all immediate tests. This is surprising because some of these patients perform at chance on yes/no recognition tests with as little as 30 sec intervening between study and test. However, this high level of accuracy on the A trials facilitates comparison with infants' performance because, as noted earlier, a high percentage of infants search correctly on A trials. More important, the amnesics' behavior on the B trial of Phase 1 closely resembled the behavior of 8- to 9-month-old infants. On the immediate test, all of the amnesics found the object at B, indicating that they had encoded B as the hiding place on that trial. But after the 2½-min delay, four of the six amnesics searched for the object at A (Figure 1A). All of the patients who erred expressed surprise—and sometimes consternation—when they found nothing hidden at A; they frequently suggested that the experimenter was "playing some kind of a trick." When asked if an object had been hidden anywhere else, patients either denied that another location had been used, made erroneous guesses about a possible location, or indicated that they were not sure whether the experimenter had placed something at a location other than A. But none of the patients who searched at A on the B trial could recall that an object had been hidden at the B location. In contrast, the control patients remembered the location of the hidden objects on all A and B trials.

The results of Phase 2 were even more compelling. Once again, amnesics performed well on the A trials: there were no errors in the immediate test, all but one of the patients found the object at A on the first delay trial, and all of them searched successfully on the second delay trial. When the object was placed at Location C, in full view of the patient and directly in front of Location A, all amnesics "found" it on the immediate test, but five of the six amnesics failed to search at C after the delay (Figure 1A). Four of these patients searched at A, and one patient, who had searched correctly at B during Phase 1, first went to B and then to A. The most striking feature of amnesics' performance became evident after the unsuccessful search at A, when the experimenter told the patients

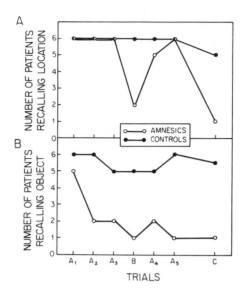

Fig. 1. Delayed recall of location and object by amnesic and control patients on consecutive trials of an object search task conducted in different places in a testing room. Objects were hidden at an initial location (A) and a second location (B) and were visible at a third location (C). A different object was used on each trial.

to look carefully at all the objects visible on the desk and to state whether the experimenter had placed any of them there. None of the amnesics chose the object that had in fact been placed at Location C. As in the B trial of Phase 1, patients either denied that an object had been placed anywhere other than Location A, or made uncertain and incorrect guesses about which objects on the desk might have been put there by the experimenter. All but one of the control patients "found" the object on the delayed test at C. The nature of this patient's error, however, was quite different from the errors made by the amnesics because he spontaneously corrected himself.

We also examined patients' delayed recall of the object on each trial (Figure 1). These data demonstrate that amnesics' delayed object recall declined sharply after the first trial and remained low, whereas the control patients consistently performed with little or no error. About half of the amnesics' errors were perseverative recalls of an object from a previous trial, and the other half were nonperseverative errors of omission or commission. The mildly impaired patients made only four object recall errors; two were omission errors, and two were perseverative.

In order to determine the generalizability of our results, we examined the performance of the same amnesics and mildly impaired patients on a

somewhat different task conducted on a separate occasion. To-be-remembered objects were hidden in one of four drawers of a square plastic
container (8½ cm × 8½ cm) that was placed on a desk directly in front
of the patient. Objects such as an elastic band or a piece of paper were
hidden in the same drawer (A) on the first three trials, and were hidden
in a different drawer (B) on the fourth trial; patients were tested immediately and after a 2½-min delay. Performance was perfect on all immediate tests, and both amnesics and controls accurately recalled the object's
location on the first three A trials (Figure 2A). On the B trial, however,
four of the six amnesics searched for the object at A, whereas all controls
performed without error. Amnesics' recall of the object declined precip-
itously after the first trial (Figure 2); control patients performed nearly
perfectly on all trials. As in the room search task, amnesics' object recall
errors were divided between perseverative and nonperseverative errors.

Our data indicate clearly that amnesic patients exhibit a phenomenon
that resembles the A$\overline{\text{B}}$ error. We call this phenomenon *mnemonic precedence*. What is the most appropriate interpretation of our results? We
can confidently rule out the possibility that mnemonic precedence ob-

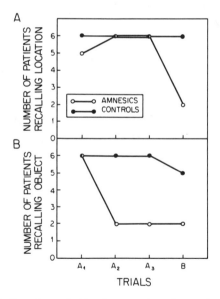

Fig. 2. Delayed recall of location and object by amnesic and control patients on consecutive
trials of an object search task conducted with a small container. Objects were hidden in
one drawer of the container (A) for three trials, and a second drawer (B) on the fourth trial.
A different object was used on each trial.

served in our tasks can be attributed to defective object concept. On immediate tests, all amnesics could describe the location and identity of the object when it was out of view. More generally, amnesic patients know fully well that objects exist independently of themselves, and can describe their homes, spouses, and possessions in the absence of their physical presence. Another possible interpretation of our data is that patients' errors can be attributed to perseverative tendencies associated with frontal lobe damage that may be independent of poor memory. Our amnesics do suffer from some perseverative tendencies, but no more so than do our control patients: the performance of the amnesics and controls is equivalent on the Wisconsin Card Sort, a task that is sensitive to perseverative tendencies associated with dorsolateral frontal lobe damage. In addition, both of our object search tasks were administered to three patients with verified bilateral frontal lobe damage, who accurately recalled the location of the displaced object on all trials.

In light of these considerations, we favor the idea that memory disorder is largely responsible for the occurrence of mnemonic precedence in amnesic patients. More specifically, we think that proactive interference generated on trials at Location A is a principal source of amnesics' errors. This interpretation is consistent with the results of other studies that have demonstrated that amnesics can be highly sensitive to the effects of proactive interference (Kinsbourne & Winocur, 1980; Warrington & Weiskrantz, 1974; Winocur & Weiskrantz, 1976). Our results do not, of course, necessarily imply that forgetting associated with sensitivity to interference is a major source of infants' A$\overline{\text{B}}$ errors, but they do lend support to this view. Moreover, the observation that amnesics exhibited mnemonic precedence in the presence of a visible object indicates that infants' A$\overline{\text{B}}$ errors in the presence of visible objects need not be inconsistent with a forgetting interpretation: infants, like amnesics, may forget the entire episode of object placement at Location B after distraction. Thus, our data, when viewed in the context of the previously reviewed studies of infants, suggest the possibility of a genuine correspondence between the mnemonic abilities of amnesics and of 8–10-month-old infants. Although further study will be necessary to determine the depth and breadth of this correspondence, we think it is reasonable to entertain the idea that A$\overline{\text{B}}$ errors produced by sensitivity to interference reflect the operation of a late memory system that is degraded in amnesics and not yet fully developed in infants.

Conclusions

The studies that were discussed in previous sections converge on the conclusion that a major change of infants' memory abilities occurs between 8 and 12 months. The work of Rose, Gottfried, and Bridger and of other researchers demonstrates clearly that performance on habituation–novelty-preference tasks prior to 8 months is highly sensitive to study–test changes of sensory modality but is virtually unaffected by them at 12 months. Conditioning studies indicate that memory performance of infants younger than about 8 months is severely disrupted by spatial displacements and temporal delays that have little or no effect on the retention of 12-month-old infants (Brody, 1981; Millar & Schaffer, 1972, 1973; Watson, 1967). Infants frequently commit the $\overline{AB}$ error during the 8–10 month period, but by 12 months they can tolerate long hiding–search delays and perform $\overline{AB}$ tasks with little or no error (e.g., Fox et al., 1979).

In addition to the foregoing results, observations reported in other situations likewise suggest a fundamental change in memory abilities between 8 and 10 months. In a study of spatial location learning, Cornell and Heth (1979) found that 4-month-old infants tended to rely on *response* cues, whereas beginning at about 8 months there is an increasing tendency to rely on *place* cues. Kagan and Hamburg (1981) demonstrated that delayed retention of the place of appearance of a puppet, as expressed by anticipatory looking, is absent at 6 months but is robust by 10–11 months. Studies of social development indicate the emergence of several memory-related phenomena at about 8–9 months. Kagan, Kearsley, and Zelazo (1978), for instance, have pointed out that studies conducted in various cultures demonstrate that separation distress (crying and other expressions of displeasure elicited by the departure of a caretaker) first appears at the age of 8 months. Kagan et al. suggested that the occurrence of separation distress depends on the ability, not present until 8 months, to recall the episode of departure. Similarly, Schaffer (1972) has noted the appearance of stranger anxiety and the onset of wariness to novel objects at about 8 months; prior to this time, infants approach unfamiliar people and objects with little or no hesitation. He suggested that the onset of these phenomena is related to maturation of mnemonic abilities: in order to express anxiety or wariness about a novel person or object, an infant must be able to gain access to stored information that can serve as a standard for judging the familiarity of the novel object. Prior to 8 months, stored information apparently does not influence the infant's awareness of a person or object as familiar or unfamiliar, although sensitivity to familiarity/unfamiliarity is evident at a much earlier age on habituation tasks (see Chapter 7 for relevant nonhuman research).

The appearance of all the aforementioned phenomena within a relatively narrow temporal window is probably not coincidental. Rather, it suggests that the period from 8–10 months represents a significant inflection point in memory development. Similar observations have been made by Schaffer (1972) and by Kagan and his colleagues (Fox et al., 1979; Kagan & Hamburg, 1981; Kagan et al., 1978), who argued that a transition from recognition to recall occurs during the critical period: Prior to 8 months, infants can recognize previously encountered stimuli but cannot recall them; after 8 months, they develop the capacity to recall information that is not available in the immediate perceptual environment.

This interpretation is consistent with many of the mnemonic changes that occur in the temporal region of 8 months. However, it is inconsistent with evidence indicating that infants exhibit a form of recall prior to 8 months (e.g., Rovee-Collier & Fagen, 1981), and does not take account of the fact that recognition, in addition to recall, changes substantially after 8 months (as demonstrated by the cross-modality studies). Thus, rather than emphasize a transition from recognition to recall, it may be more fruitful for theoretical efforts to focus on the *types* of recall and recognition abilities that are available before and after the critical temporal interval; the existing evidence suggests that they may be qualitatively different. The postulation of the early and late memory systems represents one attempt to account for such qualitative differences.

This hypothesis is, of course, a preliminary one; it is conspicuously lacking in detail and specificity. We cannot yet say very much about the properties of the postulated systems beyond the general descriptions that have been offered, nor can we point to critical experiments that have pitted the idea against competing alternatives. Moreover, the notion that the early developing system in infants corresponds to one that is preserved in amnesics requires further empirical corroboration. However, the early/late memory system hypothesis is not inconsistent with existing data, and it does have several heuristic virtues. First, it has helped us to see relations among disparate phenomena of infant memory and may serve a similar function for other investigators. Second, an ontogenetic sequence of memory systems during infancy has been postulated by Nadel and Zola-Morgan (Chapter 7) and by Bachevalier and Mishkin (1982) on the basis of observations of nonhuman primates and other animals. The similarity between their ideas and the one that we have proposed suggests the possibility of a unified theoretical approach to human and nonhuman infant memory. Third, the idea may provide a theoretical link between adult and infant memory research. Some infant memory researchers (e.g., Carter & Strauss, 1982) have expressed justified caution concerning the use of concepts and theories from the adult literature, and we do not advocate that investigators of infant memory uncritically accept ideas that derive from studies of adults. However, we do suggest that the early/late memory system hypothesis may constitute a *common problem* for the two areas. Even though the hypothesis is clearly tentative and likely to be controversial, investigation of it would give infant memory research a central role in the study of a theoretical issue that has myriad implications for the psychology and biology of memory (Schacter, 1984). In light of the largely atheoretical nature of previous infant memory research (cf. Chapter 1), such a theoretical focus would not be entirely unattractive.

One final point should be noted. We have suggested that the late memory system is available to infants by the end of the first year. What about subsequent development? Do new memory systems appear after the first year of life? At the present time, we know of no evidence that supports this contention. There is, however, a great deal of evidence that mnemonic abilities change substantially after the first year. Rather than postulate the development of new memory systems to account for these changes, it seems more likely that they are associated with the emergence of crucial cognitive abilities, such as language and self-concept, and with ongoing expansion of general knowledge and strategies. The neural machinery that underlies the ability to remember the past may be in place within a year of birth. Subsequent memory development consists of integrating this machinery with other cognitive functions.

ACKNOWLEDGMENTS

We thank Jill Moscovitch, Larry Squire, Endel Tulving, and Ken Zucker for helpful discussion, and thank Carol A. Macdonald for help in preparation of the manuscript.

References

Bachevalier, J., & Mishkin, M. *The development of memories vs. habits in infant monkeys.* Paper presented to the International Organization of Psychophysiology, 1982.

Baker, R. A., Brown, K. W., & Gottfried, A. W. Ontogeny of tactile-visual cross-modal transfer. *Infant Behavior and Development,* 1982, *5,* 14.

Barbizet, J. *Pathologie de la mémoire.* Paris: Presses Universitaires de France, 1970.

Bennett, H. L., Davis, H. S., & Giannini, J. A. *Post-hypnotic suggestions during general anesthesia and subsequent dissociated behavior.* Presented at the meeting of the Society for Clinical and Experimental Hypnosis, Portland, 1981.

Blass, E. M., Kenny, J. T., Stoloff, M., Bruno, J. P., Teicher, M. M., & Hall, W. G. Motivation, learning, and memory in the ontogeny of suckling in albino rats. In N. E. Spear & B. A. Campbell (Eds.), *The ontogeny of learning and memory.* Hillsdale, N.J.: Erlbaum, 1979.

Bremner, J. G. Egocentric versus allocentric spatial coding in nine-month-old infants: Factors influencing the choice of code. *Developmental Psychology,* 1978, *14,* 346–355. (a)

Bremner, J. G. Spatial errors made by infants: Inadequate spatial cues or evidence of egocentrism? *British Journal of Psychology,* 1978, *69,* 77–84. (b)

Bremner, J. G., & Bryant, P. E. Place versus response as the basis of spatial errors made by young infants. *Journal of Experimental Child Psychology,* 1977, *23,* 162–171.

Brody, L. R. Visual short-term cued recall memory in infancy. *Child Development,* 1981, *52,* 242–250.

Brooks, D. N., & Baddeley, A. D. What can amnesic patients learn? *Neuropsychologia,* 1976, *14,* 111–122.

Bryant, P. E., Jones, P., Claxton, V., & Perkins, G. M. Recognition of shapes across modalities by infants. *Nature,* 1972, *240,* 303–304.

Bushnell, E. W. The ontogeny of intermodal relations: Vision and touch in infancy. In R. D. Walk & H. L. Pick, Jr. (Eds.), *Intersensory perception and sensory integration.* New York: Plenum Press, 1981.

Butterworth, G. Object disappearance and error in Piaget's Stage IV task. *Journal of Experimental Child Psychology,* 1977, *23,* 391–401.

Butterworth, G., & Jarrett, N. Piaget's Stage 4 error: Background to the problem. *British Journal of Psychology,* 1982, *73,* 175–185.

Butterworth, G. E. Object identity in infancy: The interaction of spatial location codes in determining search errors. *Child Development,* 1975, *46,* 866–870.

Butterworth, G. E. Asymmetrical search errors in infancy. *Child Development,* 1976, *47,* 864–867.

Carter, P., & Strauss, M. S. Habituation is not enough, but it's not a bad start—A reply to Sophian. *Merrill-Palmer Quarterly,* 1982, *27,* 334–337.

Castelucci, V., & Kandell, E. R. An invertebrate system for the cellular study of habituation and sensitization. In T. J. Tighe & R. N. Leaton (Eds.), *Habituation.* Hillsdale, N.J.: Erlbaum, 1976.

Cermak, L. S. (Eds.). *Human memory and amnesia.* Hillsdale, N.J.: Erlbaum, 1982.

Cermak, L. S., Lewis, R., Butters, N., & Goodglass, H. Role of verbal mediation in performance of motor tasks by Korsakoff patients. *Perceptual & Motor Skills,* 1973, *37,* 259–262.

Claparède, E. Reconnaissance et moitié. *Archives de Psychologie,* 1911, *11,* 79–90. (Recognition and 'me-ness.' In D. Rapaport [Ed.], *Organization and pathology of thought.* New York: Columbia University Press, 1951.)

Cohen, L. B., & Gelber, E. R. Infant visual memory. In L. Cohen & P. Salapatek (Eds.), *Infant perception.* New York: Academic Press, 1975.

Cohen, L. B., De Loache, J. S., & Pearl, R. A. An examination of interference effects in infants' memory for faces. *Child Development,* 1977, *48,* 88–96.

Cohen, N. J. Amnesia and the distinction between procedural and declarative knowledge. In N. Butters & L. R. Squire (Eds.), *The neuropsychology of memory.* New York: Guilford Press, 1984.

Cohen, N. J., & Squire, L. R. Preserved learning and retention of pattern-analyzing skill in amnesia: Dissociation of knowing how and knowing that. *Science,* 1980, *210,* 207–210.

Corkin, S. Tactually-guided maze learning in man: Effects of unilateral cortical excisions and bilateral hippocampal lesions. *Neuropsychologia,* 1965, *3,* 339–351.

Corkin, S. Acquisition of motor skill after bilateral medial temporal-lobe excision. *Neuropsychologia,* 1968, *6,* 255–265.

Cornell, E. H. Infants' visual attention to pattern arrangement and orientation. *Child Development,* 1975, *46,* 229–232.

Cornell, E. H. Learning to find things: A reinterpretation of object permanence studies. In L. S. Siegal & C. J. Brainerd (Eds.), *Alternatives to Piaget.* New York: Academic Press, 1978.

Cornell, E. H. Infants' recognition memory, forgetting, and savings. *Journal of Experimental Child Psychology,* 1979, *28,* 359–374.

Cornell, E. H. Distributed study facilitates infants' delayed recognition memory. *Memory and Cognition,* 1980, *8,* 539–542.

Cornell, E. H., & Heth, C. D. Response versus place learning by human infants. *Journal of Experimental Psychology: Human Learning and Memory,* 1979, *2,* 188–196.

Corter, C. M., Zucker, K. J., & Galligan, R. F. Patterns in the infant's search for mother during brief separation. *Developmental Psychology*, 1980, *16*, 62–69.

Cummings, E. M., & Bjork, E. L. Perseveration and search on a five-choice visible displacement hiding task. *Journal of Genetic Psychology*, 1983, *142*, 283–291.

Diamond, R., & Rozin, P. Activation of existing memories in the amnesic syndromes. *Journal of Abnormal Psychology*, in press.

Dirks, J., & Gibson, E. J. Infants' perception of similarity between live people and their photographs. *Child Development*, 1977, *48*, 124–130.

Eich, E. Memory for versus awareness of unattended events. *Memory and Cognition*, in press.

Evans, W. F., & Gratch, G. The Stage IV error in Piaget's theory of object concept development: Difficulties in object conceptualization or spatial localization. *Child Development*, 1972, *43*, 682–688.

Fagan, J. F. Infants' recognition memory for a series of visual stimuli. *Journal of Experimental Child Psychology*, 1971, *11*, 244–250.

Fagan, J. F. Infants' delayed recognition memory and forgetting. *Journal of Experimental Child Psychology*, 1973, 16, 424–450.

Fagan, J. F. Infant recognition memory: Studies in forgetting. *Child Development*, 1977, *48*, 68–78.

Fagan, J. F. The origins of facial pattern recognition. In M. Bornstein & W. Kessen (Eds.), *Psychological development from infancy*. Hillsdale, N.J.: Erlbaum, 1979.

Fagen, J. W., & Rovee-Collier, C. K. A conditioning analysis of infant memory. In R. L. Isaacson & N. Spear (Eds.), *The expression of knowledge*. New York: Plenum Press, 1982.

Fitzgerald, H. E., & Porges, S. W. A decade of infant conditioning and learning research. *Merrill-Palmer Quarterly*, 1971, *17*, 79–117.

Fox, N., Kagan, J., & Weiskopf, S. The growth of memory during infancy. *Genetic Psychology Monographs*, 1979, *99*, 91–130.

Frye, D. Stages of development: The Stage IV error. *Infant Behavior and Development*, 1980, *3*, 115–126.

Gardner, L. E. Retention and overhabituation of a dual-component response in *Lumbricus terrestris*. *Journal of Comparative and Physiological Psychology*, 1968, 66, 315–318.

Gottfried, A. W., Rose, S. A., & Bridger, W. H. Cross-modal transfer in human infants. *Child Development*, 1977, *48*, 118–123.

Gottfried, A. W., Rose, S. A., & Bridger, W. H. Effects of visual, haptic, and manipulatory experiences on infants' visual recognition memory of objects. *Developmental Psychology*, 1978, *14*, 305–312.

Graf, P., Squire, L. R., & Mandler, G. Information that amnesic patients do not forget. *Journal of Experimental Psychology: Learning, Memory, and Cognition*, 1984, in press.

Gratch, G. On levels of awareness of objects in infants and students thereof. *Merrill-Palmer Quarterly*, 1976, *22*, 157–176.

Gratch, G., & Landers, W. F. Stage IV of Piaget's theory of infants' object concepts: A longitudinal study. *Child Development*, 1971, *42*, 359–372.

Gratch, G., Appel, K. J., Evans, W. F., LeCompte, G. K., & Wright, N. A. Piaget's Stage IV object concept error: Evidence of forgetting or object conception? *Child Development*, 1974, *45*, 71–77.

Harris, P. L. Perseverative errors in search by young infants. *Child Development*, 1973, *44*, 28–33.

Harris, P. L. Perseverative search at a visibly empty place by young infants. *Journal of Experimental Child Psychology*, 1974, *18*, 535–542.

212 Daniel L. Schacter and Morris Moscovitch

Harris, P. L. Development of search and object permanence during infancy. *Psychological Bulletin*, 1975, *82*, 332–344.

Hintzman, D. L., Block, R. A., & Inskeep, N. R. Memory for mode of input. *Journal of Verbal Learning and Verbal Behavior*, 1972, *11*, 741–749.

Hulsebus, R. C. Operant conditioning of infant behavior: A review. In H. W. Reese (Ed.), *Advances in child development and behavior* (Vol. 8). New York: Academic Press, 1973.

Jacoby, L. Knowing and remembering: Some parallels in the behavior of Korsakoff patients and normals. In L. S. Cermak (Ed.), *Human memory and amnesia*. Hillsdale, N.J.: Erlbaum, 1982.

Jacoby, L. L. Perceptual enhancement: Persistent effects of an experience. *Journal of Experimental Psychology: Learning, Memory, and Cognition*, 1983, *9*, 21–38.

Jacoby, L. L., & Dallas, M. On the relationship between autobiographical memory and perceptual learning. *Journal of Experimental Psychology: General*, 1981, *110*, 306–340.

Jacoby, L. L., & Witherspoon, D. Remembering without awareness. *Canadian Journal of Psychology*, 1982, *36*, 300–324.

Jeffrey, W. E. Habituation as a mechanism for perceptual development. In T. J. Tighe & R. N. Leaton (Eds.), *Habituation*. Hillside, N.J.: Erlbaum, 1976.

Kagan, J., & Hamburg, M. The enhancement of memory in the first year. *Journal of Genetic Psychology*, 1981, *138*, 3–14.

Kagan, J., Kearsley, R. B., & Zelazo, P. R. *Infancy: Its place in human development*. Cambridge, Mass.: Harvard University Press, 1978.

Kihlstrom, J. F. Posthypnotic amnesia for recently learned materials: Interactions with "episodic" and "semantic" memory. *Cognitive Psychology*, 1980, *12*, 227–251.

Kimble, D. P. Possible inhibitory functions of the hippocampus. *Neuropsychologia*, 1969, *7*, 235–244.

Kinsbourne, M., & Winocur, G. Response competition and interference effects in paired-associate learning by Korsakoff amnesics. *Neuropsychologia*, 1980, *18*, 541–548.

Kinsbourne, M., & Wood, F. Short-term memory and the amnesic syndrome. In D. D. Deutsch & J. A. Deutsch (Eds.), *Short-term memory*. New York: Academic Press, 1975.

Kinsbourne, M., & Wood, F. Theoretical considerations regarding the episodic-semantic memory distinction. In L. S. Cermak (Ed.), *Human memory and amnesia*. Hillsdale, N.J.: Erlbaum, 1982.

Kolers, P. A. Reading a year later. *Journal of Experimental Psychology: Human Learning and Memory*, 1976, *2*, 554–565.

Kunst-Wilson, W. R., & Zajonc, R. D. Affective discrimination of stimuli that cannot be recognized. *Science*, 1980, *207*, 557–558.

Landers, W. F. Effects of differential experience on infants' performance in a Piagetian Stage IV object concept task. *Developmental Psychology*, 1971, *5*, 48–54.

Lasky, R. E. Length of familiarization and preference for novel and familiar stimuli. *Infant Behavior and Development*, 1980, *3*, 15–28.

Lawson, K. R. Spatial and temporal congruity and auditory-visual integration in infants. *Developmental Psychology*, 1980, *16*, 185–192.

Leaton, R. N. Long-term retention of the habituation of lick suppression in rats. *Journal of Comparative and Physiological Psychology*, 1974, *87*, 1157–1164.

Luria, A. R. The directive function of speech in development and dissolution. *Word*, 1959, *15*, 341–352.

Lyons-Ruth, K. Bimodal perception in infancy: Response to auditory-visual incongruity. *Child Development*, 1977, *48*, 820–827.

Mackay-Soroka, S., Trehub, S. E., Bull, D. H., & Corter, C. M. Effects of encoding and retrieval conditions on infants' recognition memory. *Child Development*, 1982, *53*, 815–818.

Mandler, G. Recognizing: The judgment of previous occurrence. *Psychological Review*, 1980, *87*, 252–271.

McCall, R. B., Kennedy, C. B., & Dodds, C. The interfering effect of distracting stimuli on the infant's memory. *Child Development*, 1977, *48*, 79–87.

Meltzoff, A. N., & Borton, R. Intermodal matching by human neonates. *Nature*, 1979, *282*, 403–404.

Millar, W. S. A study of operant conditioning under delayed reinforcement in early infancy. *Monographs of the Society for Research in Child Development*, 1972, *37* (2, Serial No. 147).

Millar, W. S., & Schaffer, H. R. The influence of spatially displaced feedback on infant operant conditioning. *Journal of Experimental Child Psychology*, 1972, *14*, 442–453.

Millar, W. S., & Schaffer, H. R. Visual-manipulative response strategies in infant operant conditioning with spatially displaced feedback. *British Journal of Psychology*, 1973, *64*, 545–552.

Miller, D. J., Cohen, L. B., & Hill, K. T. A methodological investigation of Piaget's theory of object concept development in the sensory-motor period. *Journal of Experimental Child Psychology*, 1970, *9*, 59–85.

Milner, B., Corkin, S., & Teuber, H. L. Further analysis of the hippocampal amnesic syndrome: 14 year follow-up study of H.M. *Neuropsychologia*, 1968, *6*, 215–234.

Moore, M. K., & Meltzoff, A. Imitation, object permanence and language development in infancy: Toward a neo-development. In F. Minifie & L. Lloyd (Eds.), *Communicative and cognitive abilities*. Baltimore: University Park Press, 1978.

Morton, J. Facilitation in word recognition: Experiments causing change in the logogen model. In P. A. Kolers, M. E. Wrolstad, & H. Bouma (Eds.), *Processing of visible language* (Vol. 1). New York: Plenum Press, 1979.

Moscovitch, M. Multiple dissociations of function in amnesia. In L. S. Cermak (Ed.), *Human memory and amnesia*. Hillsdale, N.J.: Erlbaum, 1982. (a)

Moscovitch, M. A neuropsychological approach to perception and memory in normal and pathological aging. In F. I. M. Craik & S. Trehub (Eds.), *Aging and cognitive processes*. New York: Plenum Press, 1982. (b)

Moscovitch, M. Sufficient conditions for demonstrating preserved memory in amnesia: A task analysis. In N. Butters & L. R. Squire (Eds.), *The neuropsychology of memory*. New York: Guilford Press, 1984.

Nadel, L., O'Keefe, J., & Black, A. Slam on the brakes: A critique of Altman, Brunner, and Bayer's response–inhibition model of hippocampal function. *Behavioral Biology*, 1975, *14*, 151–162.

O'Keefe, J., & Nadel, L. *The hippocampus as a cognitive map*. Oxford: Clarendon Press, 1978.

Olsen, G. M. An information-processing analysis of visual memory and habituation in infants. In T. J. Tighe & R. N. Leaton (Eds.), *Habituation*. Hillsdale, N.J.: Erlbaum, 1976.

Oscar-Berman, M. Neuropsychological consequences of long-term chronic alcoholism. *American Scientist*, 1980, *68*, 410–419.

Papousek, H. Experimental studies of appetitional behavior in human newborns and infants. In H. W. Stevenson, E. H. Hess, & H. L. Rheingold (Eds.), *Early behavior*. New York: Wiley, 1967.

Parmelee, A. H. Neurophysiological and behavioral organization of premature infants in the first months of life. *Biological Psychiatry*, 1975, *10*, 501–512.

Piaget, J. *The construction of reality in the child*. New York: Basic Books, 1954.

Piaget, J., & Inhelder, B. *Memory and intelligence.* New York: Basic Books, 1973.

Prisko, L.-H. *Short-term memory in focal cerebral damage.* Doctoral thesis, McGill University, Montreal, 1963. Cited in Milner, B. Amnesia following operation on the temporal lobe. In C. W. M. Whitty & O. L. Zangwill (Eds.), *Amnesia.* London: Butterworths, 1966.

Ramey, C. T., & Ourth, L. L. Delayed reinforcement and vocalization rates of infants. *Child Development,* 1971, *42,* 291–297.

Rolfe, S. A., & Day, R. H. Effects of the similarity and dissimilarity between familiarization and test objects on recognition memory in infants following unimodal and bimodal familiarization. *Child Development,* 1981, *52,* 1308–1312.

Rose, S. A. Enhancing visual recognition memory in preterm infants. *Developmental Psychology,* 1980, *16,* 85–92.

Rose, S. A. Developmental changes in infants' retention of visual stimuli. *Child Development,* 1981, *52,* 227–233.

Rose, S. A., Gottfried, A. W., & Bridger, W. H. Cross-modal transfer in infants: Relationship to prematurity and socioeconomic background. *Developmental Psychology,* 1978, *14,* 643–652.

Rose, S. A., Gottfried, A. W., & Bridger, W. H. Effects of haptic cues on visual recognition memory in fullterm and preterm infants. *Infant Behavior and Development,* 1979, *2,* 55–67.

Rose, S. A., Gottfried, A. W., & Bridger, W. H. Cross-modal transfer in 6-month-old infants. *Developmental Psychology,* 1981, *17,* 661–669.

Rosenblatt, J. S. The sensorimotor and motivational bases of early behavioral development of selected altricial mammals. In N. E. Spear & B. A. Campbell (Eds.), *Ontogeny of learning and memory.* Hillsdale, N.J.: Erlbaum, 1979.

Rovee-Collier, C. K., & Capatides, J. B. Positive behavioral contrast in 3-month old infants on multiple conjugate reinforcement schedules. *Journal of Experimental Analysis of Behavior,* 1979, *32,* 15–27.

Rovee-Collier, C. K., & Fagen, J. W. The retrieval of memory in early infancy. In L. P. Lipsitt (Ed.), *Advances in infancy research* (Vol. 1). Norwood, N.J.: Ablex, 1981.

Ruff, H. A., & Kohler, C. J. Transfer across modalities in six-month-old infants. *Infant Behavior and Development,* 1978, *1,* 259–264.

Sameroff, A. J. Can conditioned responses be established in the newborn infant? *Developmental Psychology,* 1971, *5,* 1–12.

Scarborough, D. L., Cortese, C., & Scarborough, H. S. Frequency and repetition effects in lexical memory. *Journal of Experimental Psychology: Human Perception and Performance,* 1977, *3,* 1–17.

Scarborough, D. L., Gerard, L., & Cortese, C. Accessing lexical memory: The transfer of word repetition effects across task and modality. *Memory and Cognition,* 1979, *7,* 3–12.

Schacter, D. L. *Stranger behind the engram: Theories of memory and the psychology of science.* Hillsdale, N.J.: Erlbaum, 1982.

Schacter, D. L. Toward the multidisciplinary study of memory: Ontogeny, phylogeny, and pathology of memory systems. In N. Butters & L. R. Squire (Eds.), *The neuropsychology of memory.* New York: Guilford Press, 1984.

Schacter, D. L., & Tulving, E. Amnesia and memory research. In L. S. Cermak (Ed.), *Human memory and amnesia.* Hillsdale, N.J.: Erlbaum, 1982. (a)

Schacter, D. L., & Tulving, E. Memory, amnesia, and the episodic/semantic distinction. In R. L. Isaacson & N. Spear (Eds.), *The expression of knowledge.* New York: Plenum Press, 1982. (b)

Schacter, D. L., Tulving, E., & Wang, P. L. *Source amnesia: New methods and illustrative data.* Paper presented to a meeting of the International Neuropsychological Society, Atlanta, February 1981.

Schaffer, H. R. Cognitive components of the infant's response to strangeness. In M. Lewis & L. A. Rosenblum (Eds.), *The origins of fear*. New York: Wiley, 1972.

Schuberth, R. E., & Gratch, G. Search on a five-choice invisible displacement hiding task: A reply to Cummings and Bjork. *Infant Behavior and Development*, 1981, *4*, 61–64.

Schuberth, R. C., Werner, J. S., & Lipsitt, L. P. The Stage IV error in Piaget's theory of object concept development: A reconsideration of the spatial localization hypothesis. *Child Development*, 1978, *49*, 747–748.

Sidman, M., Stoddard, L., & Mohr, J. Some additional quantitative observations of immediate memory in a patient with bilateral hippocampal lesions. *Neuropsychologia*, 1968, *6*, 245–254.

Sigman, M., & Parmelee, A. H. Visual preferences of four-month-old premature and fullterm infants. *Child Development*, 1974, *45*, 959–965.

Sophian, C. Habituation is not enough: Novelty preferences, search, and memory in infancy. *Merrill-Palmer Quarterly*, 1980, *26*, 239–257.

Spear, N. E., & Campbell, B. A. (Eds.). *Ontogeny of learning and memory*. Hillsdale, N.J.: Erlbaum, 1979.

Spelke, E. Infants' intermodal perception of events. *Cognitive Psychology*, 1976, *8*, 553–560.

Squire, L. R. The neuropsychology of human memory. *Annual Review of Neuroscience*, 1982, *5*, 241–273.

Starr, A., & Phillips, L. Verbal and motor memory in the amnestic syndrome. *Neuropsychologia*, 1970, *8*, 75–88.

Tulving, E. *Elements of episodic memory*. Oxford: Oxford University Press, 1983.

Tulving, E., Schacter, D. L., & Stark, H. A. Priming effects in word-fragment completion are independent of recognition memory. *Journal of Experimental Psychology: Learning, Memory, and Cognition*, 1982, *8*, 336–342.

Warrington, E. K., & Weiskrantz, L. New method of testing long-term retention with special reference to amnesic patients. *Nature*, 1968, *217*, 972–974.

Warrington, E. K., & Weiskrantz, L. Amnesic syndrome: Consolidation or retrieval? *Nature*, 1970, *228*, 629–630.

Warrington, E. K., & Weiskrantz, L. The effect of prior learning on subsequent retention in amnesic patients. *Neuropsychologia*, 1974, *12*, 419–428.

Warrington, E. K., & Weiskrantz, L. Amnesia: A disconnection syndrome. *Neuropsychologia*, 1982, *20*, 233–248.

Watson, J. S. Memory and "contingency analysis" in infant learning. *Merrill-Palmer Quarterly*, 1967, *13*, 55–76.

Watson, J. S. Memory in infancy. In J. Piaget, J. P. Bronkart, & P. Mounoud (Eds.), *Encyclopédie de la pléiade: La psychologie*. Paris: Gallimard, 1980.

Webb, R. A., Massar, B., & Nadolny, T. Information and strategy in the young child's search for hidden objects. *Child Development*, 1972, *43*, 91–104.

Weiskrantz, L., & Warrington, E. K. Conditioning in amnesic patients. *Neuropsychologia*, 1979, *17*, 187–194.

Werner, J. S., & Perlmutter, M. Development of visual memory in infants. In H. W. Reese & L. P. Lipsitt (Eds.), *Advances in child development and behavior* (Vol. 14). New York: Academic Press, 1979.

Whitty, C. W. M., & Zangwill, O. L. (Eds.). *Amnesia*. London: Butterworths, 1977.

Wickelgren, W. A. Chunking and consolidation: A theoretical synthesis of semantic networks, configuring in conditioning, S-R versus cognitive learning, normal forgetting, the amnesic syndrome, and the hippocampal arousal system. *Psychological Review*, 1979, *86*, 44–60.

Williamsen, J. A., Johnson, H. J., & Eriksen, C. W. Some characteristics of posthypnotic amnesia. *Journal of Abnormal Psychology*, 1965, *70*, 123–131.

Winocur, G., & Weiskrantz, L. An investigation of paired-associate learning in amnesic patients. *Neuropsychologia,* 1976, *14,* 97–110.

Wood, R., Ebert, V., & Kinsbourne, M. The episodic-semantic memory distinction in memory and amnesia: Clinical and experimental observations. In L. S. Cermak (Ed.), *Human memory and amnesia.* Hillsdale, N.J.: Erlbaum, 1982.

Woods, R. T., & Piercy, M. A similarity between amnesic memory and normal forgetting. *Neuropsychologia,* 1974, *12,* 437–445.

Zucker, K. J. *The development of search for mother during brief separation.* Unpublished Ph.D. thesis, University of Toronto, 1982.

Index